TENNYSON'S
Maud

Come into the garden, Maud;
    For the black bat, night, has flown.
Come into the garden, Maud;
    I am here at the gate alone;
And the woodbine spices are wafted abroad,
    And the musk of the roses blown.

2

For a breeze of morning moves,
    And the planet of love is on high
Beginning to faint in the light that she loves
    On a bed of daffodil sky
To faint in the light of the sun she loves,
    To faint in his light to die.

3

All night have the roses heard
    The flute, violin, bassoon;
All night has the casement jessamine stirr'd
    To the dancers dancing in tune;
Till a silence fell with the waking bird
    And a hush with the setting moon.

I said to the lily, "There is but one
    With whom she has heart to be gay.
When will the dancers leave her alone,
    She is weary of dance & play."
Now half to the setting moon are gone,
    And half to the rising day;

'Come into the garden, Maud'
The final draft of I xxii in T36, numbered '14'
in the original series of twenty sections.

TENNYSON'S

Maud

A definitive edition

Edited with Introduction
and Commentary by
SUSAN SHATTO

THE ATHLONE PRESS
LONDON

First published in Great Britain 1986
by the Athlone Press, 44 Bedford Row, London WC1R 4LY
(C) Copyright editorial matter Susan Shatto 1986

Shatto, Susan
 Tennyson, 'Maud'.
 1. Tennyson, Alfred Tennyson, *Baron*——
 Criticism and interpretation
 I. Title
 821'.8   PR5588

 ISBN 0–485–11294–9

Typeset by Hope Services, Abingdon
Printed and bound at the University Press, Cambridge

For Philip Collins

Contents

Illustrations

Preface

The edition of *In Memoriam* on which I collaborated with
Marion Shaw (Oxford, 1982) suggested the need for a similar
treatment of *Maud*. My appointment as Hartley Fellow in the
University of Southampton enabled me to carry out most of
the work on the present edition. For this opportunity I am
extremely grateful to the University and to the Department of
English. Especially, I am indebted to James Sambrook for his
encouragement and friendship.

This edition of *Maud* provides the first complete collation of
all the known manuscripts, the surviving proofs, the privately
printed Trial issue, and the editions of the poem up to and
including 1889. The genesis and development of the poem are
reconstructed from the evidence of the manuscripts, from
Tennyson's own statements, and from the letters and reminiscences of his contemporaries. In particular, the manuscript
Journal of Tennyson's wife, Emily, has supplied a wealth of
information about the history of composition of the poem. The
work of reconstruction is greatly indebted to the revealing and
scholarly life of the poet by Robert Bernard Martin, *Tennyson:
The Unquiet Heart* (Oxford, 1980).

The Commentary serves in part to supplement and elaborate
the information on composition given in the textual apparatus.
Many of Tennyson's own comments on the poem are quoted,
as well as those of his family and friends. But for the most
part, the notes in the Commentary are original to this edition.
The Commentary is not a *variorum*: it does not attempt to
provide a survey or even a selection of notes on the poem by
other editors and scholars. The work of previous commentators
is quoted only when it is considered to identify an important
piece of information about the literary and biographical
influences on the poem or about the contemporary reception
of the poem.

More than most Tennyson scholars, an editor has particular
reason to be grateful to Christopher Ricks. His monumental

edition of the _Poems_ (1969) laid the groundwork for subsequent full-scale editions of the individual poems and greatly facilitated the work of all subsequent editors of Tennyson. I am personally indebted to Christopher Ricks for his kind and generous advice in regard to the present volume, and I look forward to the publication of his forthcoming revised edition of the _Poems_ in 1987.

I am very grateful to the British Academy for providing generous financial assistance towards the preparation and publication of this edition. I wish to thank, as well, the following institutions which have allowed me to examine their Tennyson manuscripts, printed texts and other material and have given permission to quote from or to reproduce them: Trinity College Library, Cambridge; the Houghton Library, Harvard University; the Henry E. Huntington Library and Art Gallery, San Marino, California (frontispiece and plate 3); the Henry W. and Albert A. Berg Collection, the New York Public Library, Astor, Lenox and Tilden Foundations; the Tennyson Research Centre, Lincoln Central Library; Birmingham Museums and Art Gallery (plate 2); Cambridge University Library; the University of Virginia Library; and the British Library. I am most obliged to the librarians and staff of these collections. Manuscripts in the Tennyson Research Centre collection are quoted by courtesy of Lord Tennyson and the Libraries Department of Lincolnshire Recreational Services. I am very grateful to Sir John Simeon, grandson of Tennyson's friend, for generously giving permission to quote from a hitherto unpublished manuscript in his possession, and I am pleased to acknowledge the kind assistance of William E. Fredeman in regard to information about the manuscript.

The staff of the University of Edinburgh Library and of the National Library of Scotland have patiently and courteously given me much assistance, and I am particularly indebted to them.

Many friends and colleagues have given me invaluable help and advice: Keith Ashfield; Michael Cotsell; Aidan Day; Colin Fink; Philip Gaskell; Kevin Harris; Timothy Hobbs; Wendy Jacobson; Robert Martin and W. W. Robson. This edition would not have been completed without the support and interest of Paul O'Farrell. Above all, I am indebted to Philip Collins, for many kindnesses over many years.

Edinburgh   SUSAN SHATTO

References

1 Manuscripts

Berg A *Berg B*	*Henry W. and Albert A. Berg Collection, The New York Public Library, Astor, Lenox and Tilden Foundations*
BM	*British Library BM Add. MSS 45741, 49977*
Camb	*Cambridge University Library MS add. 6346*
H13, H20, H21, *H27, H29, H148*	*Houghton Library, Harvard University MSS Eng 952 (13), (20), (21), (27), (29), and bMS Eng 952.1 (148), respectively*
H30	*Houghton Library, Harvard University MS Eng 952 (30), and two detached leaves: British Library Add. MS 45741, ff. 278, 279*
H31	*Houghton Library, Harvard University MS Eng 952 (31), and two detached leaves: bMS Eng. 952.1 (147), (149)*
Simeon MS	*MS in the possession of Sir John Simeon, Vancouver, British Columbia*
T18, T21	*Trinity College, Cambridge MSS 0.15.18, 0.15.21, respectively*
T36	*Trinity College, Cambridge MS 0.15.36, and six detached leaves (T36/H)*
T36/H	*Henry E. Huntington Library and Art Gallery HM 19495, HM 19496*
1855US	British Library c.60.f.1
1855Va	University of Virginia

2   *Printed texts*

1837   'Stanzas', by Alfred Tennyson, Esq., in *The Tribute: a Collection of Miscellaneous Unpublished Poems, by Various Authors*, ed. Lord Northampton (1837), pp. 244–50.

AR   *Annual Register . . . of . . . 1837*, pp. 402–4.

P1, 2, 3   Proofs, Henry W. and Albert A. Berg Collection, The New York Public Library, Astor, Lenox and Tilden Foundations.

Trial   Trial issue [the private printing], Tennyson Research Centre, Lincoln Central Library.

1855   *Maud, and Other Poems*, London: Edward Moxon.

1856   *Maud, and Other Poems*, 'A New Edition', London: Edward Moxon.

1857   *Maud, and Other Poems*, 'A New Edition', London: Edward Moxon.

1858   *Maud, and Other Poems*, 'A New Edition', London: Edward Moxon.

1859   *Maud, and Other Poems*, 'A New Edition', London: Edward Moxon.

1860   *Maud, and Other Poems*, 'A New Edition', London: Edward Moxon.

1861   *Maud, and Other Poems*, 'A New Edition', London: Edward Moxon

1862   *Maud, and Other Poems*, 'A New Edition', London: Edward Moxon.

1864   *Maud, and Other Poems*, 'A New Edition', London: Edward Moxon.

1865   *A Selection from the Works of Alfred Tennyson*,
Select   London: Edward Moxon.

1865   *Maud, and Other Poems*, 'A New Edition', London: Edward Moxon.

1866A	*Maud, and Other Poems*, 'Eleventh Edition', London: Edward Moxon.
1866B	*Maud, and Other Poems*, 'Twelfth Edition', London: Edward Moxon.
1867	*Maud, and Other Poems*, 'Thirteenth Edition', London: Edward Moxon.
1869A	*Maud, and Other Poems*, 'Fourteenth Edition', London: Edward Moxon.
1869B	*Maud and Other Poems*, London: Strahan.
1870 Mini	*The Works of Alfred Tennyson*, Miniature Edition, 10 vols, London: Strahan (1870; vol. 9 containing *Maud*).
1870	*Maud and Other Poems*, London: Strahan.
1872	*The Works of Alfred Tennyson*, Imperial Library Edition, 6 vols, London: Strahan (1872–3; vol. 4 containing *Maud*, 1872).
1874	*Maud and Other Poems*, London: Henry S. King.
1875	*The Works of Alfred Tennyson*, Cabinet Edition, 13 vols, London: Henry S. King (1874–7; vol. 9 containing *Maud*, 1875).
1877	*Maud and Other Poems*, London: Henry S. King.
1878	*Maud and Other Poems*, London: C. Kegan Paul.
1884	*Maud and Other Poems*, London: Macmillan.
1889	*The Works*, London: Macmillan.

3   *Symbols and expressions used in the textual apparatus and the Commentary*

T36 – *Trial–*	a dash after a MS or printed text signifies that the reading or section which first appears in that MS or printed text appears in all subsequent MSS and texts.

∧ *or* ∧	carets around a word or words signify addition or substitution in MS.
848 ∧ *849*	signifies an unadopted line between published lines.
[*illegible word*]	signifies that crossing out or erasure in MS has made a word unreadable.
[*intentional blank*]	signifies a missing word, line, or lines in MS.
alternative reading	signifies a word or words interlineated without the deletion of the original reading.

Abbreviations for Names and Works frequently cited

Alfred Tennyson	Charles Tennyson, *Alfred Tennyson* (1949; reissued with alterations, 1968)
Allingham's *Diary*	*William Allingham, A Diary,* ed. H. Allingham and D. Radford (1907)
Charles Tennyson's Notebooks	The notes of Sir Charles Tennyson in preparation for *Alfred Tennyson* (TRC)
Emily's Journal	Emily Sellwood Tennyson's Journal, two volumes condensed and transcribed by her from her original Journal (TRC)*
E.T.	Emily Tennyson
Eversley	*The Works of Alfred, Lord Tennyson,* ed. Hallam, Lord Tennyson, Eversley Edition, 9 vols. (1907), 5: 270–80, containing Tennyson's notes on *Maud*
H.T.	Hallam Tennyson
Knowles	Tennyson's extempore comments on *Maud*, as recorded in 1870–1 by James Knowles; printed *literatim* by Gordon Ray in *Tennyson Reads 'Maud'*, Sedgewick Memorial Lecture (1968), Appendix II.
Letters	*The Letters of Alfred Lord Tennyson, Volume I: 1821–1850*, ed. Cecil Y. Lang and Edgar F. Shannon, Jr (1982)
Mangles' *Diary*	Tennyson's extempore comments as recorded by his friend and neighbour

---

* *Lady Tennyson's Journal*, edited by James O. Hoge (1981), is known to be thoroughly unreliable and is not quoted in the present volume.

	during 1870–2; printed in *Tennyson at Aldworth: the Diary of James Henry Mangles*, ed. with an introduction by Earl A. Knies (1984)
Martin	Robert Bernard Martin, *Tennyson: The Unquiet Heart* (1980)
Materials	[Hallam Tennyson], *Materials for a Life of A.T.*, 4 vols. [1895]. The privately printed early stage of *Memoir*. TRC possesses the set having H.T.'s manuscript revisions
MS *Materials*	Ten manuscript volumes from which were printed *Materials* (TRC)
Memoir	Hallam, Lord Tennyson, *Alfred, Lord Tennyson: A Memoir by His Son*, 2 vols. (1897)
Rader	Ralph Wilson Rader, *Tennyson's 'Maud': The Biographical Genesis* (1963)
Ray	*See* Knowles
Ricks (1969)	Christopher Ricks, ed., *The Poems of Tennyson* (1969)
Shannon	Edgar F. Shannon, Jr 'The Critical Reception of Tennyson's "Maud"', *PMLA*, 68 (June 1953), 397–417
Shatto and Shaw	Susan Shatto and Marion Shaw, eds., *Tennyson: 'In Memoriam'* (1982)
T.	Tennyson
TRC	Tennyson Research Centre
Tennyson and His Friends	*Tennyson and His Friends*, ed. Hallam, Lord Tennyson (1911)
Van Dyke	Tennyson's extempore comments on *Maud*, as recorded in 1892 by Henry

Van Dyke, 'The Voice of Tennyson', *The Century Magazine*, 45 (1893), 539–44

Wise   T. J. Wise, *A Bibliography of the Writings of Alfred, Lord Tennyson*, 2 vols. (1908)

Introduction

1   The History of Composition

Tennyson moved into Farringford, the house on the Isle of
Wight where he composed *Maud*, on 25 November 1853. He
had taken his wife to see it a few weeks before. They crossed
from Lymington in a rowing-boat, an event Emily recorded in
her Journal: 'It was a still November evening. One dark heron
flew over the Solent backed by a daffodil sky.'

The previous October, while they were still living in the
house in Twickenham which Tennyson considered damp,
confining, and too close to London, Emily had written to her
father to request that he copy out a poem which Tennyson did
not have to hand, the poem entitled 'Stanzas' which he had
published, with considerable reluctance, in *The Tribute* in
1837. It was an extended version of a lyric he had composed in
1833–4 (H13, T21), soon after the death of Arthur Hallam,
the lyric which begins 'Oh! that 'twere possible.' Henry
Sellwood replied on 12 October with a copy of the poem and a
letter in which he looked forward to visiting his daughter and
her husband in their 'new house,' adding, 'What a trouble it is
to find one.'[1]

'Oh! that 'twere possible' became, as Tennyson said many
years later, the 'germ of the whole' of *Maud*.[2] *Maud* was to be
the first long poem he had composed since 1850, the year in
which he published *In Memoriam*, was married and was made
Poet Laureate. If the 'Ode on the Death of the Duke of
Wellington' be excepted, *Maud* was to be, moreover, the first
important poem he had composed since 1850. In the intervening
years he had not been idle, but he had not been inspired.

---

[1]   Harvard MS Eng 952.1 (145). The details of Tennyson's whereabouts
and activities between 1851–3 recorded here and in the following
paragraphs are from Martin, pp. 356–73. For a fuller account of the
composition of the lyric, see Commentary for II iv.

[2]   Allingham's *Diary*, 25 June 1865, p. 118.

Despite marriage and the birth of two children (the first stillborn), he had continued to lead the itinerant life habitual to him for more than a decade. With Emily, he had moved house three times, and paid long visits to friends. He managed to prepare a new edition of *The Princess* in 1851, and later that year they travelled to Italy. Subsequently, sometimes with Emily and sometimes without her, he visited the West Country, Yorkshire and Scotland. At the start of 1852, he was anxious about her second pregnancy and unsettled by the widespread belief that France might invade England following the *coup d'état* of Louis Napoleon. His states of mind seem reflected in the series of lame and jingoistic poems he composed and published anonymously in periodicals in January and February. The passages in *Maud* which were to receive the most severe criticism are those which echo the sentiments of these political poems. In the autumn he composed the Wellington Ode – a success, but composed nonetheless out of a sense of duty, not inspiration.[3] By the following spring, he had still not found a house, his health had deteriorated, his friends noticed he was drinking a lot and could not settle down to writing poetry, and he had to have some teeth pulled out. Emily, chronically frail, was herself in ill health and pregnant a third time (a son, Hallam, had been born the previous August). It must have come as a relief to them both when Tennyson discovered Farringford in the autumn and signed a three-year lease with an option to buy when the lease expired.

Farringford was more than the first permanent home he had known since his childhood in Somersby Rectory: in its gothicized Georgian architecture it actually resembled the Rectory. The domestic routine that Emily was quick to establish was conducive to the writing of poetry.

STAGE A: JANUARY–MARCH 1854
What had made him turn his thoughts, the month before he moved house, to a poem essentially twenty years old? No one knows for certain. Perhaps it had never been out of his

---

[3] Martin, p. 368.

thoughts, inspired as it was by the death of Arthur Hallam, echoed as it was in *In Memoriam*. Perhaps, if the details of one of the many conflicting accounts of the origins of *Maud* can be trusted, he had been encouraged by his friend Catherine Rawnsley. The second-hand account of her son does not date their conversation, but it must have occurred during Tennyson's most recent visit to Shiplake, in February 1851, when he and Emily stayed with the Rawnsleys while looking for a house:[4]

> It was at Shiplake . . . that on his casting about, as he often did, for a new subject to write on, my mother, as she herself told me, suggested his enlarging his lovely little fragment, published some years before in "The Tribute", than which she told him he had never written anything better, and which, for he acted on the suggestion, is now imbedded in "Maud."[5]

If this account is accurate, and if Mrs Rawnsley did indeed make the suggestion to Tennyson in early 1851, then it would seem that his nomadic, anxious first years of married life worked to prevent him from acting on the suggestion until almost three years later.

What is certain is that by the spring of 1854 'Oh! that 'twere possible' had occasioned a small group of poems (henceforward called sections) which Tennyson was transcribing into two notebooks (H30, T36). The notebooks were in use simultaneously, but the drafts in H30 antedate those in T36 (with one exception). At this early stage in the composition of *Maud*, H30 is of greater interest than T36, not only because its drafts are earlier, but because they are arranged in a sequence, whereas those in T36 are, as yet, only an assembly.

H30 shows the sequence in two phases. The earlier consists of a sequence of fair copies of five sections, all but one of them lyrical in nature. The sequence runs: 'Birds in the high Hallgarden' (I xii in the published poem); 'Go not, happy day' (I xvii); 'I have led her home, my love, my only friend' (I xviii); 'Strange, that I felt so gay' (I xx); and 'My life has crept so

---

[4] Martin, p. 357.
[5] H. D. Rawnsley, *Memories of the Tennysons*, 2nd ed. (1912), pp. 123–4.

long on a broken wing' (III vi *1–4*). 'O that 'twere possible' (II iv) is absent from the sequence and there is no evidence (stubs in the binding, for example) that it was included in the notebook. What is obvious is that the contents and the structure of the sequence are designed around II iv and predicate its inclusion between I xx and III. What seems probable is that Tennyson felt no need at this time to transcribe the long section into H30: T36 was taking shape as the larger repository and he would transcribe the section there.

Like the trio of ship lyrics which became the first written sections of *In Memoriam*, the H30 sequence constitutes the first written sections of *Maud*. The dramatic potential of the sequence is clear from the outset. In I xii, the narrator and Maud meet in the woods and she accepts him. He has previously suspected her of pride but now realizes his suspicions were groundless. The section ends ominously with the arrival at Maud's door of her prospective suitor, a lord. In I xvii, the narrator anticipates the moment when he and Maud will kiss. This section, incidentally, like II iv, was composed several years before the others. It is among songs composed in 1849 (Camb MS add. 6346) to be added to *The Princess* (third edition, 1850), but it was not used there. In I xviii, they have kissed and are betrothed. As she sleeps, he muses outside her window. Her love has quenched his desolation and enabled him to come to terms with his madness. He is nevertheless preoccupied by images of death and apprehensive about the future; as in I xii, the section ends ominously. In I xx, it is Maud who is melancholy. Her brother has reproved her for rejecting the advances of the lord. Tomorrow night the brother will give a grand political dinner, followed by a dance. The narrator is not invited but will await Maud in the garden.

The events narrated so far presume the location of II iv at this point in the sequence. In II iv, he now speaks of these events as taking place in the distant past. He has long suffered grief and pain. Maud is dead. He walks the city, haunted by her ghost and yearning to creep into a cavern still and deep. Finally, in III, he has recovered from his madness (prepared for in I xviii and II iv). Maud appears to him in a dream and inspires him to go to war. His love for her becomes subsumed in the higher aim of love for his country.

This early sequence of sections, the first phase in H30, constitutes a *Maud* in miniature: already, the narrative line is established, including the climax (II iv) and resolution (III), and the main figures are sketched, along with clues to the direction of the development of their characterizations and their relationships.

The three sections added later comprise the second phase of the sequence.[6] Inserted between I xii and I xvii are 'So dark a mind within me dwells' (I xv) and 'O let the solid ground' (I xi). The third added section, 'Maud has a garden of roses' (I xiv), is a fair copy transcribed from T36 and inserted between I xvii and I xviii. These inserted sections are representative of the nature of the additions Tennyson would make to the sequence as it developed further. Having established the framework of the story line and sketched the characters who would carry it out, his concerns henceforward would be to elaborate the plot, integrating and intertwining its elements; enrich the characterization; intensify the atmosphere; and increase the dramatic tension.

STAGE B: SPRING–AUTUMN 1854

A group of sections dependent on the H30 sequence appears in T36. Some of the sections may be contemporaneous with those in H30, but there is no firm evidence. Certainly, the transcription of I xiv from T36 into H30 and back again into T36 is one of the indications that both notebooks were in use at the same time. Unlike H30, T36 is a working manuscript which Tennyson used to contain, organize, revise and in some cases draft his sections. It was never intended to resemble the polished 'butcher's books' of *In Memoriam*.[7]

---

[6] Inserted drafts are easily distinguishable from drafts in the first phase of the sequence because in the use of H30 and T36 Tennyson followed his customary practice when composing and compiling long poems in notebooks. He would transcribe fair copies on to the rectos, leaving blank the versos and occasionally one or two subsequent leaves so as to allow drafts or fair copies of newly composed sections to be inserted at the appropriate place in the sequence.

[7] See Shatto and Shaw, pp. 12–17.

Stages of Composition

I   BEFORE PUBLICATION

date	mss, texts	sections
1830s		'See what a lovely shell' (II ii *1–3* only)
1833–4	H13, T21	'Oh! that 'twere possible' (II iv *1–3, 5, 7, 10, 13*)
1837	**1837**	'Stanzas' ('Oh! that 'twere possible' with added stanzas *4, 8, 9, 11, 12*)
1849	Camb	'Go not happy day' (I xvii)
STAGE A: Jan.–March 1854	H30	I xi, xii, xiv, xv, xvii, xviii, xx, III vi *1–4*
STAGE B: spring–autumn	early T36	I i, ii, xiv, iv, v, vi, II i *1* and *2* early version
	middle T36	I i *18, 19*, ix, xiii, II i *1* and *2*

STAGE C:
Aug. 1854– Feb. 1855   T36 series[1]

heading	section	heading	section
'1'	I i, ii	['11'][2]	xvii
'II'	iv	'12'	xviii
'3'	v	'13'	xx
'4'	vi	'14'	xxii
'5'	ix	'15'	II i
'6'	xi	'16'	ii
'7'	xii	['17']	['When all the scum of night . . .'][3]
'8'	xiii		
'9'	xiv		
'10'	xv	['18']	[iv]
		'19'	v
		['20']	[III vi *1–4*]

STAGE D:

Feb.–April	T36 additions	I iii, vii, viii, x, xvi, xxi

STAGE E:

25 April– 7 July	Berg A	Fair copy for printer. Contains all twenty-six sections in T36 (except for omitted '17') arranged in the published order
	P1, P2, P3	Twenty-six sections
	H148	I x *2* revisions
	Trial	Twenty-six sections (as in **1855**)

II   PUBLICATION AND AFTER

28 July	**1855**	Twenty-six sections, headed 'i'–'xxvi'
	H30⁴	I xix *2, 4–7, 9, 10*
	H31	I xix, I i *14–16*, II iii
	1855US	Contains drafts of III vi *5*
	Berg B	Fair copy of I xix for printer
1856	**1856**	Twenty-eight sections (contents of **1855** plus I xix, II iii and stanzas I i *14–16*, I x *4, 6*, III vi *5*), headed 'i'–'xxviii'
1859	**1859**	Division of poem into two parts, headed 'I i–xxii', 'II i–vi'.
1865	**1865**	Division of poem into three parts, headed 'I i–xxii', 'II i–v', 'III vi'

[ ]: Now lost but known to have existed. For details, see Appendix B.
1 The drafts listed may in some cases be the same drafts as those listed for early and middle T36. The serialization itself is understood to represent a stage of composition.
2 The heading only is torn away.
3 See Introduction, pp. 18–19.
4 Only I xix in H30 dates from 1855, not the sections listed in Stage A.

The earliest group of sections in T36 consists of the drafts which were originally fair copies which come at the front of the notebook: 'I hate the dreadful hollow behind the little wood' (I i *1–13, 17* only; Plate 3); 'Long have I sigh'd for a calm: God grant I may find it at last!' (I ii); 'The fault was mine, the fault was mine' (II i *1*), including an early version of II ii *2*; I xiv (a fair copy transcribed from H30); 'A million emeralds break from the ruby-budded lime' (I iv); 'A voice by the cedar tree' (I v); and 'Morning arises stormy and pale' (I vi). These sections are developments of the lyric sequence established in H30, and for the most part they are narratives.[8]

In I i and ii, the background to the narrator's melancholy and to his relationship with Maud is revealed, and her beauty and charm are sketched. In a stanza following I ii which remained mostly unadopted, he struggles against his growing attraction to her by reminding himself of her despised ancestry and by imagining her to be full of guile, which he vows to withstand. In II i *1*, he retrospectively describes the murder of Maud's brother in the pistol duel, and he hints that Maud herself is dead. In an unadopted early version of II i *2* he curses himself and all men moved by anger and lust: they are unfit to live, and he asks God to kill the lot of them. At this point in the notebook comes the fair copy of I xiv transcribed from H30. Then follow I iv and I v. In I iv, he dwells on his melancholy, his fascination with Maud and his despair that she will never take notice of him. He has met her with her brother and misinterprets her blush as a flash of pride. He determines to flee from the madness of love and adopt the resigned life of a philosopher. But in I v, he hears her singing a battle song and is enchanted. In I vi, his dreams that she will return his love alternate with his imagining her to be a deceitful coquette. (This passage develops the vitriolic lines otherwise unadopted following I i *2* earlier on in T36.) The character of Maud's brother is described, a contrast to her own sweetness. She reminds the narrator of his mother, since whose death he has become a misanthrope.

Many observations could be made about this group of sections, but what is most noticeable is the juxtaposition of I i

---

[8] 'T36' is understood to include six surviving folios which have become detached (T36/H). See Appendix B for details.

and ii and II i. Their location at the front of T36 suggests that they were composed about the same time as each other and may indicate that they were composed not long after III, the conclusion they prepare for. The germinal sequence of lyrics and their dramatic concluding section in H30 had given rise to two further dramatic narratives and was expanding into a dramatic poem. With the opening scenes of the first two acts and the entire third act composed, Tennyson now had the whole story before him.

Several kinds of evidence, internal and external, conspire to indicate the probable period of time in which he composed the sections in H30 and T36 described so far. The evidence suggests that those in H30 were composed by March 1854, and that at least some in T36 were composed soon afterwards. Of III (*1–4* only), Tennyson himself recorded in *Eversley*: 'Written when the cannon was heard booming from the battleships in the Solent before the Crimean War.' Emily noted in her Journal on 20 February: 'in the kitchen garden facing the down . . . . we heard the sound of the cannon practising for the Crimea. Their booming sounded somewhat knell-like.' The Baltic fleet embarked from Spithead on 11 March and Parliament declared war against Russia on 22 March. In other words, Tennyson composed III around the middle of the month. Another Journal entry is of interest in this respect. On 16 March Emily gave birth to their second son, and for this day she noted: 'Our Lionel born. A. when he heard of it was watching in the little study under the bedroom and saw Mars in the Lion culminating.' Tennyson incorporated his observation into the first stanza of III. That the contents of III presume the existence of the sections which precede it in H30 is not the only indication that the composition of these sections antedates that of III. In view of Tennyson's customary method of composition and transcription, the location of the fair copy of III at the end of the sequence of fair copies and at the end of the notebook is itself an indication that I xi, xii, xv, xviii and xx (and I xvii and II iv, of course) had all been composed by the time Tennyson composed III.[9]

A clue as to when he began work on the sequence comes at

[9] Whether the inserted section, I xiv, was composed before or after III cannot be determined.

the beginning of T36. It is an early draft of 'To the Rev. F. D. Maurice' which is located on leaves between I i and ii and II i.[10] It was published in the same volume as *Maud*, **1855**, where it is dated 'January, 1854'. The presence of the draft among the sections does not necessarily suggest that the sections were composed around the same time. For, in the first place, the date of composition of adjacent material in Tennyson's notebooks is not usually a reliable means of dating because he was in the habit of reusing old notebooks, so two adjacent poems may in fact have been composed at different times. In the second place, the first sections in T36 have been shown to postdate the composition of III, which is known to have been composed by mid-March 1854. As H30 and T36 were in use simultaneously, what the composition date of the poem does help to indicate is the time when Tennyson began to compose the sequence he completed in March. It seems reasonable to assume that the month in which he settled down to work was the same in which he composed the poem for Maurice, January 1854.

What is more interesting about the presence of the poem among sections of the developing sequence than its date of composition is what it says about Tennyson's moods and thoughts during the winter of 1853–4. The poem is an invitation to Maurice to come to Farringford to visit his godson. It reveals Tennyson's interest in the forthcoming war against Russia, and it affords a charming glimpse of Farringford and of the domestic security and tranquillity which he had finally achieved after decades of itinerancy:

> There's yet one hearth would give you welcome
> (Take it & come) to the Isle of Wight . . .
>   Your presence would be sun in winter . . .
> Listen. I see the golden ray
> Of sunrise on three headlands play,
>   Here falling over elm & ilex
> There on the curve of a lovely bay.
> And here far off from noise of town

---

[10] The draft antedates that in H.Lpr.245 quoted in Ricks (1969), pp. 1022–5.

I watch the twilight mellowing brown
    About a careless-order'd garden
Close to the ridge of a noble down.
We'll have no slander while we dine
But honest talk & wholesome wine
    And only hear the magpie gossip
Garrulous under a roof of pine.
For groves of pine on either hand
To break the blast of winter, stand
    And further on the hoary channel
Tumbles a breaker on chalk & sand
Here, if below the milky steep
Some ship of battle slowly creep . . .
We would not scruple to discuss
Our fleet that keeps the Bosporus
    Nor Oltenitza, nor Sinope,
Ottoman, Emperor, Turk and Russ.[11]

So the evidence suggests that the H30 sequence was composed between January and March 1854. As for the group of sections at the front of T36, there is no firm evidence on which to date them – only internal allusions and some vague comments by Tennyson and Hallam Tennyson. What is certain is that some of the sections take their inspiration from events in March, April and May. But to attribute their composition to these months would be presumptuous. Some sections seem to allude to articles and poems which Tennyson may have read at this time. But the same sections, and others as well, also suggest the influence of items published in the autumn (see notes I i *6–13* and I vi *6* 132–7).

In regard to the spring, Emily's Journal entry for April notes: 'I was taken to see the "wealth of Daffodils" in the wilderness and we admired the rose-coloured & green sheaths of the Lime-leaves as they lay like flowers under the trees.' The lime leaves appear in one of the many allusions to spring

[11] T36 breaks off after 'Sinope'. The last line is quoted from H.Lpr.245. War fever had seized Britain the previous November, when the Turkish fleet was entirely destroyed by a Russian bombardment. In the month Tennyson composed the poem, British and French troops entered the Black Sea. Oltenitza and Sinope were the sites of important battles.

– 'A million emeralds break from the ruby-budded lime' (I iv *1* 1) – in the trio of sections, I iv, v and vi. Emily's Journal was later used by her son when writing the biography of his father. For April and May, Hallam Tennyson notes her reference to the lime leaves, mentions the visit of Edward FitzGerald (who arrived on 25 May for a fortnight) and includes a comment by Tennyson himself: 'My father observed that his best working days were "in the early spring, when Nature begins to awaken from her winter sleep"'.[12] It is reasonable to infer that Tennyson's observation applied to the early spring of 1854, and that his 'best working days' were spent on the composition of new sections, such as some of those at the front of T36.

He alluded to the sections he had composed since January when he wrote to Coventry Patmore the following April. His characteristically querulous tone may be partly responsible for why he should contradict himself within the letter as well as contradict one of his statements later recorded in *Eversley*:

> We have hardly seen a human face since we came here, except the members of our household. Happy, I certainly have not been. I entirely disagree with the saying you quote of happy men not writing poetry. Vexations (particularly long vexations of a petty kind) are much more destructive of the "gay science," as the Troubadours (I believe) called it. I am glad to hear you have been busy. The Baltic fleet I never saw! not a vessel: not a line have I written about it or the war. Some better things I have done, I think successfully. End of my paper. Good-bye.[13]

First he implies that petty vexations have prevented him from writing poetry, mentioning he has not written about the Baltic fleet or the war, but then he says he has indeed been at work: 'Some better things I have done, I think successfully.' This denial conflicts with his account recorded in *Eversley* about the

---

[12] *Memoir* I, 374.

[13] Basil Champneys, *Memoirs and Correspondence of Coventry Patmore*, 2 vols (1900), II, 304–5. The letter can be ascribed to April by Tennyson's reference to Emily being 'a full month from her confinement': Lionel was born on 16 March.

composition of Part III: 'Written when the cannon was heard booming from the battleships in the Solent before the Crimean War.' Equally important, his denial conflicts with the textual evidence: the section referring to the Baltic fleet survives as a fair copy at the end of a sequence of fair copies shown to have been composed between January and March. The tale itself, as evidenced in the manuscript, contradicts the teller. As to which should be trusted, anyone familiar with Tennyson's chronically evasive, misleading and often conflicting responses when asked to reveal information about the genesis and sources of his poetry and about its history of composition is in no doubt. Considered in this light, his letter to Patmore is not confusing, merely characteristic. As for the 'better things' he does confess to having written, these would be the other sections (which specific ones it is impossible to say) conjectured to have been composed by this time.

After he had composed the group which ends with the sections set in springtime and had transcribed them into T36, he then transcribed fair copies of the H30 sequence, arranged as they would be in the published poem: I xi, xii, xiv, xv, xvii, xviii and xx. Interspersed among these two groups of essentially fair copies are later additions or revisions: three stanzas, I i *18* and *19*, and II i *2*; and two new sections, I ix ('I was walking a mile') and I xiii ('Scorn'd, to be scorn'd by one that I scorn'). The two stanzas added to I i develop the characterization of Maud. The revision of II i *2* clarifies a possible obscurity in II i *1* and *2* (early version). In the revision, the narrator explains that the appearance of Maud's ghost from the wood in II i *1* was not an actual event but an hallucination, 'a lying trick of the brain'. The two new sections both function as prefaces to sections previously composed. As to when Tennyson made these additions and revisions, one can only speculate. It might have been from late August onwards, when many accounts record he was hard at work on the sequence. The manuscripts give no clue. Neither are there hints to be found within the sections themselves or in any biographical information.

The one event in Tennyson's life during these months which is well known to have had a bearing on the composition of the sequence was his meeting his neighbour, Sir John

Simeon, at Lionel's christening on 6 June. This was not the first time Tennyson and Simeon had met, as Emily's Journal records. Carlyle had introduced them in London in 1838.[14] The previous year, it will be remembered, Tennyson had published 'Oh! that 'twere possible' in *The Tribute*. When they met the next time, years later at Farringford, they became intimate friends, and they spoke of this poem. Tennyson's statements about Simeon's influence on *Maud* are recorded in *Eversley* and in the notes James Knowles made when Tennyson recited all of *Maud* to him in 1870–1. Tennyson stated in *Eversley*: '"O that 'twere possible" appeared first in the *Tribute*, 1837. Sir John Simeon years after begged me to weave a story round this poem, and so *Maud* came into being'. And to Knowles he commented: 'This poem in "The Tribute" was the nucleus of all the rest of *Maud* – woven round it at the request of Sir John Simeon.'[15]

These statements have always been understood to mean that Simeon instigated the composition of *Maud*, that he was, in the words of Ralph Rader, its 'onlie begetter', and that none of the poem, or only III, had been composed by June.[16] In

[14] Emily's Journal entry for 6 June reads: 'On returning from church we found Sir John Simeon. This was my first introduction to a friend who was to be so much to us both as long as he lived. A. had met him before.' Also see *Tennyson and His Friends*, p. 307 and Martin, p. 242.

[15] Gordon Ray, *Tennyson Reads 'Maud'*, Sedgewick Memorial Lecture 1968, p. 44.

[16] P. 10. Without having examined the manuscripts of the poem, Rader was acute to detect that Tennyson could hardly have composed the stanzas of III, as he says,

> tailored as they are to the character and situation of his highly strung hero, without some idea of their place in a larger dramatic framework. And since Part III is unintelligible without reference to the story begun in "O that 'twere possible," it must from the first have been specifically intended as an extension of that poem.

Rader is not certain if Tennyson composed further sections in the spring of 1854, but he suggests that I iv may have been composed in April on account of its mention of the lime leaves. His general conclusion is that 'until an extensive collation of the widely scattered manuscripts of *Maud* is made, it would be difficult to move beyond conjecture in dating the other sections' (pp. 8, 9).

fact, of course, the evidence of the manuscripts shows otherwise. Why should Tennyson say, then, that it was Simeon who begged him to 'weave a story round this poem, and so *Maud* came into being'? Simply because he very likely had no definite plans to publish the evolving sequence. The history of all his major volumes of poetry is the history of his reluctance to publish them. A shy, arrogant man who often invited criticism but only accepted praise, he recognized the deeply personal nature of his poetry and reserved the right to hug it to himself. He had felt this way about *In Memoriam*, for example, when that sequence was substantially completed, and it was only the intervention of his publisher (and the offer of a large cheque) that determined him to complete the poem and publish it:

> Moxon, when on a visit to Alfred, asked if he had been writing anything of late, with a view to issuing a vol. for him. On which Alfred said emphatically 'No.' Moxon then said surely you have not been idle? Alfred said he had been writing for his own relief & private satisfaction some things that the public would have no interest in, and would not care to see. Moxon asked to see the Ms. It was 'In Memoriam'. Moxon was delighted, &, to Alfreds utter astonishment, offered to publish it and to hand him a cheque to a/c on the spot. If my memory serves me I think the amt. was £300.[17]

Just as Tennyson needed his friends to suggest subjects for him to write about, he needed his friends to urge him to publish. In the past, Arthur Hallam and James Spedding had provided the necessary encouragement. Now it was the turn of John Simeon. Simeon's relationship to *Maud* was not that of 'onlie begetter' but of midwife: he facilitated the emergence of the poem by prompting Tennyson to carry on developing the sequence started six months before and to publish it.

The reminiscences of Simeon's daughter, Louisa Ward, exaggerate the role her father played in the poem's history of

---

[17] An account by Charles Tennyson Turner, as reported by A. J. Symington in a letter to Hallam Tennyson, 11 January 1894, in TRC.

composition, but they provide nevertheless some details which
support this account of it:

> The writing and publication of "Maud" in 1855 was largely
> due to my father.
>   Looking through some papers one day at Farringford
> with his friend, he came upon the exquisite lyric "O that
> 'twere possible," and said, "Why do you keep these
> beautiful lines unpublished?" Tennyson told him that the
> poem had appeared years before in the *Tribute*, an
> ephemeral publication, but that it was really intended to
> belong to a dramatic poem which he had never been able to
> carry out. My father gave him no peace till he had
> persuaded him to set about the poem, and not very long
> after, he put "Maud" into his hand.[18]

The 'papers' in which Simeon came upon 'Oh! that 'twere
possible' would have been the notebook, T36, in which
Tennyson was collecting his sections and into which he had
transcribed the lyric (on leaves now lost following f.36). He
was able to tell Simeon that the lyric was 'really intended to
belong to a dramatic poem' because he had already composed
the framework of the poem, including numerous dramatic
scenes.

If he actually did say that 'he had never been able to carry
out' the poem, this could not mean that he had lost the
inspiration to compose further sections. The lyric sequence
was a form so suited to his imagination that he could generate
new lyrics, elaborating, developing and prefacing what had
gone before, as profusely as a reef of coral generates new
branches. What he surely meant was that he had not felt
compelled to complete the sequence, that he was content to
allow it to develop at the pace of his own inclinations. The
lack of confidence evident in the expression attributed to him
recalls his self-deprecatory rejoinder to Moxon's inquiry
about *In Memoriam*. Indeed, it is easy to imagine him replying
to Simeon's inquiry with the same admission: 'he had been
writing for his own relief & private satisfaction some things

---

[18] *Tennyson and His Friends*, pp. 308–9.

that the public would have no interest in, and would not care to see.'

But the depth of his feelings for Simeon, his most intimate friend in later life, obviously strengthened Simeon's persuasiveness. Henceforward, Tennyson would devote himself to rounding out the established framework of the sequence and to integrating its parts. Hardly more than a year after their reacquaintance, he would be able to put the published poem into Simeon's hand.

STAGE C: AUGUST 1854–FEBRUARY 1855

Before he set to work in earnest, he took a short holiday in August, visiting Hampshire and the West Country to gather material and ideas, as he had done on previous tours, for his long-meditated Arthurian epic. He drafted some lines on Merlin and Vivien in the notebook containing the earliest stage of his developing dramatic poem, but otherwise he did not devote attention to the epic until the next year, after the publication of the sequence in progress.

Upon his return home, he became absorbed in completing the poem, as his son describes:

> It was then that my father worked at "Maud," morning and evening, sitting in his hard high-backed wooden chair in his little room at the top of the house. His "sacred pipes," as he called them, were half an hour after breakfast, and half an hour after dinner, when no one was allowed to be with him, for then his best thoughts came to him. As he made the different poems he would repeat or read them. The constant reading of the new poems aloud was the surest way of helping him to find out any defects there might be. During his "sacred half-hours" and his other working hours and even on the Downs, he would murmur his new passages or new lines as they came to him, a habit which had always been his since boyhood.[19]

Between late August and the spring of 1855, when he transcribed a fair copy of the entire sequence for the printer,

[19] *Memoir*, I, 377–8.

Tennyson added further sections to T36. The majority of his early drafts for all the sections unfortunately no longer survive. The many stubs in T36, sometimes several whole gatherings, may well represent these 'chips of the workshop' which he either polished into the fair copies which come earlier in the notebook or decided to discard altogether. What does survive substantially is evidence of a series of twenty sections, headed with roman numerals. Three of the headed sections are now lost, but their location in the notebook can be reconstructed on the basis of what survives.

As can be seen in the Table, 'Stages of Composition', the series established is that of the poem published in **1855**, with the exception of the six sections to be added before publication. The only sections of the twenty which have not been discussed in the previous stages described above are four which come towards the end of the series.

The section headed '14', the climactic 'Come into the garden, Maud' (I xxii; frontispiece), may well have been conceived in the spring (three drafts survive in T36). It has been shown to be influenced by Persian poetry. Temperamentally defensive about suggestions that his poetry was in any way derivative, Tennyson denied the possibility of such an influence when it was suggested. But he wrote to Forster in March that he had been studying Persian, and his wife and son recorded that he was studying it in May when FitzGerald visited Farringford for a fortnight (see Commentary).

The section headed '16', 'See what a lovely shell' (II ii), includes three stanzas (*1–3*) composed in the 1830s. Clues as to when Tennyson decided to incorporate the short lyric and add six further stanzas may be the references to the Breton coast and to the 'shipwreck'd man'. He was reading Breton history and legends in December 1854. The same month he was shocked to read of the storm in the harbour at Balaclava in which a fleet of English transport ships was wrecked and a thousand men lost (see Commentary).

The section headed '17' no longer survives. The evidence indicates that Tennyson tore it out because he later substituted 'Courage, poor heart of stone!' (II iii). He mentioned the unadopted section to Knowles in 1870–1 when he paused whilst reciting *Maud* to comment on II iii: 'There was another poem about London & the streets at night – "When all the scum of night & hell boils from the cellar & the sewer" was part of it –.'[20] A section in such a desolate and caustic vein would have prepared for the dawn scene in the section headed '18' (II iv) (with its references to 'yellow vapours choke', 'drifts of lurid smoke', 'I loathe the squares and streets') and also for the mad scene in the section headed '19' (II v).

This section II v, 'Dead, long dead', can be dated by the reference to it in Emily's Journal entry for 1 February 1855 (actually an abstract of events throughout the month): 'A. reads some Edgar Poe Poems to me two or three evenings. Then the beginning of Maud & the Mad scene.' It is interesting to note the influence on the section of 'The Premature Burial', a tale by Poe in the edition Tennyson was reading from (see Commentary).

As Hallam Tennyson remarked of his father, Tennyson re-read his new poems constantly. The earliest accounts of his reading parts of the sequence aloud date from September. On the 20th Emily noted: 'A. reads his Idyll to Sir John.'[21] Francis Palgrave was a guest at Farringford during the month and years later recorded his impression of Tennyson's reading:

> 'Maud' was in course of completion . . . . the entrancement, the intoxication (I hope I may be allowed the word), with which we listened for the first time, from the author's lips, and almost in the first flush of creation, to those passionate lyrics of indignation and love and sorrow is before me even now when writing. Nor could anyone, I think, who heard them so recited wonder at the preference which, it is well known, Tennyson at times expressed for this poem.[22]

Another guest was Aubrey de Vere, who stayed through October. His recollection of his visit includes an account of the composition of the sequence. The account is interesting even

---

[20] Ray, 1968, p. 44.

[21] 'Idyll' (from the Greek for 'little poem', commonly translated 'little picture') was a term Tennyson applied broadly to many of his poems before publication.

[22] *Memoir*, II, 493.

though it cannot be trusted in every detail; it was written many years afterwards when de Vere was an old man:

> Tennyson was engaged on his new poem "Maud." Its origin and composition were, as he described them, singular. He had accidentally lighted upon a poem of his own which begins, "O that 'twere possible" . . . It had struck him, in consequence, I think, of a suggestion made by Sir John Simeon, that, to render the poem fully intelligible, a preceding one was necessary. He wrote it; the second poem too required a predecessor; and thus the whole work was written, as it were, *backwards*.[23]

The account could be understood to contradict the other accounts (by W. F. Rawnsley, Louisa Ward and Tennyson himself) about who initiated Tennyson's interest in 'Oh! that 'twere possible.'[24] This element in the history of the composition of *Maud* is one that can never be determined for certain. Moreover, it is of little importance ultimately and of no consequence here. What is interesting in de Vere's account is his description of how *Maud* was 'written, as it were, *backwards*.' That it was indeed is borne out by the evidence of H30: the first written sections which form the early lyric sequence all come from Part I, except, of course, for the final section, III. Perhaps the very first 'preceding' section to be composed was the initial one of the sequence, I xii:

> Birds in the high Hall-garden
> When twilight was falling,
> Maud, Maud, Maud, Maud,
> They were crying and calling. (1–4)

---

[23] *Memoir*, I, 379.

[24] Ralph Rader made a good attempt to reconcile the contradictions, although one need not necessarily agree with his conclusions (pp. 4–10). Another second-hand account is that of D. G. Rossetti, writing to William Allingham in August, 1855: 'I dare say that you know that *Maud* originated in the section, "Would that 'twere possible," etc., which was printed in an annual many years ago and was liked so much (as one hears) by T.'s friends that he kept it in view and gradually worked it up into the story' (quoted by M. L. Howe, 'Dante Gabriel Rossetti's Comments on "Maud"', *Modern Language Notes*, 49 (1934), 291).

How the section might have been directly occasioned by 'Oh! that 'twere possible' is apparent. Moreover, with its reiteration of Maud's name in almost every stanza, and its embryonic anticipations of many of the later developed dramatic elements, the section might at first even have seemed to Tennyson an appropriate beginning to a whole sequence.

By the time de Vere ended his stay, Tennyson had made considerable progress with the composition of his sequence. On 1 November, his publisher arrived expressly to talk business, so it seems, for he stayed only overnight. Emily recorded the reason for his visit: 'Mr Moxon comes and when told that friends wanted the Poem now nearly ready for publication to be published at once he kindly urged that they should be regardless of trouble to himself.' By 'regardless of trouble to himself', Moxon doubtless meant that he would go to the expense of printing as many successive proofs as Tennyson desired. Hallam Tennyson remarked that his father 'always liked to see his poems in print some months and sometimes some years before publication, "for," as he said, "poetry looks better, more convincing, in print."'[25] The description of the poem as 'now nearly ready for publication' probably meant that the majority of the sections in the series headed '1' to '20' had been composed and that Tennyson had the end in view. The series would not be completed until February.

Tennyson must have been motivated by Moxon's visit to compose further sections, as he had been a few years before when Moxon pressed him to prepare *In Memoriam* for publication. But the final stages in the composition of the present poem were set against the background of increasingly serious news from the Crimea. Tennyson's interest in the war even affected his sons. Emily recorded that the baby Lionel 'delights in warlike songs,' and that two-year-old Hallam would roll on the floor exclaiming: 'This is the way the Russians fall when they are killed.' Emily's letters and other Journal entries testify to how closely the Tennysons followed reports in the press throughout the autumn and winter.

---

[25] *Memoir*, I, 190.

In September, allied successes at the Battle of Alma opened
the way to the fall of Sebastopol a year later. In October at
Balaclava, Lord Cardigan, misunderstanding the confused
orders of Raglan, commanded his mounted troops to charge
into the Russian guns. Almost five hundred men were killed,
wounded or unaccounted for. The fatal blunder was swiftly
followed by the severest engagement of the war, the Battle of
Inkerman. Although a victory for the allies, they sustained
more than four thousand casualties. Only a few days later, a
huge number of ships, supplies and men were lost in the storm
that swept through the harbour at Balaclava. The whole of the
winter, British troops suffered miserably, mostly on account of
lack of supplies and absence of sanitary provisions. At home,
political opinion was deeply divided over the conduct of the
war. In January, Lord Aberdeen's government fell, and the
Roebuck Commission was established to inquire into the
conditions of the army before Sebastopol. Alternatively
'disappointed', 'excited', 'frightened', 'shocked' and 'saddened'
by all the events, Tennyson was moved to compose, in only a
few minutes one day in early December, his elegy for
Cardigan's men lost at Balaclava, 'The Charge of the Light
Brigade'.

An indication that he had not neglected his series during
these anxious months is Emily's Journal entry for 10 January:
'A. reads Maud.' Presumably he had composed some new
sections, or revised old ones, and was reading them aloud in
order to 'find out any defects'. Her entry also indicates that
since the discussion with Moxon about publication, Tennyson
had settled on a title. Perhaps it was around this time that he
contemplated a subtitle, but then abandoned the idea because
it seemed redundant, as he later explained to a correspondent:
'Before I published it I thought of calling it "Maud or the
Madness" but again it seemed to me that the countrymen of
Shakespeare are not fools.'[26]

---

[26] Letter [n.d.], TRC. He considered adopting the subtitle even after
publication. A copy of **1855** used to make revisions for **1856** has 'or the
Madness' added in his hand (**1855a**). Proof sheets of **1856** give the title as
Maud; or, the Madness (TRC). The title *Maud; A Monodrama* appeared in the
'Author's Edition' of the *Works* (Henry S. King & Co., 1875; vol. 4), but
never in any of the single-volume editions of the poem. See note 40 below.

That he had completed the entire series of twenty sections by February is evidenced by Emily's Journal entry for 1 February:

> Very cold. The snow folding in and out of the hedge like drapery. A. reads some of the Idylls of Theocritus to me . . . also the first poem of Maud in the rough. Whirling snow in the driving east wind . . . . A. reads some Edgar Poe Poems to me two or three evenings. Then the beginning of Maud & the Mad scene and one night all Maud.

By 'the first poem of Maud in the rough', Emily presumably meant the section headed '1' in T36, which includes I i *1–13, 17–19* and an early version of I ii. 'Then the beginning of Maud & the Mad scene' would comprise the sections from '1' to '14': the whole of Part I composed by then, and section '19', II v. 'All Maud' would comprise all the above sections in addition to sections '15'–'18' (II i, ii, the lost unadopted section and iv).

STAGE D: FEBRUARY–APRIL 1855

It is reasonable to conjecture that the six sections Tennyson added to the series of twenty were composed after he had read it aloud to Emily. She mentioned some of them in a letter to Thomas Woolner on 29 March: 'There are three more tiny poems added to "Maud"' (TRC). The sections are identifiable as additions to T36 because they have no heading numbers. They are drafted either at the end of the notebook, interspersed among groups of stubs (I iii, vii, x, xxi), or at approximately their location in the final order (I viii, xvi).

'Cold and clear-cut face' (I iii) is doubtless one of Emily's 'tiny poems' (with viii and xxi). The addition develops the characterization of Maud, and creates a coda for I ii and a preface for I iv. 'Did I hear it half in a doze' (I vii) enriches the story line by supplying the background to the lovers' relationship. Although some readers of the published poem found the section puzzling, its addition may also have been intended as an attempt at clarification, by explaining the apparent presumption of the narrator's attraction to Maud. 'She came to the village church' (I viii) develops both

Maud's character and the lovers' relationship and serves to
prepare for I xi. 'Sick, am I sick of a jealous dread' (I x)
develops the moody, unstable side of the narrator's character.
The caustic lines in the early drafts, vilifying the Quaker and
Maud's brother, were gradually revised out or toned down,
but the sarcasm which survives in the final version is still
strong enough to recall the slanderous comments about Maud
in the unadopted lines of I i and ii (early version).

'This lump of earth has left his estate' (I xvi) provides a
preface for I xvii. Together with I x, it serves to develop the
character of the brother, to prepare for I xx and, in the
references to the rival lover, to increase dramatic tension.
'Rivulet crossing my ground' (I xxi) creates a preface for I xxii
and also heightens the other kind of tension operative in the
first part of the sequence, the tension resolved, all too briefly
but finally, when the lovers meet in the garden.

What is noticeable about the entire group of added sections
is that all but two (I iii and xxi) are narratives. The general
effect of the additions is to develop characterization and
heighten dramatic tension, propelling the movement of the
first part of the sequence towards the climax in the garden.

STAGE E: 25 APRIL–7 JULY 1855

On the last day of March, Tennyson read 'a good deal of
Maud again' to Emily. Almost a month later, on 25 April, he
read the entire poem at Swainston, the home of Sir John
Simeon. Then he began to write it out for the press (Berg A),
transcribing the twenty-six sections from T36.[27] Moxon
obligingly printed several successive proofs, three of which
survive (P1,2,3), and a Trial issue. Correction and revision of
these took longer than anticipated. One reason for the delay
was domestic: Farringford was being redecorated during the
spring and summer, so the Tennysons vacated it in favour of
London, and then a stay with their friends the Lushingtons, at
Park House, near Maidstone. From here, Tennyson could go
up to London to read proofs, and (presumably) to ask Moxon
to print yet another state. Emily wrote from Park House in
June to Thomas Woolner: 'Alfred is with us; he came last

---

[27] Emily's Journal (25 April) and *Memoir* I, 384 (based on the Journal).

night. He seems very much fagged by London hours. It is a disappointment to find *Maud* yet where she was' (TRC).

In July, they visited Oxford, where Tennyson was awarded the honorary degree of DCL. He received it together with two heroes of the Crimea, Sir George de Lacy Evans and Sir John Burgoyne (known as 'the second man in the Eighth army'). Inside the Sheldonian, the undergraduates gave three shouts, one for *In Memoriam*, one for Alma and one for Inkerman. The Tennysons reached home on 7 July, and 'the last touch was put to *Maud* before giving it to the publisher.' As Emily noted, this 'added to the delight of returning'.[28]

The 'last touch' was that put to the Trial issue. It introduced substantive verbal changes from P3 in twenty-seven places. The proofs altogether introduced a dozen significant changes. The major revisions, in all the stages from Berg A onwards, were those to I x. Tennyson alluded to them in early July when he wrote to a friend to explain why the poem had not yet been published: 'these poems when printed I found needed considerable elision and so the book has hung on hand. It will now be ready I suppose in a week or so and I have ordered Moxon to send you a copy.'[29]

FROM PUBLICATION ONWARDS

Maud, and Other Poems, was published on 28 July.[30] Tennyson's last volume, *In Memoriam*, had been published anonymously. The new volume not only bore his name but also advertised, perhaps with a little pride, his new honorary degree and his office in the royal household: 'by Alfred Tennyson, D.C.L., Poet Laureate' (Plate 1). The 'other poems' were some he had composed since 1850: 'The Brook; an Idyl'; 'The Letters'; 'Ode on the Death of the Duke of Wellington'; 'The Daisy'; 'To the Rev. F. D. Maurice'; 'Will'; and 'The Charge of the Light Brigade'. This last poem had become a great favourite with the soldiers in the Crimea since its publication in December, and in August Tennyson arranged for it to be

[28] Emily's Journal (1 May–7 July); *Memoir* I, 384–5.
[29] To F. G. Tuckerman. A typed transcript of the letter (TRC) incorrectly ascribes it to February 1855, but Charles Tennyson's Notebooks date it July.
[30] *Athenæum*, No. 1448 (28 July 1855), 859.

M A U D,

AND OTHER POEMS.

BY

ALFRED TENNYSON, D.C.L.,

POET LAUREATE.

LONDON:

EDWARD MOXON, DOVER STREET.

1855.

1   Title-page of the first edition

printed on fly-leaves and sent out to Scutari.[31] The volume sold for five shillings and sold in the thousands: booksellers ordered 4,000 copies in advance and had sold 8,000 by October.[32] By the spring of 1856, Tennyson had made enough money from the sales to enable him to realize a dream he had long shared with Emily, the purchase of Farringford.[33]

Maud had not been published a month, however, before he began to revise it. In the first fortnight of August, he composed what Emily described as 'the saddest possible little poem', 'Courage, poor heart of stone' (II, iii) (see Commentary). It took the place of the vitriolic section he had decided not to publish. Its role in the sequence is self-evident. By September he had written a further section, as Emily noted in her Journal (18 September): 'after a glorious walk on the Down he read me a new poem in Maud.' This would have been 'Her brother is coming back to-night' (I xix). One of the stanzas may well have been influenced by the story of 'The Betrothed Children', published in *Household Words* the previous year (see Commentary).

The composition of I xix was Tennyson's immediate response to the harsh criticism of an anonymous reviewer in the *Daily Express* (11 August) and of his friend, Charles Kingsley, in the September issue of *Fraser's*.[34] Perhaps the

[31] E.T. to John Forster, 9 August [1855], TRC; *Memoir* I, 386–7.

[32] *Athenæum*, No. 1448 (28 July 1855), 859. On 1 August, *Publishers' Circular* exclaimed: 'Mr Tennyson's new work . . . was published last week by Mr Moxon, and most favourably received by the booksellers, who subscribed for upwards of 4000!' (XVIII, 305), XVIII (15 Oct. 1855), 385. In this survey of the post-publication history of *Maud*, I am very indebted to the meticulous work of Edgar F. Shannon, Jr, 'The Critical Reception of Tennyson's "Maud"', *PMLA*, 68 (June 1953), 397–417. Shannon gives further details of publication history and suggests that a subsequent drop in sales was the result of the many unfavourable reviews (p. 406).

[33] *Memoir* I, 412. In 1854 they had begun to find Farringford expensive to live in, and with the assistance of Edward Lear were reluctantly looking for another house (see E.T.'s letters to various correspondents between 1854 and June 1856, in TRC).

[34] Coventry Patmore had read Kingsley's review by 12 September (Champneys, 1900, II, 181). The causal link between these reviews and the composition of I xix was identified by Shannon (pp. 410–11), although he did not attempt to date the composition of the section. His discussion of Tennyson's response to the reviews is, of course, thorough and perceptive.

other additions he made to **1855** (I i *14–16*, I x *4, 6* and III vi *5*) were also composed during the autumn. Edgar Shannon has demonstrated how all the stanzas are responses to the unfavourable criticism of reviews published in the *Critic, Weekly Dispatch* and *Tait's Edinburgh Magazine*.[35] There were no further major changes to the poem after the addition of the new sections and stanzas in **1856** except for his final response to the reviewers: the division of the sequence into two parts in **1859** and into three parts in **1865**.[36] It is interesting to note that two of the principal objects of the reviewers' censure, the obscurities in the plot and the occasional strident tones of the narrator, were what Tennyson himself had identified as weaknesses during the course of composition and had, accordingly, revised. Clearly, he did not revise them enough before the poem was published to please the reviewers. But in responding to their criticisms he was merely reduplicating his own responses to his self-criticism.

Tennyson's reading *Maud* aloud to his friends became an activity which would haunt him like a passion for the rest of his life. He read it so often that he could even make fun of himself for doing so. One day in 1865, William Allingham walked into the drawing room at Farringford and saw Tennyson with a book in his hand: 'He accosted me, "Allingham, would it disgust you if I read 'Maud'? Would you expire?"' Even the loyalty of Emily sometimes flagged, as she herself once noted: 'Ally read Maud again. I left.'[37]

The reasons for his preoccupation with reading the poem aloud are varied and complex, but one reason, surely, was that the approval his friends would be obliged to display would help to assuage the ego wounded by the reviewers. The most famous of all the occasions on which he read *Maud* was two months after the poem had been published, at the

---

[35] Pp. 408–11.

[36] For the suggestion that the division into parts was inspired by the comments of Peter Bayne, see Shannon, p. 412. Allingham recorded that on 25 June 1865, Tennyson read him 'some additions recently made' (*Diary*, p. 118). There is no other record of the existence of these 'additions'. Either Allingham was mistaken or Tennyson changed his mind about revising the sequence and destroyed his drafts.

[37] Allingham's *Diary*, p. 118.

2 *Tennyson Reading 'Maud'*, by D. G. Rossetti
Pen and ink with grey wash, 21 × 15 cm.

This is the second of two copies Rossetti made of the original, sketched at the Brownings' on 27 September 1855. William Michael Rossetti, who was also present, described the occasion: 'Tennyson, seated on a sofa in a characteristic attitude, and holding the volume near his eyes (for he was decidedly short-sighted, though one would hardly think so from his descriptive poems), read *Maud* right through . . . So far as I remember, the Poet Laureate neither saw what Dante was doing, nor knew of it afterwards' (*Dante Gabriel Rossetti: His Family Letters*, 1895, I, 190–1).

Brownings' house in Dorset Street, Manchester Square. Browning's sister was there, and the Rossetti brothers. Tennyson sat on the sofa, one hand holding a copy of *Maud*, the other grasping his left leg which was nervously drawn up under him. Dante Rossetti sketched him unawares (Plate 2). Mrs Browning, who occupied the other end of the sofa, described the occasion for a friend soon afterwards:

> One of the pleasantest things which has happened to us here is the coming down on us of the Laureate, who, being in London for three or four days from the Isle of Wight, spent two of them with us, dined with us, smoked with us, opened his heart to us (and the second bottle of port), and ended by reading 'Maud' through from end to end, and going away at half-past two in the morning. If I had had a heart to spare, certainly he would have won mine. He is captivating with his frankness, confidingness, and un-exampled *naiveté*! Think of his stopping in 'Maud' every now and then – 'There's a wonderful touch! That's very tender. How beautiful that is!' Yes, and it *was* wonderful, tender, beautiful, and he read exquisitely in a voice like an organ, rather music than speech.[38]

A somewhat less rapturous description, given by Rossetti to Allingham, mentions the two sections recently composed, I xix and II iii, as well as Tennyson's hypersensitivity to criticism:

> I was never more amused in my life than by Tennyson's groanings and horrors over the reviews of Maud, which poem he read through to us, spouting also several sections to be introduced in a new edition. I made a sketch of him reading, which I gave to Browning, and afterwards a duplicate of it for Miss Siddall. His conversation was really one perpetual groan, and I am sure during the two long

---

[38] Virginia Surtees, *The Paintings and Drawings of Dante Gabriel Rossetti (1828–1882): A Catalogue Raisonné*, 1971, pp. 198–9; *The Letters of Elizabeth Barrett Browning*, ed. F. G. Kenyon (1897), II, 213. The letter is ascribed to October by Kenyon.

evenings I spent in his company he repeated the same stories about anonymous letters he gets, etc., at the very least 6 or 8 times in my hearing, besides an odd time or two, as I afterwards found, that he told them to members of the company in private. He also repeated them to me again, walking home together.[39]

Tennyson's apologist for the poem was his friend at Ventnor on the Isle of Wight, Dr Robert James Mann. In 1856, Mann published *Tennyson's 'Maud' Vindicated: An Explanatory Essay*, a lengthy and detailed defence which, incidentally, described the poem as a 'mono-drama'. Readers familiar with Tennyson's comments and notes on *Maud* and, indeed, with his notes on his other poems, will recognize in the tones and expressions of Dr Mann's essay those of Tennyson himself. There is hardly any doubt, as A. Dwight Culler has suggested, that both the term 'monodrama' (current in the 1850s) and the entire substance of the essay derive from Tennyson, a result of his conversations with Mann and his comments whilst reading aloud.[40]

The publication of *'Maud' Vindicated* made little impact on the critics, but Tennyson was grateful to Mann nevertheless:

Moxon was here the other day & told me he sent your essay to all the Reviews & they took no notice, the snobs. I suppose they durst not, have you lost upon it? I fear so. I have heard it praised by men who knew, & should like to learn that you are no sufferer by your chivalrous defence of the heroine.[41]

Tennyson himself, of course, continued to staunchly defend his heroine for the rest of his life. But by the time *'Maud' Vindicated* was published, he had already returned to the subject which had held his fancy since boyhood, the *Morte*

---

[39] Quoted in Howe, p. 292. The sketch reproduced in Plate 2 was made after the one Rossetti mentions.

[40] *The Poetry of Tennyson*, 1977, pp. 200–1. Also see Culler's thorough account of the history of the monodrama, 'Monodrama and the Dramatic Monologue', *PMLA*, 90 (1975), 366–85.

[41] *Materials*, II, 140.

d'Arthur. He had begun reading his new 'picture of Nimue and Merlin' to Emily during February 1856, and by March had progressed to the extent that she could note: 'He has set to work in earnest on the poem now.'

RECAPITULATION

From the germ of 'Oh! that 'twere possible' developed a lyric sequence, originally of six sections, with a dramatic structure (H30). It told a love story in which Maud and the narrator shared the foreground. Augmented by lyric prefaces and set-pieces and by narrative links, the love story itself became the emotional germ of a poetic drama. The hitherto shadowy figures of the brother and rival lover were developed, and new minor characters were introduced (the dilettante priest, the peace orator, the parents of Maud and of the narrator). Subsidiary themes of a social nature were introduced to serve as a foil for the emotions generated in the narrator by his love for Maud. These themes also became the focus for the same kind of cynical, suspicious and angry feelings which the narrator had expressed for Maud in some early drafts but which were toned down or revised out as the sequence developed. Other violent feelings were revised out, but only in the later stages of composition: the lost section containing the line 'When all the scum of night & hell boils from the cellar & the sewer'; and the virulent attacks on the aristocracy and governmental maladministration in I x.

In expanding the sequence, first into a series of twenty sections (T36), then twenty-six (**1855**) and finally twenty-eight (**1856**), Tennyson was concerned to complicate the plot and tighten the structure, increase dramatic tension, deepen character interest and intensify atmosphere. The development of these elements combined to overshadow the character of Maud. A figure of stature in the early lyric sequence, she is gradually shouldered out of the foreground by the more individualized and active minor characters and, indeed, by the narrator himself. While the characterization of Maud recedes as the sequence develops, that of the narrator increases. The subsidiary themes and incidents which are introduced all provide a field for the narrator to display and play out his own character. A scene of great dramatic potential for example, the duel with the brother and his death, is displaced from the action so as not to distract from the real drama of the poem, the chamber drama of the narrator's own interiority.

2   *Literary and Biographical Influences*

The name of Maud was not a common one in the nineteenth century until Tennyson's poem made it so. He may have derived the name, it has been suggested, from Lady Maud, a character in an anonymous neo-medieval ballad published in the same volume of *The Tribute* as his own 'Stanzas', the ballad entitled 'The Wicked Nephew'.[42] Maud would be a suitable name in such a piece, for it is a Norman-French form of the old German 'Mahthildis', a compound name meaning 'might', 'strength' and 'battle', 'strife'.[43] It would be interesting to speculate whether Tennyson had encountered this etymology during his early studies of the medieval chronicles, legends and romances associated with King Arthur and had later, perhaps inspired by the ballad of 'The Wicked Nephew', or perhaps not needing inspiration at all, adopted it as appropriate to the girl who would enchant the narrator with her singing of:

[42] See George O. Marshall, Jr, 'Gift-books, Tennyson, and *The Tribute* (1837)', *Georgia Review*, 16 (1962), 463–4. It should be remembered that, at the time Tennyson began to compose *Maud*, he did not have a copy of *The Tribute* to hand: this was why his father-in-law was asked to transcribe 'Oh! that 'twere possible' (see Introduction, p. 1 above). *Princess Maude*, incidentally, was the name of the ship on which Tennyson sailed from Ramsgate to Ostend in 1846 (*Letters*, p. 258). *Maude Talbot* was the title of a novel (1854) by Holme Lee, a lady novelist whose work was admired by Dickens. In 1854 John Greenleaf Whittier composed *Maud Müller*, the theme of which is curiously similar to *Maud*. The ballad tells of lovers whose different rank prevents them from marrying: Maud Müller is a village maiden and her lover a judge. They each make unsatisfactory marriages within their own class, and ever afterwards they look back on the past, musing: 'It might have been.' The connection between the poems is merely coincidental: *Maud Müller* was first published in the newspaper *The National Era* (Washington, DC) on 28 December 1854 and then in a collection by Whittier, *The Panorama, and Other Poems* (Boston) in 1856.

[43] E. G. Withycombe, *The Oxford Dictionary of English Christian Names*, third edition, 1977, pp. 212–13. That one of Tennyson's sisters was named Matilda would give him a reason to be familiar with the origins of the name.

> A passionate ballad gallant and gay,
> A martial song like a trumpet's call! . . .
> Singing of men that in battle array,
> Ready in heart and ready in hand,
> March with banner and bugle and fife
> To the death, for their native land.
>					(I v *1*)

It is well known that the form, tenor and content of *Maud* are generally indebted to the traditions of both German and French romanticism and to the native influences of the gothic novel and spasmodic poetry. The influence of Persian poetry on I xxii was first noticed by a contemporary reviewer. Of specific literary sources for the poem, a multitude of possibilities has been suggested. Confidence in a particular one does not preclude confidence in the rest, for as Thackeray said of Tennyson: 'he reads all sorts of things, swallows them and digests them like a great poetical boa-constrictor as he is.'[44] Among the proposed possible sources are: *Romeo and Juliet* (Tennyson himself referred to the poem as 'a little *Hamlet*'); *The Bride of Lammermoor*; Keats's 'Isabella'; and Kingsley's *Alton Locke*. To these could be added a poem by Thomas Hood and a novel by Bulwer-Lytton.

Hood's 'The Dream of Eugene Aram, the Murderer' (1829; 1831) tells of a melancholy, bookish man who murders his victim for gold, flings the body into a stream in a lonely wood, and is afterwards haunted in his sleep by his guilty deed. The murder scene contains some interesting verbal parallels with *Maud*, I i, but the most striking parallels between the poems occur in the description of Aram haunted in his sleep (see Commentary for II iv and v).

The plot of Bulwer's first novel, *Falkland* (1827), anticipates *Maud* in a remarkable number of ways. Falkland is a melancholy intellectual in the tradition of German romanticism. An orphan and a recluse, he wanders introspectively in the woods and grounds of a deserted house near his own. He falls in love with the beautiful girl who comes to live there. The owner of the house, a member of Parliament (the girl's

---

[44] Quoted in Gordon Ray, *Thackeray: The Uses of Adversity*, 1955, p. 284.

husband), invites his neighbours for a dinner followed by a dance. The lovers make a secret assignation in the grounds after dark but are discovered. The girl dies soon afterwards. Falkland suffers a period of near madness. Throughout his tortured fantasies, he is visited at his bedside by the ghost of his lost love. He recovers and goes abroad (to Spain) to fight for freedom and a just cause.[45]

The novel shares much of the same literary inheritance as *Maud* and so contains many archetypal elements and scenes characteristic of the inheritance. Nevertheless, the correspondences seem too numerous to be coincidental. It is well known that Tennyson's personal hatred of Bulwer was based on the spiteful criticisms of his poetry as effeminate and derivative that Bulwer had published since 1833. Tennyson was especially stung by 'The New Timon' (1846) for its attack on 'School-Miss Alfred' and her 'jingling medley of purloin'd conceits,/ Outbabying Wordsworth, and outglittering Keates.' His infuriated, caustic reply, 'The New Timon, and the Poets', was published in *Punch* the same year (see Commentary for I x 2). There is no doubt that Tennyson's feelings for Bulwer inspired the sarcastic description of the dandified rival lover in *Maud*.[46] In so far as *Maud* seems to appropriate and invigorate the plot of *Falkland*, it is not inconceivable that Tennyson partly intended his poem to castigate Bulwer yet again by recalling his first embarrassing attempt at novel-writing.

An important influence on the passages in *Maud* concerned with the Crimean War and other contemporary issues was Tennyson's reading of newspapers and periodicals. He was interested in politics at least as early as his years at Cambridge, and he had long harboured strong feelings against France and Russia. 'Russia has always been a bugbear to him,' a friend observed.[47] Tennyson may have retired to the remoteness of the Isle of Wight, but he kept his ear to the ground of contemporary life. A few months after the publi-

[45] This is the broad outline of the plot: it differs from *Maud* in some respects. I am indebted to Dr Jim Sait and his fellow contributors to 'The Enchanted Moan' (privately issued, TRC) for noticing the similarities between *Maud* and *Falkland*.

[46] Rader was the first to associate Bulwer with the 'sartorial excesses of Maud's brother (and her wealthy suitor)' (p. 143, n. 7).

[47] Mangles' *Diary*, 28 October 1872, p. 128.

cation of *Maud*, he described the achievement of his poem to a
correspondent: 'I took a man constitutionally diseased & dipt
him into the circumstances of the time & took him out on
fire.'[48] The hostile sentiments towards France which he
vented in his patriotic poems of 1852 were simply transferred
to Russia in the war passages of *Maud* and then supplemented
by allusions to 'the circumstances of the time' gleaned from
the press.

A number of close parallels can be found between passages
in *Maud* and articles in contemporary periodicals as well as
poems in some of the many volumes of poetry published
during 1854–5 which condemned various social evils and
extolled the virtues of war and patriotism. That Tennyson
owned copies of some of these volumes strengthens the
suspicion that they had a bearing on *Maud*. In considering the
political feelings expressed in the poem, what should of course
be remembered is that none of the attitudes about war and
peace was peculiar to Tennyson. The same ideas, imagery,
diction and violent passion appeared in periodicals and in
other poems published throughout the course of the war.
There is no doubt that the political passages in *Maud* resulted
from deeply held convictions, but Tennyson's convictions
were those of most Englishmen of his day, and the passages
merely echoes of familiar catch-phrases and popular sentiments.

In addition to his patriotic poems, several other of his
earlier poems anticipate, in different ways, aspects of *Maud*.
What he described as the 'peculiarity' of the poem, 'that
different phases of passion in one person take the place of
different characters', was for him a new direction in form.[49]
His monodrama nevertheless owes something to such earlier
monologues as 'Ulysses', 'Tiresias' and 'St Simeon Stylites'.
The situation of the lovers in the poem is reminiscent of
'Locksley Hall' and 'Edwin Morris'.

Tennyson was one of those poets, as FitzGerald said, 'who
deal in their own susceptibilities', and in many respects it is
his susceptibilities that Tennyson most deals with in *Maud*.[50]
The extent to which his own life provided a source for the

[48] To Archer Thompson Gurney, 6 December 1855.
[49] *Eversley*, p. 271.
[50] Quoted in Martin, p. 274.

poem was first brought to light by his grandson, who published details of the family history which had been excluded from the biography by Tennyson's son. In addition to revealing the mental instability and addiction to drink and drugs which contributed to the death of Tennyson's father and plagued the lives of his father's sons, Sir Charles also discussed what he quaintly termed 'Alfred's early love experiences', his relationships with Emily Sellwood, Sophy Rawnsley and Rosa Baring.

The influence these relationships may have had on the composition of *Maud* was ingeniously explored by Ralph Wilson Rader in *Tennyson's 'Maud': The Biographical Genesis* (1963), a landmark in Tennyson scholarship. Rader's concern was to propose associations between specific events and relationships of Tennyson's youth and the poem of his maturity. In particular, he proposed Rosa Baring as the foremost model for Maud. To a lesser extent, he suggested, Sophy Rawnsley and Emily Sellwood also served as models.

In many respects, the case Rader puts is convincing. The autobiographical genesis of the poem is undeniable. *Maud* was to Tennyson what *David Copperfield* was to Dickens, his 'favourite child', and for the same reason. What could be argued is that an insistence on specificity of identification not only narrows and flattens the character called Maud but also falsifies the essence of the poem.

From the earliest stages of composition onwards, Maud is as idealized a figure as the subjects of 'Claribel', 'Lilian', 'Isabel', 'Margaret', 'Madeline' and 'Adeline', Tennyson's insipid poems of the 1830s. The Dark Lady of the *Sonnets* and the Arthur of *In Memoriam* are more individualized as characters than the character of Maud. The indistinctness of her characterization suggests that her function in the poem is not as a character at all but as the obscure object of the narrator's desire. The intentional obscurity in the depiction of Maud is analogous to the ambiguous source of emotion in 'Tears, idle tears, I know not what they mean.' Considering the impregnable degree of Tennyson's self-absorption, it is difficult to believe that any woman, or synthesis of women, or indeed, anything external to Tennyson himself could have occasioned the composition of his 'favourite child'. The

combined impact on *Maud* of his wide reading, his social and
political passions and even his feelings for those he had loved
and lost was as nothing compared to the chief source of the
poem and its primary influence: the depths and unreconciled
complexities of his own self. Simply, he looked in his heart and
wrote.

3   *The Present Text*

The text of this edition is that of the poem in the one-volume
edition of the *Works* published by Macmillan in February 1889
(henceforward referred to as **1889**). This is a reprint with
slight corrections of the January 1884 edition. Hallam
Tennyson records that his father 'carefully revised' his poems
for the one-volume edition published in 1884 (*Memoir* II, 310).

In its text of *Maud*, **1889** introduces verbal changes in six
places and twenty-seven changes in punctuation. Tennyson
made no subsequent revisions. The present edition does not
alter the spelling or punctuation of the chosen text. Tennyson
was himself scrupulous in these matters, as the significant
variants and minor variants show. In the transcription of
readings from the manuscripts, however, the present edition
does not retain his use of the long 's'.

MAUD
The Text

I hate the dreadful hollow behind the little wood
Its lips in the field above are dabbled with blooded heath
The redribb'd ledges drip with a silent horror of blood
And Echo there, whatever is ask'd her, answers "death"

For there in the ghastly pit long since - a body was found
His who had given me life O father O God was it well
Mangled & flatten'd & crush'd & dented into the ground
There yet lies the crag that fell with him when he fell.

Did he slay himself? who knows? for a great speculation had fail'd
And ever he murmur'd & ever wann'd with despair
And out he walk'd when the wind like a broken worldling wail'd
And the flying gold of the woodlands drove thro' the air

I remember the time for the roots of my hair were stirr'd
By a shuffled step, by a dead weight trail'd, by a whisper'd fright
Till my pulses closed their gates on my heart as I heard
The shrill-edged shriek of a mother divide the shuddering night.

Villainy somewhere! whose? one says we are villains all.
Not he: his honest fame should at least by me be maintain'd
And that old man now lord of the broad estate & the Hall
Dropt off gorged from a scheme that had left us flaccid & drain'd

Why do they prate of the blessings of Peace: we have made them a curse
Pickpockets, each hand lusting for all that is not his own
And, lust of gain in the spirit of Cain is it better or worse
Than the heart of the citizen hissing in war on his own hearthstone

3 'I hate the dreadful hollow behind the little wood'.
Part I i in T36, numbered '1' in the original
series of twenty sections

PART I

i

1

I hate the dreadful hollow behind the little wood,
Its lips in the field above are dabbled with blood-red heath,
The red-ribb'd ledges drip with a silent horror of blood,
And Echo there, whatever is ask'd her, answers 'Death.'

I i *1–19* 1–76] H27 *(1 only)*, T36/H *(only 1–13, 17, and two drafts of 18, and 19 written as one stanza including unadopted lines)*, [Berg A] *(on now lost ff. 1, 2)*, and P1–3 *and* Trial *and* **1855** *(1–13, 17–19 only)*, H 149 *(14–16 only)*, **1856–**.

I i *1* 1–4] H27–.

H27 is an early version virtually lacking 2 *and having the other lines spaced well apart:*

(1)	O rockribb'd hollow behind the wood
(2)	The *[intentional blank]* lip
(3)	Thy redribb'd ledges ever drip
(3)	With a silent horror of blood
(4)	Whatever is ask'd her answers whispering death

2

For there in the ghastly pit long since a body was
    found,   5
His who had given me life—O father! O God! was
    it well?—
Mangled, and flatten'd, and crush'd, and dinted into
    the ground:
There yet lies the rock that fell with him when he fell.

3

Did he fling himself down? who knows? for a vast
    speculation had fail'd,
And ever he mutter'd and madden'd, and ever wann'd
    with despair,   10
And out he walk'd when the wind like a broken
    worldling wail'd,
And the flying gold of the ruin'd woodlands drove
    thro' the air.

I i *2–13* 5–52] T36/H–.

I i *2* 5–8]

6   had] P2–; has T36/H, P1.

8   rock] P2–; crag T36/H, P1.

I i *3* 9–12]

9   fling himself down?] P3–; slay himself? T36/H; kill himself? T36/H
        alternative reading, P1, 2.

     vast] **1856**–; great T36/H–**1855**.

10   mutter'd and madden'd,] P2–; murmur'd 'ruin' T36/H 1st reading;
        murmur'd & madden'd T36/H 2nd reading, murmur'd and madden'd,
        P1.

11   broken] T36/H 2nd reading–; ruin'd T36/H 1st reading.

12   ruin'd woodlands] T36/H 2nd reading–; scatter'd woodland T36/H 1st
        reading.

4

I remember the time, for the roots of my hair were
    stirr'd
By a shuffled step, by a dead weight trail'd, by a
    whisper'd fright,
And my pulses closed their gates with a shock on my
    heart as I heard   15
The shrill-edged shriek of a mother divide the
    shuddering night.

5

Villainy somewhere! whose? One says, we are
    villains all.
Not he: his honest fame should at least by me be
    maintained:
But that old man, now lord of the broad estate and
    the Hall,
Dropt off gorged from a scheme that had left us flaccid
    and drain'd.   20

I i *4* 13–16]

15 And my pulses closed their gates with a shock] P2–;

    Till my pulses closed their gates at once T36/H 1st reading;

    Till my listening pulses closed their gates T36/H 2nd reading;

    Till my pulses closed their gates with a shock P1.

16 shrill-edged] T36/H, P2–; shrill-raged P1.

I i *5* 17–20]

19 But] P2–; And T36/H, P1.

6

Why do they prate of the blessings of Peace? we have
    made them a curse,
Pickpockets, each hand lusting for all that is not its
    own;
And lust of gain, in the spirit of Cain, is it better or
    worse
Than the heart of the citizen hissing in war on his
    own hearthstone?

7

But these are the days of advance, the works of the
    men of mind,   25
When who but a fool would have faith in a tradesman's
    ware or his word?
Is it peace or war? Civil war, as I think, and that of
    a kind
The viler, as underhand, not openly bearing the sword.

8

Sooner or later I too may passively take the print
Of the golden age—why not? I have neither hope
    nor trust;   30
May make my heart as a millstone, set my face as a
    flint,
Cheat and be cheated, and die: who knows? we are
    ashes and dust.

I i *6* 21–4]

22 its] P1–; his T36/H.

I i *8* 29–32]

30 why not?] T36/H 1st reading, P2–; who knows? T36/H 2nd reading,
    P1.

32 who knows?] T36/H 1st reading, P2–; why not? T36/H 2nd reading,
    P1.

9

Peace sitting under her olive, and slurring the days
    gone by,
When the poor are hovell'd and hustled together, each
    sex, like swine,
When only the ledger lives, and when only not all
    men lie; 35
Peace in her vineyard—yes!—but a company forges
    the wine.

10

And the vitriol madness flushes up in the ruffian's
    head,
Till the filthy by-lane rings to the yell of the trampled
    wife,
And chalk and alum and plaster are sold to the poor
    for bread,
And the spirit of murder works in the very means of
    life, 40

I i *9* 33–6]

33 slurring] T36/H, P2–; cheering P1.

I i *10* 37–40]

38 filthy] T36/H 2nd reading–; reechy T36/H 1st reading.

39 And] **1865**–; While T36/H–**1864**.

11

And Sleep must lie down arm'd, for the villainous
    centre-bits
Grind on the wakeful ear in the hush of the moonless
    nights,
While another is cheating the sick of a few last gasps,
    as he sits
To pestle a poison'd poison behind his crimson lights.

12

When a Mammonite mother kills her babe for a burial
    fee,   45
And Timour-Mammon grins on a pile of children's
    bones,
Is it peace or war? better, war! loud war by land and
    by sea,
War with a thousand battles, and shaking a hundred
    thrones.

I i *11* 41–4]

41 And] T36/H 3rd reading–; When T36/H 1st reading; Poor T36/H 2nd
    reading.

43] P3–; While the chemist cheats the sick of his last poor sleep & sits
    T36/H 1st reading; While another is cheating the sick of his last few
    gasps, as he sits T36/H 2nd reading, P1 (. . . gasps . . . sits,); While
    another is cheating the sick of a last few gasps, as he sits P2.

44 a] T36/H 2nd reading–; his T36/H 1st reading.

I i *12* 45–8]

45 kills] T36/H 2nd reading–; poisons T36/H 1st reading.

46 grins] T36/H 2nd reading–; sits T36/H 1st reading.

13

For I trust if an enemy's fleet came yonder round by the hill,
And the rushing battle-bolt sang from the three-decker
    out of the foam,   50
That the smooth-faced snubnosed rogue would leap
    from his counter and till,
And strike, if he could, were it but with his cheating
    yardwand, home.——

14

What! am I raging alone as my father raged in his mood?
Must *I* too creep to the hollow and dash myself down and die
Rather than hold by the law that I made, nevermore
    to brood   55
On a horror of shatter'd limbs and a wretched
    swindler's lie?

I i *13* 49–52]

49 trust] T36/H 2nd reading–; do not doubt T36/H 1st reading.

    came yonder round] T36/H 2nd reading–; came round T36/H 1st reading.

50 battle-bolt sang] T36/H 2nd reading (battlebolt . . .), P1–; thunderbolt leapt T36/H 1st reading.

51 leap] T36/H 2nd reading–; jump T36/H 1st reading.

I i *14–16* 53–64] H31, **1855Va**, **1856**–; *not in* T36/H, Berg A, P1–3, Trial, **1855**.

I i *14* 53–6]

53 What!] **1855Va**, **1856**–; O God, H31.

    raging] **1855Va**, **1856**–; raving H31.

    raged] **1855Va**, **1856**–; raved H31.

54 hollow] **1855Va**, **1856**–; pit H31.

56] H31 2nd reading (On . . . a [*intentional blank*]), **1855Va**, **1856**–;

    On the sights that I saw [*intentional blank*] the murd [*presumably* murder *or* murderer's] work of the lie. H31 1st reading.

15

Would there be sorrow for *me?* there was *love* in the
    passionate shriek,
Love for the silent thing that had made false haste to the
    grave—
Wrapt in a cloak, as I saw him, and thought he would
    rise and speak
And rave at the lie and the liar, ah God, as he used   60
    to rave.

I i *15* 57–60]

57   Would there be] H31 2nd reading (wd . . .), **1855Va, 1856–**; Who wd
      H31 1st reading

     me?] **1855Va, 1856–**; me H31.

     love] **1855Va, 1856–**; love H31.

59   rise and speak] **1855Va** 2nd reading, **1856–**; wd stir wd speak H31 1st
      reading; would stir & speak **1855Va** 1st reading; wd rise & wd speak
      H31 2nd reading.

60   **1856–**; Wd curse with his dreadful face on his shatterd limbs & rave
      H31 1st reading; Wd rave at the lie & the liar as often he used to rave
      H31 2nd reading.

60 ∧ 61] *An unadopted stanza between 15 and 16 in* H31:

        So that I hardly believed there was nothing further to dread
        From the furious moods of the man & his ever restless eye
        But over & over again these words flasht into my head
        The work of the lie—the work of the lie—the work of the lie.

16

I am sick of the Hall and the hill, I am sick of the
　moor and the main.
Why should I stay? can a sweeter chance ever come
　to me here?
O, having the nerves of motion as well as the nerves
　of pain,
Were it not wise if I fled from the place and the pit
　and the fear?

17

Workmen up at the Hall!—they are coming back from
　abroad;　　　　　　　　　　　　　　　　　　　　　　65
The dark old place will be gilt by the touch of a
　millionaire:
I have heard, I know not whence, of the singular
　beauty of Maud;
I play'd with the girl when a child; she promised then
　to be fair.

I i *16* 61–4]

61–2] **1856–**;

> Why sd I stay? is it habit, but habit, that makes me remain?
> That, or a dream of a better chance that may come to me here? H31
> Have I a dream of a sweeter chance that may come to me here? **1855Va**

63　O, having] **1856–**; Having H31, **1855Va**.

64　wise] **1855Va** 2nd reading, **1856–**; well H31; good **1855Va** 1st
　　reading.

I i *17* 65–8] T36/H–.

65　Workmen] **1862–**; There are workmen T36/H–**1861**.

67　I know not whence,] T36/H 2nd reading–; I scarce know whence,
　　T36/H 1st reading.

68　the girl] T36/H 2nd reading–; her once T36/H 1st reading.

18

Maud with her venturous climbings and tumbles and
    childish escapes,
Maud the delight of the village, the ringing joy of the
    Hall,   70
Maud with her sweet purse-mouth when my father
    dangled the grapes,
Maud the beloved of my mother, the moon-faced
    darling of all,—

I i *18* 69–72] T36 *has two drafts (T36a, T36b [T36/H]) in which 18 is written as
one stanza with unadopted lines and 19,* P2–; *not in* P1 *so presumably not in* [Berg A].

69   venturous climbings] T36b–; crowings & creepings T36a.

     childish] T36a, P2–; pretty T36b.

70   the delight of the village,] P2–; in her aftersummers T36a, b.

71   sweet] Trial–; red T36a; pretty T36b, P2.

     father dangled] T36a, P2–; father wd dangle T36b.

72   beloved] P2–; delight T36a, b.

     the] P2–; and T36a, b.

72]   T36a *and* T36b *carry on with a group of lines (seven in* T36a, *nine in* T36b)
      subsequently unadopted:

   What is she now that to see a moment has touch'd with spite
   One that quarrels it may be with perfect sweetness and make
   Mixt with 'my love' and my dearest her best inuendo bite.
   One that has travell'd, is knowing, a beauty and ruin'd by praise
   Well I ⟨have⟩ was half afraid but I shall not die for her sake.
   Not be her savage and O the monster their delicate ways
   And finical interlarding of french and the giggle and shrug–   T36a

   What is she now that to see her a moment provokes me to spite?
   One of the monkeys who mimic wisdom, whom nothing can shake?
   One whom earthquake and deluge would touch with a feeble delight?
   One who can hate so sweetly with mannerly polish, and make
   Pointed with 'love' and 'my dearest' a sweet inuendo bite?
   One who has travell'd, is knowing? a beauty and ruin'd with praise?
   Well, I was half-afraid but I shall not die for her sake
   Not be her 'savage' and 'O the monster'! their delicate ways!
   Their finical interlarding of French and the giggle and shrug! T36b

   Immediately following on from these lines in both drafts is 19.

19

What is she now? My dreams are bad. She may
    bring me a curse.
No, there is fatter game on the moor; she will let me
    alone.
Thanks, for the fiend best knows whether woman or
    man be the worse.   75
I will bury myself in myself, and the Devil may pipe
    to his own.

I i *19* 73–6] T36 *has two drafts (*T36a, T36b [T36/H]*) in which 19 is written as one stanza with 18 and unadopted lines,* P2–; *not in* P1 *so presumably not in* [Berg A].

73] P2–; Taken with Maud no no what cd she have proved but a curse, T36a; I to be taken with Maud! it w*d* only have turn'd to a curse. *from the unadopted stanza following* I ii *in* T36/H; Taken with Maud—not so—for what cd she prove but a curse T36b.

73 ∧ 74] T36a *and* T36b *have an unadopted line:* Looking so cold, [Being so hard, T36b] she has hardly a decent regard for her pug T36a.

74 No,] P2–; True, T36a; Thanks! T36b.

75 Thanks, for the fiend best knows] P2–; For God & the Devil best know T36a; Thanks, for the Devil best knows T36b.

76 myself,] **1865**–; my books T36a, b; my books, P2–**1864**.

    pipe to his own.] T36a, b–; dance thro' his world. *from the unadopted stanza following* I ii *in* T36/H.

ii

Long have I sigh'd for a calm: God grant I may find
    it at last!
It will never be broken by Maud, she has neither
    savour nor salt,
But a cold and clear-cut face, as I found when her
    carriage past,
Perfectly beautiful: let it be granted her: where is
    the fault?   80
All that I saw (for her eyes were downcast, not to be
    seen)
Faultily faultless, icily regular, splendidly null,
Dead perfection, no more; nothing more, if it had
    not been
For a chance of travel, a paleness, an hour's defect of
    the rose,
Or an underlip, you may call it a little too ripe, too full,   85
Or the least little delicate aquiline curve in a sensitive
    nose,
From which I escaped heart-free, with the least little
    touch of spleen.

I ii 77–87] T36/H, [Berg A] (*on now lost f. 3*), P1–3, Trial, **1855–**.

---

78 never] T36/H alternative reading, P1–; not T36/H.

    she] T36/H 2nd reading–; who T36/H 1st reading.

    nor] P1–; or T36/H.

78 found] P1–; saw T36/H.

80 let . . . fault?] T36/H 2nd reading–; that, no doubt; but there is the
    fault. T36/H 1st reading.

81 (for . . . seen)] T36/H 2nd reading–; but her eyes (for they were down &
    could not be seen) T36/H 1st reading.

84 an hour's] T36/H 2nd reading (a . . .), P1–; a slight T36/H 1st reading.

84 ∧ 85] T36/H *has a line which has been deleted:* That will blossom again to
    the surface as bright, with an hour's repose.

85 you . . . full,] T36/H 2nd reading–; that may seem but a little too ripe,
    T36/H 1st reading.

87 *Following 77–87 T36/H has a stanza of eight lines. Two lines subsequently
    became 19 73, 76; the others were adapted in* I vi *4–10:*
    Comes she not out of a race that my wrongs have made me despise?
(73) I to be taken with Maud! it w^d only have turn'd to a curse.
    Now am I proof, heartproof to her unseen beautiful eyes,
    Proof for a hundred summers to whatsoever is hers
    Not to be dragg'd in her shining wake as a rustic prize
    Not to be trapt in her tresses however redundantly curl'd
    Proof to it all, thank God; so in time I may hope to be wise
(76) I will bury myself in my books & the Devil may dance thro'
        his world.

    T36/H *has another stanza which seems to have been intended to follow the above
    and which was adapted in* I vi *4–10:*

    Eyes, what care I for her eyes, those eyes that I did not behold
    Can they be more whether black or blue fullrolling or small
    More than the beldam-tutor'd Demos commonplace eyes
    Lying a splendid whoredom to full fed heirs at the Ball
    Buy me O buy me & have me for I am here to be sold

    (For both these stanzas, see Commentary, headnote to I i *1–19 and* I ii.*)*

iii

Cold and clear-cut face, why come you so cruelly
    meek,
Breaking a slumber in which all spleenful folly was
    drown'd,
Pale with the golden beam of an eyelash dead on the   90
    cheek,
Passionless, pale, cold face, star-sweet on a gloom
    profound;
Womanlike, taking revenge too deep for a transient
    wrong

I iii 88–101] T36 (*two drafts:* a, b), Berg A, P1–3, Trial, **1855–**.

T 36a *is an early draft:*
    Cold & clearcut face [*intentional blank*]
    Why have you taken a deep revenge for a trifling wrong
    Pale with a closeshut eye [*intentional blank*] without a sound
    Vexing me & the night & ~~return~~ haunting me oer & oer
    ~~Beauti~~ luminous, gemlike, ghostlike, deathlike all the night long
    Growing & fading & growing till I could bear it no more
    But waking paced by the beds of my own dark garden ground
    And heard the swell of the tide as it shriekd in a long breaker
    And walkd in a feeble [light *accidentally omitted*] & a wind like
        a wail & found
    The sweet narcissus dead & Orion low in his grave.

88]   Berg A (. . . meek), P1–; Passionless, clear-cut face, why came you so
       cruelly meek, T36b.

90   golden beam of an] Berg A–; beam of a golden T36b.

91   Passionless, pale, cold face,] P2–; Pale, how pale yet how sweet, T36b;
       Passionless, pale, cold face, Berg A 1st reading; Passionless, calm,
       cold face, Berg A 2nd reading, P1.

92   too] Berg A–; so T36b.

      transient] Berg A–; trifling T36b.

Done but in thought to your beauty, and ever as pale
    as before
Growing and fading and growing upon me without a
    sound,
Luminous, gemlike, ghostlike, deathlike, half the
    night long   95
Growing and fading and growing, till I could bear it
    no more,
But arose, and all by myself in my own dark garden
    ground,
Listening now to the tide in its broad-flung ship-
    wrecking roar,
Now to the scream of a madden'd beach dragg'd
    down by the wave,
Walk'd in a wintry wind by a ghastly glimmer, and
    found   100
The shining daffodil dead, and Orion low in his grave.

95   half] Berg A–; all T36b.

97   arose, and all by myself in] P2–; arising paced by the plots of T36b;
        arose & (arose, and P1) paced by the plots of Berg A, P1.

98–101] *Not in* T36b: *Tennyson stopped transcribing his fair copy after* 97.

98   tide in its] P2–; breaker a Berg A, P1 (breaker,).

100   P3–; [*intentional blank*] by a feeble light in a wind like a winter & found
       Berg A 1st reading; [*intentional blank*] like a phantom myself in a
       ghostly glimmer & found Berg A 2nd reading; [*intentional blank*] in a
       wintry wind by a ghastly glimmer & found Berg A 3rd reading;
       Paced in a wintry wind by a ghastly glimmer & found Berg A 4th
       reading, P1, 2 (glimmer, and).

101   shining daffodil dead,] P3–; sweet narcissus was dead, Berg A 1st
       reading; golden aconite dead, Berg A 2nd reading; sweet narcissus
       dead, Berg A 3rd reading, P1, 2 (Narcissus).

iv

1

A million emeralds break from the ruby-budded lime
In the little grove where I sit—ah, wherefore cannot
　　I be
Like things of the season gay, like the bountiful
　　season bland,
When the far-off sail is blown by the breeze of a softer
　　clime,　　　　　　　　　　　　　　　　　　　105
Half-lost in the liquid azure bloom of a crescent of
　　sea,
The silent sapphire-spangled marriage ring of the
　　land?

2

Below me, there, is the village, and looks how quiet
　　and small!
And yet bubbles o'er like a city, with gossip, scandal,
　　and spite;
And Jack on his ale-house bench has as many lies as
　　a Czar;　　　　　　　　　　　　　　　　　　110
And here on the landward side, by a red rock,
　　glimmers the Hall;
And up in the high Hall-garden I see her pass like a
　　light;
But sorrow seize me if ever that light be my leading
　　star!

I iv *1–10* 102–61] H29 (*six stanzas only: 9, 8, 5, 7, 10, 4, respectively*), T36, [Berg
A] (*on now lost f. 5*), P1 (*only 1–5 survive*), P2, 3, Trial, **1855–**.

I iv *1* 102–7] T36–; *not in* H29.

104　bountiful] T36 2nd reading–; blossoming T36 1st reading.

107　sapphire-spangled] T36 2nd reading–; sapphire-sparkling T36 1st
　　reading.

I iv *2* 108–13] T36–; *not in* H29.

3

When have I bow'd to her father, the wrinkled head
    of the race?
I met her to-day with her brother, but not to her
    brother I bow'd: 115
I bow'd to his lady-sister as she rode by on the moor;
But the fire of a foolish pride flash'd over her beautiful
    face.
O child, you wrong your beauty, believe it, in being
    so proud;
Your father has wealth well-gotten, and I am nameless
    and poor.

I iv *3* 114–19] T36–; *not in* H29.

114] T36 3rd reading (. . . father— . . .), Trial–; Her father has plunder'd
    the people & so he has wealth & place T36 1st reading; Once I met
    with her father—to him I never wd bow T36 2nd reading.

115 I met her to-day with] **1856**–; I met her abroad with T36 1st reading–
    1855–; Today I met with T36 2nd reading (*deleted*).

118 in being so proud;] P1–; in being proud T36.

119 Your] T36 2nd reading–; The T36 1st reading.

    well-gotten,] T36 2nd reading (wellgotten), P1–; & title T36 1st
    reading.

4

I keep but a man and a maid, ever ready to slander
  and steal;   120
I know it, and smile a hard-set smile, like a stoic, or
  like
A wiser epicurean, and let the world have its way:
For nature is one with rapine, a harm no preacher
  can heal;
The Mayfly is torn by the swallow, the sparrow
  spear'd by the shrike,
And the whole little wood where I sit is a world of
  plunder and prey.   125

5

We are puppets, Man in his pride, and Beauty fair in
  her flower;
Do we move ourselves, or are moved by an unseen
  hand at a game
That pushes us off from the board, and others ever
  succeed?
Ah yet, we cannot be kind to each other here for an hour;
We whisper, and hint, and chuckle, and grin at a
  brother's shame;   130
However we brave it out, we men are a little breed.

I iv *4* 120–5] H29–.

120] T36 (*no punctuation*), P1–; I keep but one little maid readyripe to
  plunder & steal H29.

121 I know it, and smile] T36 (. . . it . . .), P1–; And I smile H29.

123 nature] T36 (Nature), P1–; rapine H29.

  rapine,] T36–; Nature H29.

  a harm no preacher] T36–; [*intentional blank*] nothing H29.

124 torn by the swallow,] T36–; rent by the robin H29.

  sparrow] H29, T36 2nd reading–; swallow T36 1st reading (*error in
  transcription*).

125 a world] P2–; full H29–P1.

6

A monstrous eft was of old the Lord and Master of
    Earth,
For him did his high sun flame, and his river billowing
    ran,
And he felt himself in his force to be Nature's
    crowning race.
As nine months go to the shaping an infant ripe for
    his birth,   135
So many a million of ages have gone to the making of
    man:
He now is first, but is he the last? is he not too base?

127 Do we move ourselves, or are moved] T36 (. . . ourselves . . .), P1–;
      We do not play but are play'd H29.

     a] T36–; the H29.

128 off from the] T36 2nd reading–; off the H29, T36 1st reading.
     ever] T36–; for ever H29.

129 Ah yet,] P2–; And yet, H29, T36; Yet, ah! P1.
     other here] H29 2nd reading–; other H29 1st reading.

130 grin] T36–; laugh H29.

I iv *6* 132–7] T36–; *not in* H29.

133 river billowing] P2–; billowing river T36.

137 He] P2–; Who T36.

7

The man of science himself is fonder of glory, and
    vain,
An eye well-practised in nature, a spirit bounded and
    poor;
The passionate heart of the poet is whirl'd into folly
    and vice.   140
I would not marvel at either, but keep a temperate
    brain;
For not to desire or admire, if a man could learn it,
    were more
Than to walk all day like the sultan of old in a garden
    of spice.

8

For the drift of the Maker is dark, an Isis hid by the
    veil.
Who knows the ways of the world, how God will bring
    them about?   145
Our planet is one, the suns are many, the world is
    wide.
Shall I weep if a Poland fall? shall I shriek if a
    Hungary fail?
Or an infant civilisation be ruled with rod or with
    knout?
I have not made the world, and He that made it will
    guide.

I iv 7 138–43] H29–.

138   fonder of glory, and vain,] T36 (*no punctuation*), P2–; greedy of glory &
      selfish & vain H29.

139   spirit bounded and poor;] T36 (. . . poor), P2–; soul that is narrow &
      poor H29.

141   would] T36–; will H29.

142   learn] T36–; hold H29.

9

Be mine a philosopher's life in the quiet woodland ways, 150
Where if I cannot be gay let a passionless peace be my
    lot,
Far-off from the clamour of liars belied in the hubbub of
    lies;
From the long-neck'd geese of the world that are ever
    hissing dispraise
Because their natures are little, and, whether he heed it
    or not,
Where each man walks with his head in a cloud of
    poisonous flies. 155

I iv *8* 144–9] H29–.

144 For the] T36–; The H29.

146 Our planet is one, the suns are many,] T36–; We are not first, our
    planet is one, H29.

    world is] T36–; worlds are H29.

147 weep] T36–; shriek H29.

    shriek] T36–; weep H29.

148 or] T36–; and H29.

149 *I*] **1889**; I H29–**1884**.

I iv *9* 150–5] H29–.

150–2] T36–;
        O green little wood O quiet of winding woodland ways
              yet here   be my lot
        If I cannot be merry at least shall peace ~~sleep~~ [?]
        I shall hear no more the liar belied in the hubbub of lies

153 geese of the world] T36–; gander & goose H29.

154 natures are little,] T36–; nature is little H29.

    it] T36–; them H29.

155 Where each man walks] T36–; Each man walks on H29.

10

And most of all would I flee from the cruel madness
    of love,
The honey of poison-flowers and all the measureless
    ill.
Ah Maud, you milkwhite fawn, you are all unmeet
    for a wife.
Your mother is mute in her grave as her image in
    marble above;
Your father is ever in London, you wander about at
    your will;   160
You have but fed on the roses and lain in the lilies of
    life.

I iv *10* 156–61] H29–.
158   Ah] T36–; O H29.

v

1

A voice by the cedar tree
In the meadow under the Hall!
She is singing an air that is known to me,
A passionate ballad gallant and gay,   165
A martial song like a trumpet's call!
Singing alone in the morning of life,
In the happy morning of life and of May,
Singing of men that in battle array,
Ready in heart and ready in hand,   170
March with banner and bugle and fife
To the death, for their native land.

2

Maud with her exquisite face,
And wild voice pealing up to the sunny sky,
And feet like sunny gems on an English green,   175
Maud in the light of her youth and her grace,
Singing of Death, and of Honour that cannot die,
Till I well could weep for a time so sordid and mean,
And myself so languid and base.

I v *1–3* 162–89] T36 (*two drafts:* a, b), [Berg A] (*on now lost f. 6*), [P1], P2, 3, Trial, **1855–**.

I v *1* 162–72]

166 martial] T36b 2nd reading–; passionate T36a 1st reading; fiery T36a 2nd reading, T36b 1st reading.

I v *2* 173–9

174 And wild voice] P2–; And her wild voice T36a, b.

175] P2–; And unto the woodland green T36a, b.

178] T36b 3rd reading (... mean), P2–; Till I feel the foolish tears running [coming T36b 1st reading] over my face T36a, T36b 1st reading; To think that I live in a time so sordid & mean T36b 2nd reading.

3

Silence, beautiful voice!   180
Be still, for you only trouble the mind
With a joy in which I cannot rejoice,
A glory I shall not find.
Still! I will hear you no more,
For your sweetness hardly leaves me a choice   185
But to move to the meadow and fall before
Her feet on the meadow grass, and adore,
Not her, who is neither courtly nor kind,
Not her, not her, but a voice.

I v *3* 180–9]

180   beautiful] T36a 2nd reading–; exquisite T36a 1st reading.

186   move] T36b–; run T36a.

188   nor] P2–; or T36a, b.

vi

1

Morning arises stormy and pale,   190
No sun, but a wannish glare
In fold upon fold of hueless cloud,
And the budded peaks of the wood are bow'd
Caught and cuff'd by the gale:
I had fancied it would be fair.   195

2

Whom but Maud should I meet
Last night, when the sunset burn'd
On the blossom'd gable-ends
At the head of the village street,
Whom but Maud should I meet?   200
And she touch'd my hand with a smile so sweet,
She made me divine amends
For a courtesy not return'd.

3

And thus a delicate spark
Of glowing and growing light   205
Thro' the livelong hours of the dark
Kept itself warm in the heart of my dreams,
Ready to burst in a colour'd flame;
Till at last when the morning came
In a cloud, it faded, and seems   210
But an ashen-grey delight.

I vi *1–10* 190–284] BM (*9 and 10 only*), T36, [Berg A] (*on now lost ff. 7–9*),
[P1], P2, 3, Trial, **1855–**.

4

What if with her sunny hair,
And smile as sunny as cold,
She meant to weave me a snare
Of some coquettish deceit,   215
Cleopatra-like as of old
To entangle me when we met,
To have her lion roll in a silken net
And fawn at a victor's feet.

5

Ah, what shall I be at fifty   220
Should Nature keep me alive,
If I find the world so bitter
When I am but twenty-five?
Yet, if she were not a cheat,
If Maud were all that she seem'd,   225
And her smile were all that I dream'd,
Then the world were not so bitter
But a smile could make it sweet.

6

What if tho' her eye seem'd full
Of a kind intent to me,   230
What if that dandy-despot, he,
That jewell'd mass of millinery,
That oil'd and curl'd Assyrian Bull
Smelling of musk and of insolence,
Her brother, from whom I keep aloof,   235
Who wants the finer politic sense
To mask, tho' but in his own behoof,
With a glassy smile his brutal scorn—
What if he had told her yestermorn
How prettily for his own sweet sake   240
A face of tenderness might be feign'd,
And a moist mirage in desert eyes,
That so, when the rotten hustings shake

In another month to his brazen lies,
A wretched vote may be gain'd.   245

7

For a raven ever croaks, at my side,
Keep watch and ward, keep watch and ward,
Or thou wilt prove their tool.
Yea, too, myself from myself I guard,
For often a man's own angry pride   250
Is cap and bells for a fool.

8

Perhaps the smile and tender tone
Came out of her pitying womanhood,
For am I not, am I not, here alone
So many a summer since she died,   255
My mother, who was so gentle and good?
Living alone in an empty house,
Here half-hid in the gleaming wood,
Where I hear the dead at midday moan,
And the shrieking rush of the wainscot mouse, 260
And my own sad name in corners cried,
When the shiver of dancing leaves is thrown
About its echoing chambers wide,
Till a morbid hate and horror have grown
Of a world in which I have hardly mixt,   265
And a morbid eating lichen fixt
On a heart half-turn'd to stone.

I vi *8* 252–67]
259 midday] P2–; noonday T36.

9

O heart of stone, are you flesh, and caught
By that you swore to withstand?
For what was it else within me wrought   270
But, I fear, the new strong wine of love,
That made my tongue so stammer and trip
When I saw the treasured splendour, her hand,
Come sliding out of her sacred glove,
And the sunlight broke from her lip?   275

10

I have play'd with her when a child;
She remembers it now we meet.
Ah well, well, well, I *may* be beguiled
By some coquettish deceit.
Yet, if she were not a cheat,   280
If Maud were all that she seem'd,
And her smile had all that I dream'd,
Then the world were not so bitter
But a smile could make it sweet.

I vi *10* 276–84]

278   *may*] **1865**–; may BM–**1864**.

280   T36 2nd reading (Yet), P2–; But T36 1st reading; *not in* BM.
281]   T36 (*no punctuation*), Trial–; But if she were all she seemd BM.

vii

1

Did I hear it half in a doze   285
  Long since, I know not where?
Did I dream it an hour ago,
  When asleep in this arm-chair?

2

Men were drinking together,
  Drinking and talking of me;   290
'Well, if it prove a girl, the boy
  Will have plenty: so let it be.'

I vii *1–4* 285–300] T36 *(two drafts:* a, b*)*, Berg A, [P1], P2, 3, Trial, **1855–**.
T36a *lacks 3 and runs 2, 1, 4, respectively.*

I vii *1* 285–8]

285–6] T36b (. . . since . . .), Berg A–;
                    Did I hear it, long years back
                      Half-dozing who knows where   T36a

288 When asleep] T36b–; Sleeping T36a.

I vii *2* 289–92]

289   Men] T36a, Berg A–; Who T36b.

        together,] T36b (together), Berg A–; & talking T36a.
291   the] T36b–; my T36a.

3

Is it an echo of something
  Read with a boy's delight,
Viziers nodding together   295
  In some Arabian night?

4

Strange, that I hear two men,
  Somewhere, talking of me;
'Well, if it proves a girl, my boy
  Will have plenty: so let it be.'   300

I vii *3* 293–6]

Not in T36a.

293 an echo of something] T36b 2nd reading–; a part of a tale T36b 1st
     reading.

I vii *4* 297–300]

297 I hear two men,] T36b *and* Berg A (. . . men), P2–; the words come
     back T36a.

298 T36b 2nd reading *and* Berg A (*no punctuation*), P2–; With such a force
     upon me T36a; Talking & talking of me T36b 1st reading.

299 my] T36b–; the T36a.

viii

She came to the village church,
And sat by a pillar alone;
An angel watching an urn
Wept over her, carved in stone;
And once, but once, she lifted her eyes, 305
And suddenly, sweetly, strangely blush'd
To find they were met by my own;
And suddenly, sweetly, my heart beat stronger
And thicker, until I heard no longer
The snowy-banded, dilettante, 310
Delicate-handed priest intone;
And thought, is it pride, and mused and sigh'd
'No surely, now it cannot be pride.'

I viii 301–13] T36, Berg A, [P1], P2, 3, Trial, **1855–**.

T36 1st reading *is a fair copy of an early version:*

> I went to the village church.
>   She was there: she was not alone
> A silent angel watching an urn
>   Wept over her carved in stone.
> Suddenly strangely sweetly she blush'd
>   When her eyes met once with my own
> Suddenly sweetly my heart beat stronger
> And thicker until I heard no longer
> The snowy-banded, dilettante,
> Delicate-handed priest intone;
> She look'd no more but I thought & sigh'd

306 sweetly, strangely] Berg A–; strangely sweetly T36 2nd reading.

313 'No surely, now] T36 3rd reading *and* Berg A ('No, surely . . .), P2–;
     'What is it? no T36 2nd reading.

ix

I was walking a mile,
More than a mile from the shore,   315
The sun look'd out with a smile
Betwixt the cloud and the moor,
And riding at set of day
Over the dark moor land,
Rapidly riding far away,   320
She waved to me with her hand.
There were two at her side,
Something flash'd in the sun,
Down by the hill I saw them ride,
In a moment they were gone: 325
Like a sudden spark
Struck vainly in the night,
Then returns the dark
With no more hope of light.

I ix 314–29] T36, [Berg A] (*on now lost f. 11*), [P1], P2, 3, Trial, **1855**–.

316   The] T36 2nd reading–; And T36 1st reading.

322   T36 2nd reading (. . . side.), P2–; There were two at her side. T36 1st
        reading.

328   Then] **1865**–; And back T36–**1864**.

I x *1–6* 330–97] T36 (*1, 2* early version, *three unadopted stanzas, 3, 4* early
version), Berg A *and* P1–3 (*all the above, plus 5, but* P1 *now lost for 1 and 5*),
H148 (*2 only*), Trial *and* **1855** (*1–3, 5 only*), **1856**–.

x

1

Sick, am I sick of a jealous dread?   330
Was not one of the two at her side
This new-made lord, whose splendour plucks
The slavish hat from the villager's head?
Whose old grandfather has lately died,
Gone to a blacker pit, for whom   335
Grimy nakedness dragging his trucks
And laying his trams in a poison'd gloom
Wrought, till he crept from a gutted mine
Master of half a servile shire,
And left his coal all turn'd into gold   340
To a grandson, first of his noble line,
Rich in the grace all women desire,
Strong in the power that all men adore,
And simper and set their voices lower,
And soften as if to a girl, and hold   345
Awe-stricken breaths at a work divine,
Seeing his gewgaw castle shine,
New as his title, built last year,
There amid perky larches and pine,
And over the sullen-purple moor   350
(Look at it) pricking a cockney ear.

I x *1* 330–51] T36–.

330] Berg A–; I think I am sick of a jealous dread T36.

331   Was] Berg A–; For was T36.

335   Gone to] Berg A–; Now in T36.

341   a] Berg A–; his T36.

      his] Berg A–; a T36.

342   Berg A (. . . desire), P2–; Rich in the beauty all maidens admire T36.

344–7] Berg A (. . . Awe-stricken 2nd reading, Awe-struck 1st reading, . . .
    no punctuation), P2–;
            Who address him sweet like a woman & hold
            Their breath but to see his castle shine T36

349] Berg A (. . . pine), P2–; ~~There~~ on a knoll of perky larch & pine T36.

2

What, has he found my jewel out?
For one of the two that rode at her side
Bound for the Hall, I am sure was he:
Bound for the Hall, and I think for a bride.   355
Blithe would her brother's acceptance be.
Maud could be gracious too, no doubt
To a lord, a captain, a padded shape,
A bought commission, a waxen face,
A rabbit mouth that is ever agape—   360
Bought? what is it he cannot buy?
And therefore splenetic, personal, base,
A wounded thing with a rancorous cry,
At war with myself and a wretched race,
Sick, sick to the heart of life, am I.   365

I x 2 early version *and unadopted stanzas* A, B, C] T36, Berg A, P1–3.

T36 *has two drafts (*a, b*) of 2 early version.* T36a *has sixteen lines:*

> What has he found my jewel out
> This bantam lord—I am sure it was he—
> Blithe w*d* her brother's acceptance be
> Maud could be gracious too no doubt,
> Maud could be very gracious too
> To the rabbit mouth & the baby face.
> ~~O Lord~~ What ails me that I cannot be cool
> Harsh splenetic, personal, base
> I am not worthy of her—a fool
> And most unworthy—yet it is true
> That I check'd [*illegible letter deleted*] my maid who wantonly smild
> As at some fair jest when she call'd him wild
> Poor worm she meant it half in his praise
> For there is nothing he may not do;
> And sick to the heart of life am I
> To think there is nothing he may not buy.

T36b *has nine lines;* Berg A *and* P1–3 *have ten lines:*

> What, has he found my jewel out,
> This bantam lord—[babe-faced lord, Berg A, P1–3] I am sure it was he
> Bound for the hall & perhaps for a bride
> ∧ Blithe would her brother's acceptance be∧ (*additional line in* Berg A, P1–3)
> Maud will [could Berg A, P1–3] be gracious too no doubt
> To the dawdling drawl of the tender ape
> His bought commission his [and Berg A, P1–3] padded shape

His one half grain of sense & his three
Straw colour'd hairs ~~on~~ upon either side
Of a baby [rabbit Berg A, P1–3] mouth that is ever agape T36b

Following the above, T36b, Berg A, *and* P1–3 *have three stanzas (*A, B, C*), here numbered consecutively:*

[A]
1) Now is she smiling up at the hall   [Will she smile if he presses her hand]
2) Now this new soldier presses her hand   [This lord-captain up at the Hall?] Berg A
           [Now are they serf-like, horribly bland,
            To this lord-captain up at the Hall:
            Will she smile if he presses her hand?] P1–3
3) Commission! [Captain! Berg A, P1, 3] he to hold a command!
   He can hold a cue, he can pocket a ball
5) For I know [And, sure, Berg A, P1–3] not a bantam-cockrel lives
   With a weaker crow upon English land
   Whether he boast of a horse that gains
   Or cackle his own applause when he gives
   A filthy story at second hand
10) And [Where Berg A, P1–3] the point is miss'd & the filth remains

[B]
   His bought commission! [Bought commission! Berg A, P1–3] can such as he
   Be wholesome guards for an ancient [English Berg A, P1–3] throne
   When if France but make a lunge—why she
   God knows—might prick us to the backbone.

[C]
15) What use for a single mouth to rage
    At the rotten creak of the state [old P1–3] machine
    Which [Tho it Berg A, P1–3] makes friend weep & enemy smile
    Here in the [The sons of a Berg A, P1–3] graybeard-ridden isle
20) Should dance in a round of old routine
    While [~~And~~ While Berg A; And P1–3] a few great families lead the reels
    And [While P1–3] pauper manhood lies in the dirt
    ~~Wh~~ And [And Berg A, P1–3] Favour & Wealth with gilded heels
    Trample service & tried desert. T36

I x 2 352–65] H148–; *not in* T36, Berg A, P1–3.

358   a lord, a captain,] Trial–; the lord of land & H148.

359   waxen] Trial–; baby H148.

360   A] H148 2nd reading (a), Trial–; And a H148 1st reading.

363–4] **1855Va** (*interlineated lines in reverse order*), **1856**–; *not in* H148–**1855**.

3

Last week came one to the county town,
To preach our poor little army down,
And play the game of the despot kings,
Tho' the state has done it and thrice as well:
This broad-brimm'd hawker of holy things,   370
Whose ear is cramm'd with his cotton, and rings
Even in dreams to the chink of his pence,
This huckster put down war! can he tell
Whether war be a cause or a consequence?
Put down the passions that make earth Hell!   375
Down with ambition, avarice, pride,
Jealousy, down! cut off from the mind
The bitter springs of anger and fear;
Down too, down at your own fireside,
With the evil tongue and the evil ear,   380
For each is at war with mankind.

I x *3* 366–81] (*two drafts:* a, b)–.

366–74] T36a *has these lines cancelled.* T36b *is a revision of this cancelled passage.*
Both drafts have lines out of order:

368   We tickle the lust of tyrant kings

366   Last week there came to the county town (*revised to*)
      One came last week to the county town

370   A broad brimm'd hawker of holy things

367   To preach our poor little army down

369   The state has done it & thrice as well

371   His ear is stuff'd with his cotton & rings

372   Ev'n in a dream to the chink of his pence

373   He put down war! can the huckster tell

374   Whether war be a cause or a consequence T36a

366   One came last week to the county town

368   Playing the game of the despot kings

367   Preaching our poor little army down.

369 The state has done it & thrice as well.

370 This broadbrim hawker of holy things,

373 This ~~hawker~~ huckster put down war! can he tell

374 Whether war be a cause or a consequence,

371 His ear is stuff'd with his cotton & rings

372 Ev'n in a dream to the chink of his pence T36b

366 Last week] H148 *has these words only below a fair copy of* I x 2.

368–9] Trial–;
> Playing the game of the despot kings,
> Preaching our poor little army down,
> > Berg A 1st reading, P1

> To preach our poor little army down,
> Playing the game of the despot kings,
> > Berg A 2nd reading, P2, 3

370 This] Berg A 2nd reading–; As Berg A 1st reading.

375–81] *Not in* T36b.

371 cramm'd] **1859**–; stuft Berg A, P1–3, Trial, **1855Va**, **1856**; stuff'd **1855, 1855Va**.

376 avarice,] Trial–; envy T36a; envy, Berg A, P1–3.

377 Jealousy,] Trial–; Avarice T36a, P1–3; Avarice, Berg A.

378 anger and fear;] Berg A–; hate & of fear T36a.

4

I wish I could hear again
The chivalrous battle-song
That she warbled alone in her joy!
I might persuade myself then   385
She would not do herself this great wrong,
To take a wanton dissolute boy
For a man and leader of men.

5

Ah God, for a man with heart, head, hand,
Like some of the simple great ones gone   390
For ever and ever by,
One still strong man in a blatant land,
Whatever they call him, what care I,
Aristocrat, democrat, autocrat—one
Who can rule and dare not lie.   395

I x *4* 382–8] T36, Berg A, P1–3, **1855Va**, **1856**–; *not in* Trial, **1855**.

Early version in T36, Berg A, *and* P1–3:

    And Maud who when I had languish'd long [Maud, P1–3]
    Reach'd me a shining hand of help
    To ~~up~~ arouse me that May morning when [morning, P1–3]
    She chanted a chivalrous battle song [battle-song, P1–3]
5) Can [Maud, can Berg A, P1–3] she do herself so much wrong
    As take [As to take Berg A, P1–3] this waxen effeminate whelp
    For a man & leader of men T36 [and P1–3; men. P1; men? P2, 3]

382 I wish] **1856**–; O, would **1855Va**.

386 this] **1856**–; that **1855Va**.

387 To] **1856**–; As to **1855Va**.

I x *5* 389–95] Berg A, [P1], P2–; *not in* T36.

389] H148 *has* Ah God for a man & , *an isolated phrase below a fair copy of I x*
    2.
    Ah] Berg A, Trial–; Oh P2, 3.

6

And ah for a man to arise in me,
That the man I am may cease to be!

I x *6* 396–7] **1856**–; *not in* T36, Berg A, Pl–3, Trial, **1855**.

xi

1

O let the solid ground
  Not fail beneath my feet
Before my life has found   400
  What some have found so sweet;
Then let come what come may,
What matter if I go mad,
I shall have had my day.

2

Let the sweet heavens endure,   405
  Not close and darken above me
Before I am quite quite sure
  That there is one to love me;
Then let come what come may
To a life that has been so sad,   410
I shall have had my day.

I xi *1, 2* 398–411] BM (*two drafts:* a, b) H30, T36, [Berg A] (*on now lost f.14*),
[P1], P2, 3, Trial, **1855–**.

I xi *1* 398–404]

398   Trial–; Let not the sound earth fail BMa *and* H30 1st reading;
      Let not the solid ground BMa 2nd reading, BMb, H30 2nd reading–
        T36 1st reading;
      Let the solid ground T36 2nd reading; O Let . . . T36 3rd reading,
      deleted

399] T36 2nd reading–; And open under my feet BMa *and* H30 1st reading;
      Fail beneath my feet BMa 2nd reading, BMb, H30 2nd reading–T36
      1st reading.

400   has found] BMa 2nd reading, BMb, H30 2nd reading–; finds out BMa
      and H30 1st reading.

401   some] BMa 2nd reading, BMb, H30 2nd reading–; others BMa *and*
      H30 1st reading.

403   BMa 2nd reading, BMb, H30 2nd reading–T36 (. . . mad), Trial–; To
      a life that has been so sad BMa *and* H30 1st reading.

xii

1

Birds in the high Hall-garden
  When twilight was falling,
Maud, Maud, Maud, Maud,
  They were crying and calling.   415

2

Where was Maud? in our wood;
  And I, who else, was with her,
Gathering woodland lilies,
  Myriads blow together.

I xi *2* 405–11]

405 BMb *and* T36 (. . . Heavens endure), P2–; Let not the sweet Heaven
     fail BMa *and* H30 1st reading; Let the sweet Heaven endure BMa
     and H30 2nd reading.

406 Not close] BMa 2nd reading, BMb, H30 2nd reading (. . . Close)
     T36–; Close BMa *and* H30 1st reading.

408 there is one to] BMa 2nd reading, BMb, H30 2nd reading–; Maud
     does BMa *and* H30 1st reading.

410 BMa 2nd reading, BMb, H30 2nd reading, T36 (. . .sad), Trial–;
     What matter if I go mad BMa *and* H30 1st reading.

411 had] P2–; lived BMa–T36.

I xii *1–8* 412–43] BM, H30, T36, [Berg A] (*on now lost f.15*), P1–3 (*but* P1 *now
lost for 1–6*), Trial, **1855**–.

3

Birds in our wood sang   420
   Ringing thro' the valleys,
Maud is here, here, here
   In among the lillies.

4

I kiss'd her slender hand,
   She took the kiss sedately;   425
Maud is not seventeen,
   But she is tall and stately.

5

I to cry out on pride
   Who have won her favour!
O Maud were sure of Heaven   430
   If lowliness could save her.

6

I know the way she went
   Home with her maiden posy,
For her feet have touch'd the meadows
   And left the daisies rosy.   435

7

Birds in the high Hall-garden
   Were crying and calling to her,
Where is Maud, Maud, Maud?
   One is come to woo her.

I xii *4, 5*] *Transposed in* BM, H30 1st reading.

I xii *4* 424–7]

426   not seventeen,] P2–; but sixteen BM–T36.

8

Look, a horse at the door,   440
　And little King Charley snarling,
Go back, my lord, across the moor,
　You are not her darling.

I xii *8* 440–3]

441　Charley] **1864**–; Charles is BM–**1862**.

xiii

1

Scorn'd, to be scorn'd by one that I scorn,
Is that a matter to make me fret?   445
That a calamity hard to be borne?
Well, he may live to hate me yet.
Fool that I am to be vext with his pride!
I past him, I was crossing his lands;
He stood on the path a little aside;   450
His face, as I grant, in spite of spite,
Has a broad-blown comeliness, red and white,
And six feet two, as I think, he stands;
But his essences turn'd the live air sick,
And barbarous opulence jewel-thick   455
Sunn'd itself on his breast and his hands.

I xiii *1–4* 444–88] T36 *(two drafts:* a, b*; see Commentary)*, Berg A, P1–3 *(but* P1
now lost for 2–4), Trial, **1855–**.

T36a *and* T36b *represent three stages of composition. Stage 1 (*T36a) reads:*

[*3*]
468   Is he ashamed to be seen

467   That he never comes to his Place.

469   Only once in the street

470   I caught a glimpse of his face,

471   A gray old wolf & a lean.

472   I will not call him a cheat

473   For then might Maud be untrue

475   And Maud is as true as sweet

478   ~~She must have been a thing complete~~

479   ~~However she came~~ [*intentional blank*]

476   But this, I doubt not is due

477   To her blood on the other side

478   Her mother has been a thing complete

479   However she came to be so allied

482   I think that some peculiar grace

480 Made my Maud without & within

483 Only the child of a gracious mother

484 But heapt the whole inherited sin

485 On that huge scapegoat of the race

486 All all upon the brother.

*Stage 2 (*T36b, *fair copy) reads:*
[1]
449 I met him walking over his lands;

451 His face is a servant maid's delight

452 A vulgar comeliness, red & white

454 A gust of his essences made me sick

455 And those fat fingers, foolishly thick

456 With jewels, stunted obstinate hands!
[2]
460 While I past he was humming an air

461 But stopt, & then with a riding-whip

462 Leisurely tapt on a polish'd boot

463 And making a supercilious lip

464 Gorgonized me from head to foot

465 With a stony execrable stare.
[3]
466 Why sits he here in his father's chair.

467 That old man never comes to his Place.

468 What is he ashamed to be seen?

469 For only once in the village street

470 I caught, long since, a glimpse of his face

471 A gray old wolf & a lean.

472 I dare not call him a cheat

473/4 Then might Maud be untrue.

475 Maud is as true as sweet

476 But I fancy her sweetness due

477 To the blood by the other side

478 And think her mother too was some
     Ideal, as mother & bride

2

Who shall call me ungentle, unfair,
I long'd so heartily then and there
To give him the grasp of fellowship;
But while I past he was humming an air,   460
Stopt, and then with a riding whip
Leisurely tapping a glossy boot,
And curving a contumelious lip,
Gorgonised me from head to foot
With a stony British stare.   465

I xiii *1* 444–56]

444–8] *Added in* Stage 3.

447   hate] Stage 3, Berg A 2nd reading–; curse Berg A 1st reading.

448   Fool] Trial–; Ass Stage 3, Berg A, P1–3.

      vext with] Berg A–; hurt by Stage 3.

449   past] Stage 3–.

450   *Added in* Stage 3.

451–3] *Revisions made in* Stage 3.

454   Trial–; But a gust of his essences made me sick Stage 3, Berg A, P1;
      But his essences made the morning sick, P2, 3.

455   Trial–; Stage 3, Berg A *and* P1–3 *agree with* Stage 2, *except* Berg A *has no*
      comma.

456]   Trial–; Stage 3, Berg A *and* P1 *agree with* Stage 2, *except* Berg A *has*
      hands; P1 hands; Flash'd on his obstinate-finger'd hands. P2, 3.

I xiii *2* 457–65]

457–9] P2–; *not in* Stage 3, Berg A.

458   heartily] **1856**–; earnestly P2, 3, Trial, **1855**.

459   grasp] Trial–; hand P2, 3.

460   But] P2–; Berg A *agrees with* Stages 2, 3.

462   P2–; Berg A *agrees with* Stages 2, 3.

463   Stage 3 *and* Berg A (. . . lip), P2, 3, Trial–.

465   British] Berg A–; execrable Stages 2, 3.

3

Why sits he here in his father's chair?
That old man never comes to his place:
Shall I believe him ashamed to be seen?
For only once, in the village street,
Last year, I caught a glimpse of his face,   470
A gray old wolf and a lean.
Scarcely, now, would I call him a cheat;
For then, perhaps, as a child of deceit,
She might by a true descent be untrue;
And Maud is as true as Maud is sweet: 475
Tho' I fancy her sweetness only due
To the sweeter blood by the other side;
Her mother has been a thing complete,
However she came to be so allied.

468   Shall I believe him] Stage 3–.

470   Last year, I caught] Trial–; Stage 3 *transposes* Stage 2 reading; Berg A
      (*fair copy of* Stage 3) *and* P2, 3 *read* Long since I caught
      (. . . since, . . . P2, 3).

472   P2–; For now I dare not call him a cheat Stage 3; Now not now would
      I call him a cheat. Berg A.

473–4]   P2–; Then perhaps might Maud be untrue. Stage 3, Berg A.

475]   P2–; Maud is as true as Maud is sweet Stage 3, Berg A.

476]   P2–; But I fancy her sweetness only due Stage 3, Berg A.

477]   sweeter] Stage 3–.

478]   Stage 3 (her . . . complete), Berg A–.

479–86]   Stage 3 *adapts lines from* Stage 1 *which were not incorporated in* Stage 2.
      To them is added 481. Stage 3 *agrees with* Stage 1 *unless otherwise noted.*

And fair without, faithful within,   480
Maud to him is nothing akin:
Some peculiar mystic grace
Made her only the child of her mother,
And heap'd the whole inherited sin
On that huge scapegoat of the race,   485
All, all upon the brother.

                        4

Peace, angry spirit, and let him be!
Has not his sister smiled on me?

480–1] P2–;

      Fair without, faithful within
      Maud to him is nothing akin
          Stage 3 1st reading

      And Maud to him is nothing akin
      She is Fair [fair Berg A] without, faithful within [within: Berg A]
          Stage 3 2nd reading, Berg A

482] Stage 3–.

484   And] Stage 3–.

I xiii *4* 487–8]

Introduced in Stage 3.

xiv

1

Maud has a garden of roses
And lilies fair on a lawn;   490
There she walks in her state
And tends upon bed and bower,
And thither I climb'd at dawn
And stood by her garden-gate;
A lion ramps at the top,   495
He is claspt by a passion-flower.

2

Maud's own little oak-room
(Which Maud, like a precious stone
Set in the heart of the carven gloom,

I xiv *1–4* 489–526] H20 (489–90 *only*), T36a (*1, 2, 4 only*), BM (*adds 3*), H30,
T36b, [Berg A] (*on now lost f.17*), [P1], P2, 3, Trial, **1855–**.

I xiv *1* 489–96] H20 (489–90 *only*), T36a–.

490   fair] BM–; bright H20, T36a.

491–2] *Transposed in* T36a.

492   And tends upon bed and] BM–; Bright is the bed and the T36a.

I xiv *2* 497–510] T36a–.

497–9] BM *and* H30 (*no round bracket*), T36b (. . . oak-room, | Which . . .
pretious . . .), P2–;

> Maud's little carven room
> Which, set like a precious stone
> In pannels of oaken gloom T36a

> Maud has an old oak-room
> A room that is all her own
>   T36b *false start, deleted*

Lights with herself, when alone   500
She sits by her music and books
And her brother lingers late
With a roystering company) looks
Upon Maud's own garden-gate:
And I thought as I stood, if a hand, as white   505
As ocean-foam in the moon, were laid
On the hasp of the window, and my Delight
Had a sudden desire, like a glorious ghost, to glide,
Like a beam of the seventh Heaven, down to my side,
There were but a step to be made.   510

3

The fancy flatter'd my mind,
And again seem'd overbold;
Now I thought that she cared for me,
Now I thought she was kind
Only because she was cold.   515

500   Lights] BM–; She lights T36a.

501   by] BM–; with T36a.

503   With a roystering company)] BM, H30 *and* T36b (. . . company,),
        P2–; By his bacchanal company, T36a.

505]   BM, H30 (. . . thought, . . . stood . . . hand . . .), T36b (*no commas*),
        P2–; And I thought if a hand as white T36a.

507   hasp of the window,] BM, H30 (. . . window), T36b–; window handle
        T36a.

508–9]   T36b 2nd reading (*substantives only; see Minor Variants*)–;

> Had a sudden desire to glide
> Like a glorious ghost to my side T36a

> Had a sudden desire to glide (glide, T36b)
> Like a beam of the seventh Heaven down to my side
>   (Heaven, T36b)
>   BM, H30 *and* T36b 1st reading

4

I heard no sound where I stood
But the rivulet on from the lawn
Running down to my own dark wood;
Or the voice of the long sea-wave as it swell'd
Now and then in the dim-gray dawn;   520
But I look'd, and round, all round the house I beheld
The death-white curtain drawn;
Felt a horror over me creep,
Prickle my skin and catch my breath,
Knew that the death-white curtain meant but sleep,   525
Yet I shudder'd and thought like a fool of the sleep
      of death.

I xiv *4* 516–26] T36a– (BM *breaks off after* 520).

516   where] T36a, T36b–; as BM, H30.

517   on from] BM, H30–; over T36a.

518   my own dark wood;] T36b 2nd reading–; my little wood. T36a; the
          little wood BM, H30, T36b 1st reading (wood;).

518 ∧ 519] T36a *has a line between*:

                    And so by the village out to the sea;

519   voice] T36a, T36b–; sound H30.

      long sea-wave] BM *and* H30 (. . . seawave), T36b–; sea itself T36a.

520 ∧ 521 T36a *has a line between*:

                    But a morbid fancy belongs to me:

521   But I look'd,] H30 (. . . lookd), T36b–; I lookd T36a.

523   Felt] T36b–; And I felt T36a, H30.

525   Knew] T36b 2nd reading–; For I knew T36a, H30, T36b 1st reading.

526] T36b 2nd reading–;

      Yet I shudderd & thought of the sleep of death. (shudder'd H30,
          T36b) (Death. H30)
                              T36a 1st reading, H30, T36b 1st reading

      Yet I shudderd & thought of the sleep but sleep of death.
                              T36a 2nd reading

XV

So dark a mind within me dwells,
  And I make myself such evil cheer,
That if *I* be dear to some one else,
  Then some one else may have much to fear;   530
But if *I* be dear to some one else,
Then I should be to myself more dear.
Shall I not take care of all that I think,
Yea ev'n of wretched meat and drink,
If I be dear,   535
If I be dear to some one else.

I xv 527–36] BM, H30, T36, [Berg A] (*on now lost f.18*), P1–3, Trial, **1855–**.

P1 *has three lines preceding* 527 *which may also have been in now lost* Berg A:

        If a man desire his marriage bells
          He will count at least on a happy year;
        But a mind so dark,

529 *I*] P3, Trial, **1864–**; I BM–T36, P1, 2, **1855–1862**.

530 may have] T36 2nd reading–; has BM–T36 1st reading.

531 *I*] P3, Trial, **1864–**; I BM H30, T36, P1, 2, **1855–1862**.

532 I should] T36, **1855–**; should BM, I H30; P1–3, *I* should Trial.

533 Shall I not] T36 2nd reading–; I will BM–T36 1st reading.
      all that] T36–; what BM, H30.

534 wretched meat] T36 2nd reading–; what I eat BM–T36 1st reading.

535 I] BM, H30, T36, **1855–**; *I* P1–3, Trial.

536 I] BM, H30, T36, **1855–**; *I* P1–3, Trial.

xvi

1

This lump of earth has left his estate
The lighter by the loss of his weight;
And so that he find what he went to seek,
And fulsome Pleasure clog him, and drown   540
His heart in the gross mud-honey of town,
He may stay for a year who has gone for a week:
But this is the day when I must speak,
And I see my Oread coming down,
O this is the day!   545
O beautiful creature, what am I
That I dare to look her way;
Think I may hold dominion sweet,
Lord of the pulse that is lord of her breast,
And dream of her beauty with tender dread,   550

I xvi *1–3* 537–70] T36, Berg A, Pl–3; Trial, **1855–**.

I xvi *1* 537–59]

537] T36 2nd reading–; This clod has left his broad estate T36 1st reading.

539] *interlineated in* T36 (. . . seek), Berg A–.

540   And] T36 2nd reading–; Let T36 1st reading.

542   He may] T36 2nd reading–; Till he T36 1st reading.

543   when] T36 2nd reading–; that T36 1st reading.

544–5] *transposed in* T36.

544   And] T36, Pl–; For Berg A.

548   Think I may hold] Trial–; To think of holding T36; That I think of holding Berg A; Pl–3.

549] Berg A–; Lord of the pulses that move her breast; T36.

550   And] Berg A–; To T36.

From the delicate Arab arch of her feet
To the grace that, bright and light as the crest
Of a peacock, sits on her shining head,
And she knows it not: O, if she knew it,
To know her beauty might half undo it.   555
I know it the one bright thing to save
My yet young life in the wilds of Time,
Perhaps from madness, perhaps from crime,
Perhaps from a selfish grave.

2

What, if she be fasten'd to this fool lord,   560
Dare I bid her abide by her word?
Should I love her so well if she
Had given her word to a thing so low?
Shall I love her as well if she
Can break her word were it even for me?   565
I trust that it is not so.

3

Catch not my breath, O clamorous heart,
Let not my tongue be a thrall to my eye,
For I must tell her before we part,
I must tell her, or die.   570

552] T36 1st reading (. . . grace, that . . .), Berg A (. . . that . . .), P1–; To
    the splendid grace, that light as the crest T36 2nd reading.

556–9] *Added in the margin in* T36.

559   a selfish grave.] Berg A–; the grave. T36.

I xvi 2 560–6] *Run on as one stanza with* 1 *in* Berg A *and* P1.

562–6] P1–; *not in* T36 *or* Berg A, *but evidence suggests these lines were once in* T36
    and have been torn out.

I xvi 3 567–70] *Run on as one stanza with* 1 *and* 2 *in* Berg A and P1.

567   breath,] T36, P2–; heart, Berg A, P1.

    heart,] T36 (heart), P2–; breath, Berg A, P1.

xvii

Go not, happy day,
   From the shining fields,
Go not, happy day,
   Till the maiden yields.
Rosy is the West,   575
   Rosy is the South,
Roses are her cheeks,
   And a rose her mouth.
When the happy Yes
   Falters from her lips,   580
Pass and blush the news
   Over glowing ships;
Over blowing seas,
   Over seas at rest,
Pass the happy news,   585
Blush it thro' the West;
Till the red man dance
   By his red cedar-tree,
And the red man's babe

I xvii 571–98] Camb, H30 (571–8 *only*), T36, [Berg A] (*on now lost f.20*),
Pl–3, Trial, **1855**–.
578] H30 *is torn away after this line.*

582] **1865 Select, 1872, 1875, 1889**; Oer the blowing ships Camb, T36;
   O'er the blowing ships. Pl–Trial, *all single-volume editions from* **1855**
   to **1884, 1870 Mini**.

585] T36 (. . . news), Pl–; Round the rosy world. Camb (*fills in an intentional
   blank*).

588   his red] T36–; the Camb.

Leap, beyond the sea.   590
Blush from West to East,
  Blush from East to West,
Till the West is East,
  Blush it thro' the West.
Rosy is the West,   595
  Rosy is the South,
Roses are her cheeks,
  And a rose her mouth.

595] Camb *reads* Rosy is the west & a *and then breaks off, omitting* 596–8.

xviii

1

I have led her home, my love, my only friend.
There is none like her, none.   600
And never yet so warmly ran my blood
And sweetly, on and on
Calming itself to the long-wish'd-for end,
Full to the banks, close on the promised good.

2

None like her, none.   605
Just now the dry-tongued laurels' pattering talk
Seem'd her light foot along the garden walk,
And shook my heart to think she comes once more;
But even then I heard her close the door,
The gates of Heaven are closed, and she is gone.   610

I xviii *1–8* 599–683] H30 (*1–5, 6 647–50 only, 8*), T36, [Berg A] (*on now lost ff.21, 22*), P1–3, Trial, **1855–**.

I xviii *1* 599–604] H30–.

599   led] T36–; brought H30.

601   warmly] P2–; sweetly H30, T36, P1.

602] P2–; So like a sunwarm river on & on H30; And warmly, on & on T36, P1.

I xviii *2* 605–10] H30–.

607   Seem'd her light foot] T36–; Like her light feet H30.

608   And shook my heart] T36–; Made my heart shake H30.

3

There is none like her, none.
Nor will be when our summers have deceased.
O, art thou sighing for Lebanon
In the long breeze that streams to thy delicious East,
Sighing for Lebanon,   615
Dark cedar, tho' thy limbs have here increased,
Upon a pastoral slope as fair,
And looking to the South, and fed
With honey'd rain and delicate air,
And haunted by the starry head   620
Of her whose gentle will has changed my fate,
And made my life a perfumed altar-flame;
And over whom thy darkness must have spread
With such delight as theirs of old, thy great
Forefathers of the thornless garden, there   625
Shadowing the snow-limb'd Eve from whom she came.

I xviii *3* 611–26] H30–.

616] *Written continuously as one stanza with* 615 *in* P1, *and so, presumably, in now
      lost* Berg A.

      limbs have here increased,] *In* H30 limbs *is an isolated word filling in part
      of an intentional blank. In* T36 *an intentional blank has been completely filled
      in with this whole phrase.*

617   Upon] H30, P2–; Here on T36, P1.

619   honey'd rain and delicate] T36 2nd reading–; honeyd showers &
      tender H30; honey'd shower & delicate T36 1st reading.

620   by] T36–; with H30.

4

Here will I lie, while these long branches sway,
And you fair stars that crown a happy day
Go in and out as if at merry play,
Who am no more so all forlorn,   630
As when it seem'd far better to be born
To labour and the mattock-harden'd hand,
Than nursed at ease and brought to understand
A sad astrology, the boundless plan
That makes you tyrants in your iron skies,   635
Innumerable, pitiless, passionless eyes,
Cold fires, yet with power to burn and brand
His nothingness into man.

5

But now shine on, and what care I,
Who in this stormy gulf have found a pearl   640
The countercharm of space and hollow sky,
And do accept my madness, and would die
To save from some slight shame one simple girl.

I xviii *4* 627–38] H30–.

627 these] P2–; thy H30, T36, P1.

628 you fair] P2–; watch the H30, T36, P1.

633 at] T36–; with H30.

634–5] P2–;   Some cheerless fragment of the boundless plan
                     Which is the despot of your iron skies H30

                     The huge uncomfortable plan
                     Of your tyrannic iron skies, T36 1st reading

                     A cheerless fragment of the boundless plan
                     That is the tyrant of your iron skies, (skies,– P1)
                                       T36 2nd reading *and* P1

636 pitiless, passionless] T36 (pityless. . .), P1–; passionless, pitiless H30.

I xviii *5* 639–43] H30–.

640 stormy gulf] T36–; gulf H30.

641 hollow sky,] T36 (. . . sky), P1–; sky H30.

6

Would die; for sullen-seeming Death may give
More life to Love than is or ever was   645
In our low world, where yet 'tis sweet to live.
Let no one ask me how it came to pass;
It seems that I am happy, that to me
A livelier emerald twinkles in the grass,
A purer sapphire melts into the sea.   650

7

Not die; but live a life of truest breath,
And teach true life to fight with mortal wrongs.
O, why should Love, like men in drinking-songs,
Spice his fair banquet with the dust of death?
Make answer, Maud my bliss,   655
Maud made my Maud by that long loving kiss,
Life of my life, wilt thou not answer this?
'The dusky strand of Death inwoven here
With dear Love's tie, makes Love himself more dear.'

I xviii *6* 644–50] H30 (647–50 *only*), T36–.

644–6] *Not in* H30; *added to* T36 *after the draft had been completed.*

644   Would die;] T36 2nd reading (. . . Die,), P1–; Die, yes T36 1st
      reading.

645] T36 2nd reading–; Some sweeter life to love than ever was T36 1st
      reading.

646   low] T36 2nd reading–; sweet T36 1st reading.

647   Let no one] H30, T36 2nd reading–; For let none T36 1st reading.

I xviii *7* 651–9] T36–; *not in* H30.

652   fight with] T36 2nd reading–; conquer T36 1st reading.

653   O,] T36 2nd reading (O), P1–; For T36 1st reading.

656   loving] **1889**; lover's T36–**1884**.

657   Life of my life,] T36 2nd reading (. . . life), P1–; Maud my true T36
      1st reading.

658, 659 'The . . . dear.'] P1–; The . . . dear. T36.

659   dear Love's tie, makes] T36 2nd reading (. . . love's tie . . .), P1–;
      love's ~~life~~ tie made T36 1st reading.

8

Is that enchanted moan only the swell   660
Of the long waves that roll in yonder bay?
And hark the clock within, the silver knell
Of twelve sweet hours that past in bridal white,
And died to live, long as my pulses play;
But now by this my love has closed her sight   665
And given false death her hand, and stol'n away
To dreamful wastes where footless fancies dwell
Among the fragments of the golden day.
May nothing there her maiden grace affright!
Dear heart, I feel with thee the drowsy spell.   670
My bride to be, my evermore delight,
My own heart's heart, my ownest own, farewell;
It is but for a little space I go:
And ye meanwhile far over moor and fell
Beat to the noiseless music of the night!   675
Has our whole earth gone nearer to the glow
Of your soft splendours that you look so bright?
I have climb'd nearer out of lonely Hell.
Beat, happy stars, timing with things below,
Beat with my heart more blest than heart can tell,   680
Blest, but for some dark undercurrent woe
That seems to draw—but it shall not be so:
Let all be well, be well.

I xviii *8* 660–83] H30 (*two drafts:* a, b)–.

H30a *is an early version which Tennyson deleted. It lacks most lines* (660–71, 673, 680–3):

672　Farewell ʌ dear love, my ownest own, farewell.

　　　　　own（above line before 672）

676　Has the whole Earth gone nearer to the glow

677　Of these sweet fires that all things seem so bright

678　I have climb'd nearer out of lonely Hell

674　Beat high & low far over frith & fell

675　Beat to the noiseless music of the night

679　Beat on sweet stars timing with things below

To H30a, H30b *adds all lines except* 660, 661, 664, 670. *Its lines up to* 669 *are out of order:*

662　The clock within strikes twelve, the silver knell

663　Of twelve sweet hours for ever mark'd with white
　　　And yet I scarce have heart to break the spell

665　But by this my love has closed her sight

　　　　　now（above line before 665）

666　And given false death her hand and stol'n away

669　May nothing there her maiden heart affright

667　To dreamful wastes where footless Fancies dwell

668　Among the golden fragments of the day.

H30b *has* 671–83 *in the final order. The following collation includes* H30b (671–83), T36, *and printed texts.*

660]　T36 3rd reading–; I scarce can think this music but the swell T36 1st reading; What threefold meaning echoes from the swell T36 2nd reading.

663　that past in bridal] T36 2nd reading–; for ever mark'd in T36 1st reading.

664　And died to live,] T36 2nd reading (. . . died . . . live), P1–; So mark'd at least T36 1st reading.

666–70]　T36 *runs:* 666, 669, 667, 668, 670.

669　there] H30b, T36 1st reading, P1–; rude T36 2nd reading.

670]　T36 2nd reading–; I likewise droop & feel the drowsy spell. T36 1st reading.

672　My own heart's heart,] P1–**1884** (. . . heart), **1889**; My life's own life, H30b, T36 1st reading; Dear heart's mid-heart T36 2nd reading.

672　my] H30b, T36 2nd reading, **1889**; and T36 1st reading, P1–**1884**.

674 ye] P1–; you H30b, T36.

    moor] T36–; fold H30b.

677 you look] T36–; they stream H30b.

678 *I*] H30b, T36, P2–; I P1.

679 Beat, happy] T36–; Beat on, true H30b.

681] T36 (Blest . . .), P1–; But for some strange & misconjectured woe H30.

682 That seems to draw—] T36–; Some undercurrent— H30b.

    but it shall not] T36 2nd reading–; may it not H30b; but it may not T36 1st reading.

xix

1

Her brother is coming back to-night,
Breaking up my dream of delight.   685

2

My dream? do I dream of bliss?
I have walk'd awake with Truth.
O when did a morning shine
So rich in atonement as this
For my dark-dawning youth,   690
Darken'd watching a mother decline
And that dead man at her heart and mine:
For who was left to watch her but I?
Yet so did I let my freshness die.

I xix *1–10* 684–786] H30 (*2, 4–7, 9, 10 only*), H31, Berg B, **1856–**; *not in* T36,
Berg A, P1–3; Trial, **1855**.

I xix *1* 684–5] H31–; *not in* H30.

I xix *2* 686–94] H30–.

686] **1856–**; I am not dreaming of bliss H30; Yet I am not dreaming of
bliss: H31, Berg B 1st reading; Yet it is no dream of bliss: Berg B
2nd reading.

687] H31 2nd reading (. . . Truth:), Berg B–; It was here she sat: it is truth:
H30; Here she sat: it is truth. H31 1st reading.

688 O] *added in margin in* H30.

690 dark-dawning] Berg B 2nd reading–; long wasted H30; long-wasted
H31 1st reading; long-darken'd H31 2nd reading, Berg B 1st
reading.

691] Berg B 3rd reading (Darkend), **1856–**; Watching a mother decline
H30 1st reading; Spent in Watching a mother decline H30 2nd
reading, H31 2nd reading (. . . watching . . .), Berg B 1st reading
(. . . mother's . . .); Wasted in . . . H31 1st reading; Long-darken'd
watching . . . Berg B 2nd reading.

3

I trust that I did not talk   695
To gentle Maud in our walk
(For often in lonely wanderings
I have cursed him even to lifeless things)
But I trust that I did not talk,
Not touch on her father's sin: 700
I am sure I did but speak
Of my mother's faded cheek
When it slowly grew so thin,
That I felt she was slowly dying
Vext with lawyers and harass'd with debt: 705
For how often I caught her with eyes all wet,
Shaking her head at her son and sighing
A world of trouble within!

692   And] Berg B 2nd reading–; With H30, H31, Berg B 1st reading.

693–4] *Not in* H30.

693]   Berg B 2nd reading–; Not wasted—who was to watch her but I? H31,
        Berg B 1st reading.

694   freshness] H31 2nd reading–; own youth H31 1st reading.

I xix *3* 695–708] H31–; *not in* H30.

695–704] H31 *has only the second half of these lines, the leaf having been torn away.*

702   faded] Berg B–; wasted H31 1st reading; fading H31 2nd reading.

703   so] H31 2nd reading–; more H31 1st reading.

704   slowly] H31 1st reading, Berg B–; daily H31 2nd reading.

708]   *Following this line* H31 *has a deleted line:* And thus I remember her yet.

4

And Maud too, Maud was moved
To speak of the mother she loved   710
As one scarce less forlorn,
Dying abroad and it seems apart
From him who had ceased to share her heart,
And ever mourning over the feud,
The household Fury sprinkled with blood   715
By which our houses are torn:
How strange was what she said,
When only Maud and the brother
Hung over her dying bed—
That Maud's dark father and mine   720
Had bound us one to the other,
Betrothed us over their wine,
On the day when Maud was born;
Seal'd her mine from her first sweet breath.
Mine, mine by a right, from birth till death.   725
Mine, mine—our fathers have sworn.

I xix *4* 709–26] H30 (*four drafts*: a, b, c, d)–.

H30a *is an early version, lacking* 709, 711–16, 718, 724–6:

710   She ~~has~~ too has loved her mother

717   What was it her mother said

719   To Maud on her death-bed?

720   That our two fathers had ever

721/2   Betrothed us one to the other

       On
723   ~~From~~ the day when Maud was born.

To H30a, H30b (*which has been deleted*) *adds* 709, 711, *but still lacks* 712–16, 718, 724–6:

709/10 Maud too spoke of her mother

711   Whose death had left her forlorn:

717   What was it her mother said

719   When lying on her death bed

720   What! that her father & mine

722   Betroth'd us over their wine

721   Bound us one to the other

723   The day when Maud was born.

To H30b, H30c *adds* 714, 716, 718, *but still lacks* 712, 713, 715, 724–6:

709/10 Maud too spoke of a mother

       Who living a life
711   ~~Whose death had left~~ her forlorn;

       Often weeping
714   ~~Who sorrow'd~~ over the feud

            are
716   By which our houses were torn.

       Strange, what was it she
717   ~~What was it her mother~~ said,

718   When only Maud & the brother

719   Hung over her dying bed.

       That my Maud's
720   ~~What, that her~~ father & mine

722   Had betrothed us over their wine

721   Bound us one to the other

723   The day when Maud was born.

To H30c, H30d *adds* 715 *and two lines not adopted in later stages; still lacking are* 712, 713, 724–6. *Quoted here are only* 709–15, *for* 716–23 *agree substantively with the final reading.*

709/10 Maud too spoke of her mother

       Nay when I ask'd of the father

710   Would speak of the mother rather,

       And then as of a being imbued

711   With a fixed sorrow, living forlorn

714   And ever mourning over the feud

715   Is it a wonder? was there not blood

To H30d, H31 *adds all the lines hitherto lacking. Quoted here are* 709–15:

709   Maud too, was she not moved?

        To speak
710   ~~She too spoke~~ of the mother she loved,

711   As one scarce less forlorn;

712   Dying abroad & it seems, apart

        him
713   From ~~one~~ who had ceased to share her heart,

714   And ever mourning over the feud

715   The household fury sprinkled with blood,

The following collation gives variants in Berg B *and printed texts (for lines* 709–26), *in* H30d *(*716–23*), and in* H31 *(*716–26*):*

709]   **1856**–; Maud also, she was moved Berg B.

717   what] H30d, H31 2nd reading–; that which H31 1st reading.

724–6] *Not in* H30.

724   her first sweet breath.] Berg B 2nd reading (. . . breath), **1856**–; the dawn of her life H31, Berg B 1st reading.

725   from birth till death.] Berg B 2nd reading (. . . death,), **1856–1886** (. . . death,), **1889**; my Maud, my wife, H31, Berg B 1st reading.

5

But the true blood spilt had in it a heat
To dissolve the precious seal on a bond,
That, if left uncancell'd, had been so sweet:
And none of us thought of a something beyond,   730
A desire that awoke in the heart of the child,
As it were a duty done to the tomb,
To be friends for her sake, to be reconciled;
And I was cursing them and my doom,
And letting a dangerous thought run wild   735
While often abroad in the fragrant gloom
Of foreign churches—I see her there,
Bright English lily, breathing a prayer
To be friends, to be reconciled!

I xix 5 727–39] H30 (*three drafts*: a, b, c)–.

H30a *is a very early version which lacks most of the lines (727–35) and includes others subsequently unadopted. The spacing between the lines suggests they were written down almost at random:*

> A nature as undefiled
> As the heart of a maiden child

736	And oft abroad in the fragrant gloom
737/8	Of foreign minsters a dream & a prayer
739	That we should be reconciled

> This has been the dream of her life.
> I used to call her my little wife

Opposite H30a, *on the verso of the preceding leaf, is written a phrase and then, after a gap*, 734:   It was so then

> When I was cursing them & my doom

To H30a, H30b *adds* 731, 733, 734, *but still lacks* 727–30, 732, 735:

733   So, to be friends to be reconciled

734   While I was cursing them & my doom

731   Had been the dream of the maiden child

736   Often ~~abroad~~ alone in the fragrant gloom

737   Of foreign churches—I see her there

738   My blessing on her—breathing a prayer

739   To be friends, to be reconciled

To H30b, H30c *adds* 735, *but still lacks* 727–30, 732:

731 Then rose in the heart of the child

733 A desire to be reconciled;

734 When I was cursing them & my doom

735 And letting a dangerous thought run wild,

736 Often alone in the fragrant gloom

737 Of foreign churches—I see her there,

    White
738 ~~My~~ lily—she was breathing a prayer

739 To be friends, to be reconciled.

To H30c, H31 *adds all the lines hitherto lacking, except* 729. H31 *agrees, for the most part, with the final reading. However,* 727 *is preceded by five deleted lines:*

> ~~Was he not bound the more,~~
> ~~After the horrible end~~
> ~~Of the man that he called his friend,~~
> ~~By the promise sworn to before?~~
> ~~Were his feelings then so fine & sweet~~

The following collation includes H31, *Berg* B, *and printed texts.*

727 But] H31 2nd reading–; That H31 1st reading.

728 precious] *interlineated in* H31. *Berg* B *originally read* the precious, *but Tennyson deleted this and interlineated a 2nd reading. He then reverted to the 1st reading, cancelling and erasing the 2nd reading. Of this, only the following is legible:*

> , [*erasure*], the

    a] Berg B 2nd reading–; the H31, Berg B 1st reading.

729] *interlineated in* Berg B (That, left . . .), **1856**–; *not in* H31.

730 And] H31 2nd reading–; But H31 1st reading.

731 A] H31 2nd reading–; The H31 1st reading.

6

But then what a flint is he! 740
Abroad, at Florence, at Rome,
I find whenever she touch'd on me
This brother had laugh'd her down,
And at last, when each came home,
He had darken'd into a frown, 745
Chid her, and forbid her to speak
To me, her friend of the years before;
And this was what had redden'd her cheek
When I bow'd to her on the moor.

I xix *6* 740–9] H30 (*two drafts:* a, b)–.

742   I find whenever] H31 (. . . find, . . .), Berg B–; Whenever H30a, b.

743] H30b *and* H31 (. . . down;), Berg B–; H30a *has two lines alternating with two lines of* 744 (*the first of* 744 *is interlineated*):

743   He ever had laugh'd her down

744   And at last when both came home
743   This brother of hers but when

744   They came to the hall had met

744] H31 *and* Berg B (*no punctuation*), **1856**–; H30a *has two lines (see above);* And last when both came home H30b.

745] H30b *and* Berg B (. . . frown), H31, **1856**–; Her brother exprest with a frown H30a.

746] H31 *and* Berg B (*no punctuation*), **1856**–; And at last forbid her to speak H30a; They quarrell'd; he forbad her to speak H30b.

747] H31 *and* Berg B (. . . before,), **1856**–; To him who had been ~~the~~ her [*intentional blank*] before *interlineated in* H30a; To me her friend of the days before H30b.

748   what had] H30b–; that which H30a.

7

Yet Maud, altho' not blind   750
To the faults of his heart and mind,
I see she cannot but love him,
And says he is rough but kind,
And wishes me to approve him,
And tells me, when she lay   755
Sick once, with a fear of worse,
That he left his wine and horses and play,
Sat with her, read to her, night and day,
And tended her like a nurse.

I xix *7* 750–9] H30–.

750, 751, 753] *Adapted from a draft of* I xix *9 in* H30 (H30b) *where they begin
that stanza:*

       She loves him
   750 ~~Maud the she is~~ not blind

   751 Loves him with heart & mind

   753 Says, he is rough but kind

The isolated phrase rough but kind *is part of an uncompleted line which begins the
earliest draft of* I xix *9 in* H30 (H30a).

753 And says] H31 2nd reading (. . . Says), Berg B–; Says H30, H31 1st
     reading.

754 And wishes] H31–; Wishes H30.

755 tells] H31–; told H30.

757 That he] H31–; He had H30.

758] H31–; Came & read to her night & day H30.

759 And tended] H31–; Tended H30.

8

Kind? but the deathbed desire   760
Spurn'd by this heir of the liar—
Rough but kind? yet I know
He has plotted against me in this,
That he plots against me still.
Kind to Maud? that were not amiss.   765
Well, rough but kind; why let it be so:
For shall not Maud have her will?

I xix *8* 760–7] H31–; *not in* H30.

761   the] H31, Berg B 2nd reading–; a Berg B 1st reading.

766   Well, rough] H31, Berg B 2nd reading–; Rough Berg B 1st reading.

767] Berg B 2nd reading (. . . will.), **1856**–; My lady shall have her will.
       H31, Berg B 1st reading.

9

For, Maud, so tender and true,
As long as my life endures
I feel I shall owe you a debt,   770
That I never can hope to pay;
And if ever I should forget
That I owe this debt to you
And for your sweet sake to yours;
O then, what then shall I say?—   775
If ever I *should* forget,
May God make me more wretched
Than ever I have been yet!

I xix 9 768–78] H30 (*three drafts:* a, b, c)–.

H30a *is an early version which lacks* 771, 775, 776. *It begins with a phrase later adopted in* I xix 7:

    [intentional blank] rough but kind

768/9 Sweet Maud while life endures

770   I ever owe you a debt
772   And when *[intentional blank]* I forget *[interlineated]*
773/4 ~~Of~~ To you 9 even to yours

774   To be tender to you & yours

777   May God make me more wretched

778   Than ever I have been yet.

H30b *adds all the lines not in* H30a. Moreover, H30b *begins with three lines (*750, 751, 753*) later adopted in* I xix 7 (*see* 7).

768–9] H30b *reads:*   O Maud, while life endures
                      Sweet Maud, so tender & true

768   For,] Berg B 2nd reading–; O H30c; Ah H31, Berg B 1st reading.

769   As long as my] H31 2nd reading–; I swear while H30c, H31 1st
        reading.

770   I feel I shall] Berg B–; I shall ever H30b, H31; ~~That~~ I shall ever H30c.

771]   *Interlineated in* H30b.

773   That I owe this debt] H30b 2nd reading–; To be tender *[intentional
        blank]* H30b 1st reading.

774   your sweet sake] Berg B 2nd reading–; your sake H30b–Berg B 1st
        reading.

10

So now I have sworn to bury
All this dead body of hate,   780
I feel so free and so clear
By the loss of that dead weight,
That I should grow light-headed, I fear,
Fantastically merry;
But that her brother comes, like a blight   785
On my fresh hope, to the Hall to-night.

775] H31 3rd reading (. . . say?), Berg B–; I have but one thing to say,
    H30b, c; I have but this to say, H31 1st reading; Oh then, what then
    should I say? H31 2nd reading.

776 *should*] H30c–; should H30b.

I xix *10* 779–86] H30 (*two drafts:* a, b)–.

H30a *is an early draft lacking* 780–2. H30b *adds these lines but has them in this
order:* 779, 780, 783, 784, 782, 785, 786.

779 So now] H30b–; Now H30a.

780–2] *Not in* H30a.

781 So clear] II31–; clear H30b.

782–3] *Transposed in* H31 1st reading; H31 2nd reading *has final order.*

782 By] H31 3rd reading–; From H30b, H31 1st, 2nd readings.

783] H31 2nd reading–; Should grow light-headed perhaps H30a; I shall
    grow lightheaded I fear H30b, H31 1st reading (. . . light-headed, . . .).

785] H31–; But that her brother H30a; Save that her brother comes, like a
    blight H30b.

786 On my fresh hope,] H30b–; Is coming back H30a.

XX

1

Strange, that I felt so gay,
Strange, that *I* tried to-day
To beguile her melancholy;
The Sultan, as we name him,—   790
She did not wish to blame him—
But he vext her and perplext her
With his worldly talk and folly:
Was it gentle to reprove her
For stealing out of view   795
From a little lazy lover
Who but claims her as his due?
Or for chilling his caresses
By the coldness of her manners,
Nay, the plainness of her dresses?   800
Now I know her but in two,
Nor can pronounce upon it
If one should ask me whether
The habit, hat, and feather,
Or the frock and gipsy bonnet   805
Be the neater and completer;
For nothing can be sweeter
Than maiden Maud in either.

I xx *1–4* 787–836] T18 (*1* 802–8 *only*), H30, T36, Berg A, P1–3, Trial,
1855–.

I xx / 787–808] T18 (802–8 *only*), H30 (*two drafts:* a, b)–.
787–800] H3Qa *runs:* 789, 810, 793, 794, 798, 796, 799, 800. H30a *lacks* 787,
788, 790–2, 795, 797. H30b *adds* 787, 788, 790, 792, *and runs:* 787–90, 792–4,
798, 796, 799, 800. H30b *lacks* 791, 795, 797. T36 *has the lines in the same order
as* H30b *but adds* 797 *after* 796. T36 *lacks* 791 *and* 795. Berg A *and* P1–3
transpose 787 *and* 788 *but have the remaining lines in the same order as* T36. *Like* T36
they lack 791 *and* 795. Trial *adds* 791 *and* 795 *and has all the lines in the final order.*
787–8] Trial–**1864** (. . . I tried . . .), **1865–**;

> I am not often gay, (gay T36)
> Yet so I seem'd today H30b, T36

I tried, for an hour today,
Why not, I have grown so gay, Berg A 1st reading

(today *and* so gay *fill in intentional blanks*)

Strange, that I tried today,
I felt myself so gay, Berg A 2nd reading

Strange, that I tried,
To-day I felt myself so gay, P1

Strange, that I tried to-day,
Strange that I felt so gay, P2, 3

789] H30b *and* T36 (melancholy), Berg A (melancholy,), P1–3 (melancholy;), Trial–; He has made her melancholy H30a.

790] P3–; Because the lubber dandy H30b, T36; For it seems the lubber dandy Berg A, P1, 2.

792 But he] P3–; Had H30b–P1, 2.

her and] T36 *has* her *interlineated.*

794 Was it gentle] P3–; O the booby, H30a; Ah booby H30b, T36; Ah the booby, Berg A (the *is interlineated*), P1, 2.

796–8] P1 *and* P2 *run* 798, 796, 797.

796] P3–; Of the little lord, [lord H30b, T36] her lover, H30a, H30b, T36 1st reading; Of a little lazy lover T36 2nd reading, Berg A, P1 (lover,), P2.

798] P3–; For slighting the caresses H30a, b; For chilling the caresses T36, Berg A, P1, 2.

799 By] T36–; And H30a; For H30b.

800 Nay,] H30b *and* T36 2nd reading (Nay), Berg A–; And H30a, T36 1st reading.

801–8] *Not in* H30b (*a revision of only* 789–800 *in* H30a).

801 Now I know] P3–; I have seen H30a; For I know T36–P1, 2.

802–8] *Early version in* T18:

803) O Maud I know not whether

802) Had I to pronounce upon it

804) The habit, hat & feather

805) Or the frock & gipsy bonnet

Is the dearer to ~~the~~ my mind

808) For I love you well in either

802 can pronounce] T36–; can I pronounce H30a.

803 If one should ask me] T36–; If a man should ask one, H30a.

2

But to-morrow, if we live,
Our ponderous squire will give   810
A grand political dinner
To half the squirelings near;
And Maud will wear her jewels,
And the bird of prey will hover,
And the titmouse hope to win her   815
With his chirrup at her ear.

3

A grand political dinner
To the men of many acres,
A gathering of the Tory,
A dinner and then a dance   820
For the maids and marriage-makers,
And every eye but mine will glance
At Maud in all her glory.

I xx *2* 809–16]

809]   T36 (*substantive reading; see Minor Variants*)–; But tomorrow night he
       gives H30.

810]   T36–; The ponderous squire her brother H30 (*which has the line between*
       789 *and* 793).

812   near;] T36, Berg A (near), Trial–; here, H30.

814]   Trial–; *not in* H30–P1; That her gentle mother left her, P2, 3.

815   titmouse] H30 2nd reading–; young Lord H30 1st reading.

       hope] P3–; hopes H30–P1, 2.

816   his chirrup at] H30 2nd reading–; a whisper in H30 1st reading.

I xx *3* 817–23]

817   grand] T36–; great H30.

818   To] T36–; For H30.

819   A] T36 1st reading–; And a H30; At A T36 2nd reading, *deleted*.

820   A dinner and then] T36–; And after that H30.

823   At] T36 *has an illegible letter revised to* At.

4

For I am not invited,
But, with the Sultan's pardon,   825
I am all as well delighted,
For I know her own rose-garden,
And mean to linger in it
Till the dancing will be over;
And then, oh then, come out to me   830
For a minute, but for a minute,
Come out to your own true lover,
That your true lover may see
Your glory also, and render
All homage to his own darling,   835
Queen Maud in all her splendour.

I xx *4* 824–36]

824] T36 *and* Berg A (. . . invited), P1–; *not in* H30.

825   the Sultan's] P3–; her brother's H30–P1, 2.

826] T36, Berg A (. . . delightd), P1–; *not in* H30.

827   For I know] T36–; I know H30.

828   And mean] T36–; And I mean H30.

   linger] T36–; loiter H30.

828 ∧ 829] *Between these lines* H30 *has*

            Till the rising of the sun
            And the waking of the linnet

829] T36 *and* Berg A (. . . over), P1–; When the dances will be done— H30.

830] T36 *and* Berg A 2nd reading (*no punctuation*), P1–; And then slip out, slip out to me H30; And then oh then slip out to me Berg A 1st reading.

832] Berg A 2nd reading (come . . . lover), P1–; Come if you can to your lover T36 1st reading; O Come . . . T36 2nd reading; Oh come to your own true lover Berg A 1st reading.

833   your true lover] T36–; I your lover H30.

835   his] T36–; my H30.

xxi

Rivulet crossing my ground,
And bringing me down from the Hall
This garden-rose that I found,
Forgetful of Maud and me,   840
And lost in trouble and moving round
Here at the head of a tinkling fall,
And trying to pass to the sea;
O Rivulet, born at the Hall,
My Maud has sent it by thee   845
(If I read her sweet will right)
On a blushing mission to me,
Saying in odour and colour, 'Ah, be
Among the roses to-night.'

I xxi 837–49] T36 (*three drafts:* a, b, c), Berg A, Trial, **1855**–. T36a *and* T36b
are fragmentary, the leaves having been torn away.

837   crossing my] T36b–; crossing over T36a.

838] T36b–; *not in* T36a.

839   This] T36b–; Here is a T36a.

840–2] Berg A 2nd reading *and* P1–3 (. . . poppling fall,), Trial–;

    841)   In doubt & trouble & round

    840)   Forgetful of Maud of me

    842)   Caught at the head of a poppling fall T36a

    840)   Forgetful of Maud & me,

    841)   In trouble & doubt, & round

    842)   Moved at the head of a [*leaf torn away*] T36b 1st reading

    841)   In doubt & trouble, & m[*leaf torn away*]

    840)   Forgetful of Maud & me,

    842)   Here at the head of a [*leaf torn away*] T36b 2nd reading

842) Here at the head of a poppling fall

841) In doubt & trouble & moving round T36c *(omits 840)*

840) Forgetful of Maud & me,

842) Here at the head of a poppling fall,

841) And lost in trouble & moving round Berg A 1st reading

844 O Rivulet,] T36b 1st reading, T36c *and* Berg A (. . . Rivulet), P1–; But O Rivulet T36a; Rivulet, T36b 2nd reading.

845] T36c–; [Has] not Maud [*leaf torn away*] T36a 1st reading; [Has] Maud not sent it by thee T36a 2nd reading; Has Maud not sent [*leaf torn away*] T36b 1st reading; My Maud has sent [*leaf torn away*] T36b 2nd reading.

846–9] *Torn away in* T36a.

846] T36b (*omits brackets*), T36c–.

847] *Interlineated in* T36b (*which has only* . . . mission *because of torn leaf*).

848 Saying] T36c–; And saying T36b.

848–9 'Ah, be . . . to-night.'] P1–; 'O . . . tonight T36c; 'O Be . . . tonight' Berg A 1st reading; 'Ah, be . . . tonight' Berg A 2nd reading; *torn away in* T36b.

849 the] T36b, P2–; our Berg A, P1.

849] *Below this line* T36b *has, after a gap, an alternative reading:* Among my sisters.

xxii

1

Come into the garden, Maud,   850
   For the black bat, night, has flown,
Come into the garden, Maud,
   I am here at the gate alone;
And the woodbine spices are wafted abroad,
   And the musk of the rose is blown.   855

2

For a breeze of morning moves,
   And the planet of Love is on high,
Beginning to faint in the light that she loves
   On a bed of daffodil sky,
To faint in the light of the sun she loves,   860
   To faint in his light, and to die.

3

All night have the roses heard
   The flute, violin, bassoon;
All night has the casement jessamine stirr'd
   To the dancers dancing in tune;   865
Till a silence fell with the waking bird,
   And a hush with the setting moon.

I xxii *1–11* 850–923] T36 *has two drafts:* T36a *has only 1, 2;* T36/H *adds 3–11,*
[Berg A] *(on now lost ff. 25, 26),* P1–3, Trial, **1855–**.

I xxii *1* 850–5] T36a–.

855   rose is] **1872, 1889**; roses T36/H–Trial, *all single-volume editions from*
     1855*to* **1884, 1865 Select, 1870 Mini**.

4

I said to the lily, 'There is but one
  With whom she has heart to be gay.
When will the dancers leave her alone?   870
  She is weary of dance and play.'
Now half to the setting moon are gone,
  And half to the rising day;
Low on the sand and loud on the stone
  The last wheel echoes away.   875

I xxii *3–11* 862–923] T36/H–; *not in* T36a.

I xxii *3* 862–7]

866 fell] T36/H alternative reading–; came T36/H 1st reading.

      waking] T36/H 2nd reading–; morning T36/II 1st reading.

I xxii *4* 868–75]

868–9] *Added to* T36/H *after* 870–5 *had been written down.*

870] T36/H 2nd reading (. . . alone,), P1–; 'O dancers leave my darling
    alone, T36/H 1st reading.

873 rising] T36/H 2nd reading–; breaking T36/H 1st reading.

874 sand] T36/H 2nd reading–; grass T36/H 1st reading.

5

I said to the rose, 'The brief night goes
    In babble and revel and wine.
O young lord-lover, what sighs are those,
    For one that will never be thine?
But mine, but mine,' so I sware to the rose,   880
    'For ever and ever, mine.'

6

And the soul of the rose went into my blood,
    As the music clash'd in the hall;
And long by the garden lake I stood,
    For I heard your rivulet fall   885
From the lake to the meadow and on to the wood,
    Our wood, that is dearer than all;

I xxii *5* 876–81]

877] T36/H 3rd reading–;

           'O leave her a little to sweet repose.
             You are merry with feast & wine.
                    T36/H 1st reading
           For babble & revel & wine.
                  T36/H 2nd reading

878   sighs] T36/H 2nd reading–; looks T36/H 1st reading.

879   one] T36/H 2nd reading–; a heart T36/H 1st reading.

880   so I sware] T36/H 2nd reading–; I said T36/H 1st reading.

881   ever,] T36/H (~~fo~~ ever), P1–.

7

From the meadow your walks have left so sweet
   That whenever a March-wind sighs
He sets the jewel-print of your feet   890
   In violets blue as your eyes,
To the woody hollows in which we meet
   And the valleys of Paradise.

8

The slender acacia would not shake
   One long milk-bloom on the tree;   895
The white lake-blossom fell into the lake
   As the pimpernel dozed on the lea;
But the rose was awake all night for your sake,
   Knowing your promise to me;
The lilies and roses were all awake,   900
   They sigh'd for the dawn and thee.

I xxii *7* 888–93]

888   your . . . left] T36/H 2nd reading–; you pace & have made T36/H 1st reading.

889–90] T36/H 2nd reading (. . . march-wind . . . It sets The . . .), P1–;

         That it sets when a march-wind sighs
         The dewy jewel-print of your feet
               T36/H 1st reading

I xxii *8* 894–901]

894–5] *Added to* T36/H *after* 896–901 *had been written down.*

896   white lake-blossom] T36/H 2nd reading–; water blossom T36/H 1st reading.

897   As the pimpernel] T36/H 2nd reading–; The daisy T36/H 1st reading.

898   all night for your] T36/H 2nd reading–; for thy sweet T36/H 1st reading.

899   Knowing your] T36/H 2nd reading–; And felt thy T36/H 1st reading.

901   sigh'd for the dawn] T36/H 2nd reading–; waited for dawn T36/H 1st reading.

9

Queen rose of the rosebud garden of girls,
  Come hither, the dances are done,
In gloss of satin and glimmer of pearls,
  Queen lily and rose in one;   905
Shine out, little head, sunning over with curls,
  To the flowers, and be their sun.

10

There has fallen a splendid tear
  From the passion-flower at the gate.
She is coming, my dove, my dear;   910
  She is coming, my life, my fate;
The red rose cries, 'She is near, she is near;'
  And the white rose weeps, 'She is late;'
The larkspur listens, 'I hear, I hear;'
  And the lily whispers, 'I wait.'   915

11

She is coming, my own, my sweet;
  Were it ever so airy a tread,
My heart would hear her and beat,
  Were it earth in an earthy bed;
My dust would hear her and beat,   920
  Had I lain for a century dead;
Would start and tremble under her feet,
  And blossom in purple and red.

I xxii *9* 902–7]

902   rosebud] T36/H 2nd reading–; muskrose T36/H 1st reading.

906   Shine out,] T36/H 2nd reading–; Shine, sweet T36/H 1st reading.

I xxii *11* 916–23]

918,920 her] T36/H 2nd reading–; it T36/H 1st reading.

919   earth] T36/H 2nd reading–; hush'd T36/H 1st reading.

920   and beat,] T36/H 2nd reading–; & beat, & beat; T36/H 1st reading.

PART II

i

1

'The fault was mine, the fault was mine'—
Why am I sitting here so stunn'd and still,
Plucking the harmless wild-flower on the hill?—
It is this guilty hand!—
And there rises ever a passionate cry   5
From underneath in the darkening land—
What is it, that has been done?
O dawn of Eden bright over earth and sky,
The fires of Hell brake out of thy rising sun,
The fires of Hell and of Hate;   10
For she, sweet soul, had hardly spoken a word,
When her brother ran in his rage to the gate,
He came with the babe-faced lord;

II i *1, 2,* 1–48] T36 (*two drafts:* a, b), [Berg A] (*on now lost f.27*), P1–3, Trial,
1855–.

II I *1* 1–35]

1   was . . . was] T36b–; is . . . is T36a.

2] T36b (. . . still), P1–; T36a *has two lines:*

> Why do I stare at the far sea-line?
> Why sit I here so stunn'd & still

5–6] T36b–;

> And I seem to hear a passionate cry
> That rings about the darkening land. T36a

127

Heap'd on her terms of disgrace,
And while she wept, and I strove to be cool,   15
He fiercely gave me the lie,
Till I with as fierce an anger spoke,
And he struck me, madman, over the face,
Struck me before the languid fool,
Who was gaping and grinning by: 20
Struck for himself an evil stroke;
Wrought for his house an irredeemable woe;
For front to front in an hour we stood,
And a million horrible bellowing echoes broke
From the red-ribb'd hollow behind the wood,   25
And thunder'd up into Heaven the Christless code,
That must have life for a blow.
Ever and ever afresh they seem'd to grow.
Was it he lay there with a fading eye?
'The fault was mine,' he whisper'd, 'fly!'   30
Then glided out of the joyous wood
The ghastly Wraith of one that I know;
And there rang on a sudden a passionate cry,
A cry for a brother's blood:
It will ring in my heart and my ears, till I die, till I die.   35

17] T36b–; *not in* T36a.

anger] T36b 2nd reading–; answer T36b 1st reading.

18–19] T36b–;

> And struck me, madman, over the face
> Before the languid fool, T36a.

21] T36b–; Laid on me an unbearable load, T36a.

22   Wrought] T36b–; And wrought T36a.

23–32] T36a *reads:*

> For he fell at noon, by the Christless code
> That must have life for a blow,
> Poor angry wretch—in the little wood;
> 'The fault is mine' he whisper'd fly.'

33   And] T36b–; But T36a.

2

Is it gone? my pulses beat—
What was it? a lying trick of the brain?
Yet I thought I saw her stand,
A shadow there at my feet,
High over the shadowy land. 40
It is gone; and the heavens fall in a gentle rain,
When they should burst and drown with deluging
    storms
The feeble vassals of wine and anger and lust,
The little hearts that know not how to forgive:
Arise, my God, and strike, for we hold Thee just, 45
Strike dead the whole weak race of venomous worms,
That sting each other here in the dust;
We are not worthy to live.

II i *2* 36–48]

T36a *is an early version:*

> Break forth in earthquake & in storms
> Kill kill the feeble vassals of anger & lust
> That know not how to forgive.
> Strike dead, O God, for we hold thee just,
> The whole weak race of venomous worms,
> That sting each other in the dust.
> We are not fit to live.

38   her] T36b 2nd reading–; it T36b 1st reading.

45–6] Pl–;

> Rise, strike, my God, strike dead, for we hold Thee just,
> The whole weak race of venomous worms, T36b

48   worthy] Pl–; fit T36b.

ii

1

See what a lovely shell,
Small and pure as a pearl,   50
Lying close to my foot,
Frail, but a work divine,
Made so fairily well
With delicate spire and whorl,
How exquisitely minute,   55
A miracle of design!

2

What is it? a learned man
Could give it a clumsy name.
Let him name it who can,
The beauty would be the same.   60

II ii *1–9* 49–131] H27 (*9 only*), T36 (*except 8: see Commentary*), [Berg A] (*on now lost ff. 28, 29*), P1–, Trial, **1855**–.

II ii *1* 49–56]

53   Made] T36 2nd reading–; And T36 1st reading.

II ii *2* 57–60]

57   What is it?] T36 2nd reading–; If I were T36 1st reading.

58   Could] T36 2nd reading–; I could T36 1st reading.

3

The tiny cell is forlorn,
Void of the little living will
That made it stir on the shore.
Did he stand at the diamond door
Of his house in a rainbow frill?   65
Did he push, when he was uncurl'd,
A golden foot or a fairy horn
Thro' his dim water-world?

4

Slight, to be crush'd with a tap
Of my finger-nail on the sand,   70
Small, but a work divine,
Frail, but of force to withstand,
Year upon year, the shock
Of cataract seas that snap
The three decker's oaken spine   75
Athwart the ledges of rock,
Here on the Breton strand!

II ii *3* 61–8]

67   golden] P2–; rosy T36, P1.

5

Breton, not Briton; here
Like a shipwreck'd man on a coast
Of ancient fable and fear—   80
Plagued with a flitting to and fro,
A disease, a hard mechanic ghost
That never came from on high
Nor ever arose from below,
But only moves with the moving eye,   85
Flying along the land and the main—
Why should it look like Maud?
Am I to be overawed
By what I cannot but know
Is a juggle born of the brain?   90

II ii *5* 78–90] T36 (*two drafts:* a, b)–.

T36a *is an early version*:

> Here on the Breton coast
> Pacing beside the main
> Vext with a hard mechanic ghost
> That looks a little like Maud
> But I will not be overawed
> By a juggle born of the brain

82, 90] *Adopted from lines in the four stanzas in* **1837** *which Tennyson did not
    incorporate into* II iv:

> By a dull mechanic ghost
>   And a juggle of the brain.

For the complete stanzas, see the Commentary for II iv.

88, 89] *Between these lines* T36b *has a deleted line:* By a juggle born of the
    brain?, *probably an error in transcription.*

6

Back from the Breton coast,
Sick of a nameless fear,
Back to the dark sea-line
Looking, thinking of all I have lost;
An old song vexes my ear;   95
But that of Lamech is mine.

7

For years, a measureless ill,
For years, for ever, to part—
But she, she would love me still;
And as long, O God, as she   100
Have a grain of love for me,
So long, no doubt, no doubt,
Shall I nurse in my dark heart,
However weary, a spark of will
Not to be trampled out.   105

II ii *6* 91–6]

T36 *has only an early version:*

> Back from the Breton coast
>   to
> Back ~~over~~ the dark sea-line
> Looking & sighing for all I have lost,
> The song of Lamech is mine

For the later draft, now lost, see Commentary.

II ii *7* 97–105]

97   measureless] P2–; meanless P1 (*error?*).

104] P2–; One spark of a fiery will T36, P1.

8

Strange, that the mind, when fraught
With a passion so intense
One would think that it well
Might drown all life in the eye,—
That it should, by being so overwrought,   110
Suddenly strike on a sharper sense
For a shell, or a flower, little things
Which else would have been past by!
And now I remember, I,
When he lay dying there,   115
I noticed one of his many rings
(For he had many, poor worm) and thought
It is his mother's hair.

II ii *8* 106–18] [Berg A?], P1–; *only fragments of a fair copy survive on a stub in* T36 (*see Commentary*).

II ii *9* 119–31] H27, T36–.

H27 *is an early draft lacking* 128 *and having the lines out of order:*

119   Perhaps he is not dead

120   Perhaps I need not have fled

121   I may not be guilty of blood

122   But howsoever it be

123   Comfort her, comfort her, all things good

124   While I am over the sea

126   Speak to her all things holy & high

127   Whatever happen to me.

125   Let me & my passionate love go by

123   But comfort her comfort her all things good

129   Visit her waking find her asleep

130   Powers of the hight & powers of the deep

131   Comfort her tho' I die

9

Who knows if he be dead?
Whether I need have fled? 120
Am I guilty of blood?
However this may be,
Comfort her, comfort her, all things good,
While I am over the sea!
Let me and my passionate love go by, 125
But speak to her all things holy and high,
Whatever happen to me!
Me and my harmful love go by;
But come to her waking, find her asleep,
Powers of the height, Powers of the deep, 130
And comfort her tho' I die.

Tennyson has marked 124 and 127 to be transposed. To H27 T36 adds no new lines but repeats 126. It transposes 124 and 127 so that the lines are in this order: 119–23, 127, 126, 124, 125, 123, 126, 129–31. T36 originally contained a later draft (see Commentary).

119] T36 2nd reading (. . . dead), P1–; I have not heard he is dead T36 1st reading.

120 Whether I need] P1–; Perhaps I need not T36.

121 Am I] P2–; I may not be T36; For am I P1.

122] P1–; But howsoever it be T36.

123] T36 *repeats 123 after 125, as in H27. But* T36 *has the repeated 123 together with the next line, 126 (also repeated), deleted.*

126 But speak] P1–; Speak T36 (*both lines*).

128] P1–; *not in* T36.

129 But come] T36 2nd reading (. . . Come), P1–; Come T36 1st reading.

130 Powers] P1–; & powers T36.

131 And comfort] P1–; Comfort T36.

iii

Courage, poor heart of stone!
I will not ask thee why
Thou canst not understand
That thou art left for ever alone: 135
Courage, poor stupid heart of stone.—
Or if I ask thee why,
Care not thou to reply:
She is but dead, and the time is at hand
When thou shalt more than die.   140

II iii 132–40] H31, **1856**–; *not in* T36, Berg A, P1–3, Trial, **1855**.

139   time is at] H31 *has* is *interlineated.*

iv

1

O that 'twere possible
After long grief and pain
To find the arms of my true love
Round me once again!

2

When I was wont to meet her   145
In the silent woody places
By the home that gave me birth,
We stood tranced in long embraces
Mixt with kisses sweeter sweeter
Than anything on earth.   150

II iv *1–13* 141–238] H21 *and* H13 *(six stanzas only: 1–3, one stanza conflating 5 and 7, 10, 13)*, T21 *1st reading (eight stanzas only: 1–3, one stanza conflating 5 and 7, 8, 10, 11, 13)*, T21 *2nd reading (ten stanzas only) adds 4 and 9,* **1837** *(adds all remaining stanzas, except 6, in this order: 1–5, 7 (184, 191–5 only), 9–11, 13, 8, 12, followed by four stanzas unadopted in any stage in the composition of 'Maud',* **AR** *(agrees with* **1837** *except for minor variants, a result of editorial intervention: see Minor Variants. In the textual apparatus,* **1837** *includes* **AR**, *except for minor variants, listed separately),* [T36] *(on now lost leaves following f. 36,* [Berg A] *(on now lost ff. 30, 31),* P1–3, Trial *(adds 6 and has all the stanzas in the final order),* **1855–**.

II iv *1* 141–4] H21–.

II iv *2* 145–50] H21–.

147   By the home] **1856–**; Of the land H21–**1855**.

3

A shadow flits before me,
Not thou, but like to thee:
Ah Christ, that it were possible
For one short hour to see
The souls we loved, that they might tell us   155
What and where they be.

4

It leads me forth at evening,
It lightly winds and steals
In a cold white robe before me,
When all my spirit reels   160
At the shouts, the leagues of lights,
And the roaring of the wheels.

II iv *3* 151–6] H21–.

153   Ah] H21 *and* H13 (Ah!), **1837**–; Oh T21.

   Christ,] H21–T21 (*no comma*), P1–; God! **1837**.

II iv *4* 157–62] T21–; *not in* H21, H13.

157–62] T21 *originally had* 156 *followed by* 163. *Tennyson added 4 for insertion after* 156.

5

Half the night I waste in sighs,
Half in dreams I sorrow after
The delight of early skies;   165
In a wakeful doze I sorrow
For the hand, the lips, the eyes,
For the meeting of the morrow,
The delight of happy laughter,
The delight of low replies.   170

II iv *5 163–70 and 7 184–95]* H21–.
*H21, H13, and T21 have only 163, 164 and versions of 167, 169. These lines are
conflated with a version of 7 (184, 191–5 only). In regard to 191–5, the MSS order
these lines variously. In H13 (transcribed below) Tennyson has added numerals in round
brackets to indicate that 192–5 are to be transposed from the original reading. The order
of these lines in H21 agrees with H13 1st reading, while the order in T21 agrees with
H13 2nd reading. In all other respects H21 and T21 agree with H13 unless stated
otherwise. For minor variants see Appendix C.*

163] Half the night I waste in sighs

     Half
164]   O̶r̶ [Or H21, Half T21] in dreams I sorrow after

167] Her hands, her lips, her eyes [The hand, the lips, the eyes, T21]

169]   Her [The T21] winsome laughter,

       I hear
184] And t̶h̶e̶ ̶s̶o̶u̶n̶d̶ ̶o̶f̶ [And the sound o' H21, I hear T21]
      the pleasant ditty

184]   She was wont to [That I heard her T21] chaųnt of old.

     But
191]   I ɟwake—[I awake— H21, But I wake— T21] my dream is
      fled

192] 2) In the glimmering [shuddering T21] gray behold

194] 3)   By the curtains of my bed

193] 1) Without knowlege, without pity

195] 4)   That dreadful phantom cold. H13

II iv *5 163–70]* H21, H13, T21 *(for all of which, see above)*–.

164–5] P1–; *not in* **1837**.

168 the morrow,] P1–; to-morrow, **1837**.

6

'Tis a morning pure and sweet,
And a dewy splendour falls
On the little flower that clings
To the turrets and the walls;
'Tis a morning pure and sweet,   175
And the light and shadow fleet;
She is walking in the meadow,
And the woodland echo rings;
In a moment we shall meet;
She is singing in the meadow   180
And the rivulet at her feet
Ripples on in light and shadow
To the ballad that she sings.

7

Do I hear her sing as of old,
My bird with the shining head,   185
My own dove with the tender eye?
But there rings on a sudden a passionate cry,
There is some one dying or dead,
And a sullen thunder is roll'd;
For a tumult shakes the city,   190
And I wake, my dream is fled;
In the shuddering dawn, behold,
Without knowledge, without pity,
By the curtains of my bed
That abiding phantom cold.   195

II iv 6 171–83] P1–; *not in* H21, H13, T21, **1837**.

II iv 7 184–95] H21, H13, T21 *and* **1837** *(*184, 191–5 *only)*, P1–3, Trial–. *The MSS* have the lines conflated with lines from 5. For this early version, see above. **1837** has the lines in this order: 184, 191, 193, 192, 194, 195.

184] P1–; **1837** *has two lines:*

> Do I hear the pleasant ditty,
> That I heard her chant of old?

8

Get thee hence, nor come again,
Mix not memory with doubt,
Pass, thou deathlike type of pain,
Pass and cease to move about!
'Tis the blot upon the brain   200
That *will* show itself without.

9

Then I rise, the eavedrops fall,
And the yellow vapours choke
The great city sounding wide;
The day comes, a dull red ball   205
Wrapt in drifts of lurid smoke
On the misty river-tide.

185–90] P1–; *not in* **1837**.

191   And] P1–; But **1837**.

192–3] *Transposed in* **1837**.

II iv 8 196–201] T21–; *not in* H21, H13. **1837** *has the lines in this order*: 196, 199, 198, 197, 200, 201.

197   Mix not] **1837**–; Mixing T21.

201   *will*] **1837**–; will T21.

II iv 9 202–7] T21–; *not in* H21, H13. *Run on as one stanza with 8 in* P3.

202–7] T21 *originally had* 201 *followed by* 208. *Tennyson added* 9 *for insertion after* 201.

205   The day] **1837**–; Day T21; And Day *autograph revision of* Heath MS, *a scribal transcript of* T21.

206   Wrapt in drifts] **1837**–; In a drift T21.

10

Thro' the hubbub of the market
I steal, a wasted frame,
It crosses here, it crosses there,   210
Thro' all that crowd confused and loud,
The shadow still the same;
And on my heavy eyelids
My anguish hangs like shame.

11

Alas for her that met me,   215
That heard me softly call,
Came glimmering thro' the laurels
At the quiet evenfall,
In the garden by the turrets
Of the old manorial hall.   220

12

Would the happy spirit descend,
From the realms of light and song,
In the chamber or the street,
As she looks among the blest,
Should I fear to greet my friend   225
Or to say 'Forgive the wrong,'
Or to ask her, 'Take me, sweet,
To the regions of thy rest'?

II iv *10* 208–14] H21–.

210   crosses . . . crosses] P1–; crosseth . . . crosseth H21–**1837**.

II iv *11* 215–20] T21–; *not in* H21, H13.

II iv *12* 221–8] **1837**–; *not in* H21, H13, T21.

222] P1–; *not in* **1837**.

226] P1–; *not in* **1837**.

228   regions] P1–; region **1837**.

228] *Following this line,* **1837** *and* **AR** *continue with four more stanzas not adopted in 'Maud' (see Appendix A).*

13

But the broad light glares and beats,
And the shadow flits and fleets 230
And will not let me be;
And I loathe the squares and streets,
And the faces that one meets,
Hearts with no love for me:
Always I long to creep 235
Into some still cavern deep,
There to weep, and weep, and weep
My whole soul out to thee.

II iv *13* 229–38] H21–.

229–31] *Not in* H21, H13.

229 But the] P1–; The T21; Then the **1837**.

230 shadow] P1–; sunk eye T21, **1837**.

232 And I] P1–; I H21–**1837**.

236 Into] P1–; To H21–**1837**.

237 There] P1–; And H21–**1837**.

v

1

Dead, long dead,
Long dead!   240
And my heart is a handful of dust,
And the wheels go over my head,
And my bones are shaken with pain,
For into a shallow grave they are thrust,
Only a yard beneath the street,   245
And the hoofs of the horses beat, beat,
The hoofs of the horses beat,
Beat into my scalp and my brain,
With never an end to the stream of passing feet,
Driving, hurrying, marrying, burying,   250
Clamour and rumble, and ringing and clatter,
And here beneath it is all as bad,
For I thought the dead had peace, but it is not so;
To have no peace in the grave, is that not sad?
But up and down and to and fro,   255
Ever about me the dead men go;
And then to hear a dead man chatter
Is enough to drive one mad.

II v *1–11* 239–342] Simeon MS (*detached from* T36?), T36 (*having 1–3, 4 and 7 written as one stanza, 8–11, omitting 5, 6*), Berg A, P1–3 Trial, **1855**–.

II v *1* 239–58] Simeon MS (*only a fragment has been examined; see p. 240*), T36–.

241   heart] T36 2nd reading–; brain T36 1st reading.

243] T36 2nd reading *and* Berg A (. . . pain), P1–; And my bones tho' dead are full of pain T36 1st reading.

248] *Following* 248 *in* T36 *is a line which has been deleted*: All the roar of the street.

249–50] T36 *originally had these lines transposed, but Tennyson revised them to the final order.*

249   With never an] T36 2nd reading–; There is no T36 1st reading.

2

Wretchedest age, since Time began,
They cannot even bury a man;   260
And tho' we paid our tithes in the days that are gone,
 Not a bell was rung, not a prayer was read;
It is that which makes us loud in the world of the
      dead;
There is none that does his work, not one;
A touch of their office might have sufficed,   265
But the churchmen fain would kill their church,
As the churches have kill'd their Christ.

251] T35 2nd reading (. . . rumble . . . clatter;), Berg A (. . . rumble. . .
    clatter,), P1–; Clamour & gabble & cackle & clatter; T36 1st reading.

252   beneath] T36 2nd reading–; in the grave T36 1st reading.

256] T36 2nd reading (. . . The . . . go), Berg A (. . . go,), P1–; The dead
    men trample as they go T36 1st reading.

II v *2* 259–67] T36–.

261] Berg A (. . . gone), P1–; We paid our tithes in the days that are gone
    T36.

262] Berg A–; But over us not a prayer ~~not~~ was read T36.

263] Trial–; That makes us so loud in the world of the dead. T36; That
    makes us now so loud in the world of the dead; Berg A, P1–3.

265   their] Berg A–; his T36.

3

See, there is one of us sobbing,
No limit to his distress;
And another, a lord of all things, praying   270
To his own great self, as I guess;
And another, a statesman there, betraying
His party-secret, fool, to the press;
And yonder a vile physician, blabbing
The case of his patient—all for what?   275
To tickle the maggot born in an empty head,
And wheedle a world that loves him not,
For it is but a world of the dead.

4

Nothing but idiot gabble!
For the prophecy given of old   280
And then not understood,
Has come to pass as foretold;

II v *3* 268–78] T36–.

268 See,] T36 1st reading *and* Berg A (See . . .), P1–; Lo! T36 2nd reading.

270–1] Berg A (. . . Lord . . . self . . . guess), P1–; And another musical puppet
      ~~fool~~ is playing T36.

                another
272] Berga A–; And ~~a silly~~ statesman there betraying T36.

273] T36 2nd reading (. . . party-secret fool . . .), Berg A–; His party secret
      to the press; T36 1st reading.

                 ailment
275] Berg A (. . . what), P1–; His patient's ~~case~~—& all for what T36.

           tickle   loves
276–8] Berg A (*no commas*), P1–; To ~~please~~ a world of the dead that ~~heeds~~
      him not T36.

II v *4* 279–90] T36–.

281 T36 3rd reading *and* Berg A (. . . understood), P1–; ~~Discredited~~ by the
      rabble T36 1st reading; Is now fulfill'd by ye rabble T36 2nd
      reading.

282 Has] T36 1st reading, Berg A–; It Has T36 2nd reading.

Not let any man think for the public good,
But babble, merely for babble.
For I never whisper'd a private affair   285
Within the hearing of cat or mouse,
No, not to myself in the closet alone,
But I heard it shouted at once from the top of the
    house;
Everything came to be known.
Who told *him* we were there?   290

5

Not that gray old wolf, for he came not back
From the wilderness, full of wolves, where he used
    to lie;
He has gather'd the bones for his o'ergrown whelp
    to crack;
Crack them now for yourself, and howl, and die.

283–6] T36 *originally read:*

> But not virtue's sake, merely for babble
> But tell not thou thy secret to the mouse

Tennyson added an alternative reading:

> Not,
> ~~But not~~ let any man think, for the public good
> But babble merely for babble
> Wilt
> ~~Darest~~ thou whisper a private affair

287   myself] Berg A–; thyself T36.

288] Berg A (*no punctuation*), P1–; It is shouted at once from the top of the house T36.

289] Berg A–**1884** (. . . known:), **1889**; And everything is known *deleted in* T36.

290] P1–; For who told him we were there. T36; Who told him we were there? Berg A.

II v 5 291–4] Berg A–; *not in* T36.

6

Prophet, curse me the blabbing lip,   295
And curse me the British vermin, the rat;
I know not whether he came in the Hanover ship,
But I know that he lies and listens mute
In an ancient mansion's crannies and holes:
Arsenic, arsenic, sure, would do it,   300
Except that now we poison our babes, poor souls!
It is all used up for that.

7

Tell him now: she is standing here at my head;
Not beautiful now, not even kind;
He may take her now; for she never speaks her   305
    mind,
But is ever the one thing silent here.
She is not *of* us, as I divine;
She comes from another stiller world of the dead,
Stiller, not fairer than mine.

II v *6* 295–302] Berg A–; *not in* T36.

300   sure,] **1856**–; Sir, Berg A; sir, P1–**1855B**.

301   babes,] Trial–; wives, Berg A, P1–3.

II v *7, 8* 303–20] Simeon MS *is an early version with a heading*:

    prophecy
      She is here at my bed.
      She is ghastly [ghostly?] now she is not kind—
             not
        What ails her she never tells her mind
      She alone is silent here
        She comes from another world of the dead
           not sweeter
      That is stiller than mine.

      I know   Garden where the rose tree shoots
        More sweeter than in all the world wide
      That is when the season is good.
        A garden of flowers: it has no fruits

8

But I know where a garden grows,   310
Fairer than aught in the world beside,
All made up of the lily and rose
That blow by night, when the season is good,
To the sound of dancing music and flutes:
It is only flowers, they had no fruits,   315
And I almost fear they are not roses, but blood;
For the keeper was one, so full of pride,
He linkt a dead man there to a spectral bride;
For he, if he had not been a Sultan of brutes,
Would he have that hole in his side?   320

        I fear
And ∧ they are not roses but blood
    For there a dead man woo'd a dying bride

        If he had not been the prince of brutes
Wd. he have that hole in his side

                                    deep enough

II v *7* 303–9] T36–.

303] Berg A–; T36 *has* They may tell him now *interlineated above* Why is she
    always standing at my head.

304] T36 2nd reading (not. . . now . . . kind), Berg A–; She is not beautiful
    now she is not kind T36 1st reading.

305] Berg A (. . . mind), P1–; T36 *has* Let him take her now *interlineated
    above* What ails her that she never tells her mind.

306] Berg A–; But is the one thing silent here T36.

307 *of*] **1889**; of T36–**1884**.
    as] *interlineated in* T36.

308 stiller] *interlineated in* T36.

309] Berg A–; T36 *has* But it seems no fairer *interlineated above* That is stiller
    not sweeter than mine.

II v *8* 310–20] T36 (*two drafts*: a, b)–.

310 grows,] Berg A (grows), P1–; blows T36a, b.

311] T36b 2nd reading *and* Berg A (. . . beside), P1–; Sweeter than all in the
    whole world wide T36a; Sweeter than aught in the world beside
    T36b 1st reading.

312] T36b–; *not in* T36a.

    the] *interlineated in* T36b.

313–15] T36a *reads*:

    (314)   Blows to the sound of dancing & flutes:

    (315)   ~~A garden of flowers for it had no fruits~~

    (313)   That is when the season is good:

    (315)   A garden of flowers for it had no fruits

313] T36b *and* Berg A (*no punctuation*), P1.

314] T36b (. . . flutes.), Berg A–.

315] T36b (. . . flowers: . . . fruits:), Berg A (. . . fruits), P1.

316   And I almost fear] T36b–; And I fear T36a.

317] T36b *and* Berg A (*no punctuation*), P1–; *not in* T36a.

318] T36b (. . . link'd . . . bride), Berg A–; For there did a dead man woo for a spectre bride T36a.

319   For he,] T36b, Berg A (. . . he—), P1–; And he— T36a.

    a Sultan] Trial–; the prince T36a–P3.

9

But what will the old man say?
He laid a cruel snare in a pit
To catch a friend of mine one stormy day;
Yet now I could even weep to think of it;
For what will the old man say   325
When he comes to the second corpse in the pit?

10

Friend, to be struck by the public foe,
Then to strike him and lay him low,
That were a public merit, far,
Whatever the Quaker holds, from sin;   330
But the red life spilt for a private blow—
I swear to you, lawful and lawless war
Are scarcely even akin.

II v *9* 321–6] T36–.

322] Berg A–; He that a snare in a pit T36.

324   weep] Berg A–; cry T36.

326   comes to] Berg A–; finds T36.

II v *10* 327–33] T36–.

327   Friend, to be struck by] Trial–; To kill T36 1st reading; Sir To be
       struck by T36 2nd reading, Berg A *and* P1–3 (Sir, to . . .).

328   Then to] T36 2nd reading (. . . To), Berg A–; To T36 1st reading.

329]   T36 3rd reading (. . . Were . . . merit far), Berg A–; Is a public merit I
       hold & far T36 1st reading; Were a public merit far T36 2nd
       reading.

330   holds,] T36 2nd reading–; says, T36 1st reading.

331   the red life spilt] T36 2nd reading–; murder done T36 1st reading.

332   swear to] T36 2nd reading–; tell T36 1st reading.

11

O me, why have they not buried me deep enough?
Is it kind to have made me a grave so rough,   335
Me, that was never a quiet sleeper?
Maybe still I am but half-dead;
Then I cannot be wholly dumb;
I will cry to the steps above my head
And somebody, surely, some kind heart will come   340
To bury me, bury me
Deeper, ever so little deeper.

II v *11* 334–42] T36–.

334   O me, why have they] T36 2nd reading (. . . me . . .), Berg A–; O me
      they have not T36 1st reading.

335] Berg A (. . . rough), P1–; Or they have made a grave too rough T36
      1st reading; Was it kind to have made me a grave too rough T36 2nd
      reading.

336] Berg A–; For one that never was a quiet sleeper T36 1st reading; Me
      that never was never a quiet sleeper T36 2nd reading.

337   Maybe still] T36 2nd reading (maybe . . .), Berg A–; Or maybe yet
      T36 1st reading.

338   Then] Berg A–; And then T36.

339   steps] T36 2nd reading–; feet T36 1st reading.

340   surely,] *interlineated in* T36; T36 *and* Berg A (surely), P1–.

      will] *alternative reading in* T36, Berg A–; may T36.

341] *interlineated in* T36; T36 *and* Berg A (. . . me, . . .me,), P1–.

342   Deeper,] Berg A–; And bury me T36 1st reading; Bury me T36 2nd
      reading.

PART III

vi

1

My life has crept so long on a broken wing
Thro' cells of madness, haunts of horror and fear,
That I come to be grateful at last for a little thing:
My mood is changed, for it fell at a time of year
When the face of night is fair on the dewy downs,   5
And the shining daffodil dies, and the Charioteer
And starry Gemini hang like glorious crowns
Over Orion's grave low down in the west,
That like a silent lightning under the stars
She seem'd to divide in a dream from a band of the
    blest,   10
And spoke of a hope for the world in the coming
    wars—
'And in that hope, dear soul, let trouble have rest,
Knowing I tarry for thee,' and pointed to Mars
As he glow'd like a ruddy shield on the Lion's breast.

III vi *1–5 1–59*] *4 only:* Camb, *1–4 only:* H30, [T36?] *(on now lost leaves following f. 42),* [Berg A] *(on now lost f. 34),* P1–3 *(and so presumably* [Berg A]*) have 2 and 3 run together as one stanza,* Trial, **1855**, **1855US** *(only line 50 and 5);* **1856** *introduces 5.*

III vi *1* 1–14] H30–.

  6 shining daffodil] Trial–; sweet narcissus H30, P1–3 (. . . Narcissus).

 10 divide] P2–; slide H30, P1.

     from a band of the blest,] H30 alternative reading (. . . blest), P1–; to the couch of my rest H30 1st reading.

 11 spoke] P2–; speak H30, P1.

 12 have rest,] H30 1st reading, P1–; be blest H30 2nd reading.

2

And it was but a dream, yet it yielded a dear delight   15
To have look'd, tho' but in a dream, upon eyes so
          fair,
That had been in a weary world my one thing bright;
And it was but a dream, yet it lighten'd my despair
When I thought that a war would arise in defence of
          the right,
That an iron tyranny now should bend or cease,   20
The glory of manhood stand on his ancient height,
Nor Britain's one sole God be the millionaire:
No more shall commerce be all in all, and Peace
Pipe on her pastoral hillock a languid note,
And watch her harvest ripen, her herd increase,   25
Nor the cannon-bullet rust on a slothful shore,
And the cobweb woven across the cannon's throat
Shall shake its threaded tears in the wind no more.

III vi *2* 15–28] H30–.

15] H30 1st reading (. . . dream . . .), P1–;

> And I woke & found no Mars in the Lion there
> Nor a star in the heaven, yet it yielded a dear delight
>   H30 2nd reading

16   To have look'd,] H30 2nd reading (. . . look'd), P1–; To look H30 1st reading

19   When I thought] H30 2nd reading–; To think H30 1st reading.

3

And as months ran on and rumour of battle grew,
'It is time, it is time, O passionate heart,' said I   30
(For I cleaved to a cause that I felt to be pure and
      true),
'It is time, O passionate heart and morbid eye,
That old hysterical mock-disease should die.'
And I stood on a giant deck and mix'd my breath
With a loyal people shouting a battle cry,   35
Till I saw the dreary phantom arise and fly
Far into the North, and battle, and seas of death.

III vi *3* 29–37] H30–. *Run together as one stanza with 2 in* P1–3, *and so,
presumably in* [Berg A].

29   months] P1–; weeks H30.

30–3] *Inverted commas introduced in* Trial.

34   And] P1–; Till H30.

36   Till] P1–; And H30.

4

Let it go or stay, so I wake to the higher aims
Of a land that has lost for a little her lust of gold,
And love of a peace that was full of wrongs and   40
    shames,
Horrible, hateful, monstrous, not to be told;
And hail once more to the banner of battle unroll'd!
Tho' many a light shall darken, and many shall weep
For those that are crush'd in the clash of jarring
    claims,
Yet God's just wrath shall be wreak'd on a giant liar;   45
And many a darkness into the light shall leap,
And shine in the sudden making of splendid names,
And noble thought be freer under the sun,
And the heart of a people beat with one desire;
For the peace, that I deem'd no peace, is over and
    done,   50
And now by the side of the Black and the Baltic deep,
And deathful-grinning mouths of the fortress, flames
The blood-red blossom of war with a heart of fire.

III vi *4* 38–53] Camb, H30–.

> For many shall trumpet & some shall fall & sleep
> In wreaking Heaven's just doom on a crafty liar
>   [*intentional blank*]   claims
> [*intentional blank*] sudden making of splendid names
>   [*intentional blank*]   higher
> And noble thought be freer under the sun
> For the long long canker of peace is over & done
> And now by the shore of the Black & Baltic deep
> And the deathful-grinning mouths of the fortress, flames
> The bloodred blossom of war with a heart of fire Camb

44   jarring] P2–; warring H30, P1.

45   wrath] **1856**–; doom H30–**1855**.

     giant] P1–; crafty H30.

50   For the peace, that I deem'd no peace,] **1855US** 3rd reading (*Tennyson's
     revision in an American copy of* **1855**), **1856**–; For the peace, that I
     thought no peace, **1855US** 2nd reading; For the peace that had
     nothing noble **1855US** 1st reading; For the long, long canker of
     peace H30–**1855**.

5

Let it flame or fade, and the war roll down like a
    wind,
We have proved we have hearts in a cause, we are
    noble still,   55
And myself have awaked, as it seems, to the better
    mind;
It is better to fight for the good than to rail at the ill;
I have felt with my native land, I am one with my
    kind,
I embrace the purpose of God, and the doom assign'd.

III vi 5 54–9] **1855US** (*except for minor variants*), **1856–**; *not in* H30, T36,
Berg A, P1–3, Trial, **1855**.

1855US 1st draft *(deleted):*

>   walk
> Let it go or stay so I ~~live~~ henceforth resigned
> By the light of a love not lost, with a purer mind
> And rejoice in my native land & am one with my kind.

1855US 2nd draft *(deleted):*

> And I rise from
> ~~So after~~ a life half-lost with a better mind
> I embrace the purpose of God & the doom assign'd
> And rejoice in my native land & am one with my kind

1855US 3rd draft *agrees with* **1856** *except for minor variants.*

Commentary

Introduction

Information on dating the sections, when such information exists, is not usually given in the Commentary but can be found discussed in the context of the entire poem in the Introduction. Information given about other poems of Tennyson is usually derived from Ricks. Poems first published by Christopher Ricks are quoted from his 1969 edition of the poems, but Tennyson's other poems are quoted from **1889** unless noted otherwise. The biographical information is derived from Martin. Most of the comments on the poem by Tennyson and Hallam Tennyson are quoted from *Eversley*, in which case no source is given. Tennyson's comments to Knowles are quoted from Ray.

Part I

I i *1–19* and ii 1–87

Composition: T36/H is a lightly revised draft consisting of three sections (set off from one another by the short dash which T. customarily used to divide one part from the next):

> *Section 1:* I i *1–13, 17* (ff. [1]–[3ʳ])
> *Section 2:* I ii (f. [3ʳ])
> *Section 3:* stanza of eight lines: two lines became *19* 73, 76; the other lines (f. [3ʳ]) were adapted (and tempered in tone) in I vi *4–10* (see textual notes).

Apparently dissatisfied with this sequence, T. revised it by adding (on the blank f. [2ᵛ]) two further stanzas (fair copies of now lost intermediate drafts). He did not indicate whether he intended these stanzas to supplement or to replace some of those in the original sequence, nor where the new stanzas should be located. The two stanzas consist of:
(1) five lines which follow on from Section 2 and Section 3 and which were adapted in I vi *4–10*.

(2) eighteen lines composed of: *18*; nine lines not subsequently adopted; *19* (including one line between 73 and 74 not adopted).

These lines are a revision of an earlier draft in T36 (f. 49ᵛ).

To summarize the results of T.'s pre-publication revisions: Section 3 was for the most part unadopted, and Section 1 was expanded by the addition of two stanzas (*18* and *19*). (For the stanzas added in **1856**, see *14–16* below.) T. comments:

> This poem of 'Maud or the Madness' is a little *Hamlet*, the history of a morbid, poetic soul, under the blighting influence of a recklessly speculative age. He is the heir of madness, an egoist with the makings of a cynic, raised to a pure and holy love which elevates his whole nature, passing from the height of triumph to the lowest depth of misery, driven into madness by the loss of her whom he has loved, and, when he has at length passed through the fiery furnace, and has recovered his reason, giving himself up to work for the good of mankind through the unselfishness born of a great passion. The peculiarity of this poem is that different phases of passion in one person take the place of different characters.

H. T. comments:

> The passion in the first Canto was given by my father in a sort of rushing recitative through the long sweeping lines of satire and invective against the greed for money, and of horror at the consequences of the war of the hearth. (*Memoir* I, 396)

1–3 1–12

Cf. the murder of Montague Tigg in *Martin Chuzzlewit* (1843–4), (note 'hollow', the repetition of 'wood', 'fallen headlong down', 'abhorrence' (with line 3, 'horror of blood') and the diction and image in the final sentence (with line 12)):

> . . . but before going down into a hollow place, he looked round once upon the evening prospect sorrowfully. Then he went down, down, down, into the dell.

It brought him to the wood; a close, thick, shadowy wood
. . . the stillness of this spot almost daunted him . . .

As the sunlight died away, and evening fell upon the
wood, he entered it . . . then he was seen or heard no more
. . . one man excepted. That man . . . came leaping out soon
afterwards.

What had he left within the wood, that he sprang out of
it, as if it were a Hell!

The body of a murdered man. In one thick solitary spot,
it lay among the last year's leaves of oak and beech, just as
it had fallen headlong down. Sopping and soaking in
among the leaves that formed its pillow; oozing down into
the boggy ground, as if to cover itself from human sight;
forcing its way between and through the curling leaves, as if
those senseless things rejected and foreswore it, and were
coiled up in abhorrence; went a dark, dark stain that dyed
and scented the whole summer night from earth to Heaven.

The doer of this deed came leaping from the wood so
fiercely, that he cast into the air a shower of fragments of
young boughs, torn away in his passage, and fell with
violence upon the grass. (Ch. 47)

Rader observes that the fall to death may have been
suggested by some wild adventures which T.'s father claimed
he experienced in Italy in 1830 (p. 142). Dr Tennyson's son
Charles recorded his father's account:

Once he was nearly buried alive by an avalanche; once,
being overcome with giddiness on the edge of a precipice,
he was only saved from destruction by his neighbour
seizing hold of him. Finally, when he was driving over the
mountains in a small carriage, a dog sprang out and
frightened the horses, which ran away and hurled the whole
equipage over the edge of a sheer rock. The Doctor saved
himself from death by convulsively grasping a pine, while
carriage, driver and horses were dashed to death thousands
of feet below. (*Alfred Tennyson*, p. 97)

1 1–4
2 blood-red heath] T. commented to Van Dyke: 'There is no

such thing in nature; but he sees the heather tinged like blood because his mind has been disordered and his sight discoloured by the tragedy of his youth.' Once when reading the poem aloud, T. paused here and remarked: '"Blood-red heath"! The critics might have known by *that* that the man was mad; there's no such thing' (W. J. Rolfe, ed. *Tennyson's Poetical Works*, 1898, IV, 350).

4 And Echo there, whatever is ask'd her, answers 'Death'] Cf. *Paradise Lost* II 787–9:

> I fled, and cried out *Death!*
> Hell trembled at the hideous name, and sighed
> From all her caves, and back resounded *Death!*

(Noted by John Churton Collins, ed. *'In Memoriam', 'The Princess', and 'Maud'*, 1902, p. 285).

3 9–12
9 a vast speculation had fail'd] Usually understood as an allusion to Matthew Allen's scheme to make wood-carvings by steam-driven machine. T. and his family invested £8000 in the project in 1840, but it collapsed two years later and the Tennysons lost all their money. More generally, a surge in company flotations, share-holding and speculation took place in the 1850s and continued for more than a decade. Thousands of small investors, unfamiliar with the commercial world, invested their capital in companies offering high returns and limited risks. The crash of such companies, many of them dishonest, often brought financial ruin to their shareholders.

12 And the flying gold of the ruin'd woodlands drove thro' the air] 'My father pointed out that even Nature at first presented herself to the man in sad visions' (H.T., *Memoir* I, 396).

6–13 21–52
Since early 1852, T. had been expressing his attitudes towards the social evils which seemed to him, and to a great number of

his contemporaries, the consequences of the last twenty-five predominantly peaceful years. (The public conscience chose to ignore the wars waged on behalf of British interests in India, China, Afghanistan and South Africa.) Although it, too, was fought in a distant land, the Crimean War served to foment at home the criticisms of the status quo which had been developing during the previous decade. The commonly blamed cause of discontent with a variety of social and domestic issues was selfish materialism. The groups widely accused of Mammon-worship were the pacifists and the Manchester School radicals who denounced the war partly on the grounds that it would arrest commercial development and bring economic disaster (see Olive Anderson, *A Liberal State at War*, 1967, pp. 98, 101, 163). T. gave vent to his social criticism and patriotism in a series of poems published anonymously in periodicals: 'The Penny-Wise', 'Rifle-Clubs!!!', 'Riflemen Form!' (published 1859), 'Britons, Guard Your Own', 'For the Penny-Wise', 'The Third of February, 1852', 'Hands All Round!' and 'Suggested by Reading an Article in a Newspaper'. Most of the poems were occasioned by the threat of an invasion from France. Their ideas and diction anticipate much of *Maud*.

T.'s political attitudes broadly agreed with those of Carlyle, and the influence of *Sartor Resartus* and *Past and Present* (both 1843) is unmistakable (see A. MacMechan, ed. *Sartor Resartus*, 1896, quoted in Ricks (1969), pp. 1041–2; John Churton Collins, ed. *'In Memoriam', 'The Princess', and 'Maud'*, 1902, p. 286; Valerie Pitt, *Tennyson Laureate*, 1962, p. 175). Most interesting is the comparison (by MacMechan) with *Sartor Resartus* III v:

'Call ye that a Society,' cries [Teufelsdrockh] again, 'where there is no longer any Social Idea extant; not so much as the Idea of a common Home, but only of a common, over-crowded Lodging-house? Where each, isolated, regardless of his neighbour, turned against his neighbour, clutches what he can get, and cries "Mine!" and calls it Peace, because, in the cut-purse and cut-throat Scramble, no steel knives, but only a far cunninger sort, can be employed?'

Such sentiments were widely echoed in the 1850s, but close parallels with *Maud* occur in a poem, 'The Muster of the Guards', by Franklin Lushington. He gave a copy to the Tennysons on 15 May 1854 (TRC):

> Peace, peace, peace, with the vain and silly song,
> That we do no sin ourselves, if we wink at others'
>   wrong;
> That to turn the second cheek is *the* lesson of
>   the Cross,
> To be proved by calculation of the profit and the
>   loss:
> Go home, you idle teachers! you miserable creatures!—
> The cannons are God's preachers, when the time is ripe
>   for War.
>
> Peace is no peace, if it lets the ill grow stronger,
> Merely cheating destiny a very little longer;
> War, with its agonies, its horrors, and its crimes,
> Is cheaper if discounted and taken up betimes:
> When the weeds of wrath are rank, you must plough the
>   poisoned bank,
> Sow and reap the crop of Peace with the implements
>   of war.
>
> God, defend the right, and those that dare to
>   claim it!
> God, cleanse the earth from the many wrongs that
>   shame it!
> Give peace in our time, but not the peace of
>   trembling,
> Won by true strength, not cowardly dissembling;
> Let us see in pride returning, as we send them forth
>   in yearning,
> Our Grenadier Guards from earning the trophies of
>   the War.

(in Henry Lushington, *La Nation Boutiquière and Other Poems Chiefly Political*, 1855, pp. 70–1; see Winston Collins, '"Maud": Tennyson's Point of War', *TRB* 2 (Nov. 1974), 126–8.)

Another and similar expression of the popular sentiments in these stanzas appeared in 'Peace and War: A Dialogue', *Blackwood's Edinburgh Magazine*, 76 (Nov. 1854) 589–98. An advocate of the moral superiority of war over peace argues against a Quaker:

What is called peace is too often a misnomer: only another name for internecine and most uncivil war. It is war at home, civil or uncivil, I especially deprecate . . .

When the Quaker suggests that a war undertaken to further commercial intercourse is perhaps excusable, the advocate of war replies:

I think it, of all reasons for war, the one involving the greatest moral guilt . . . . least of all will Mammon-worship excuse it [war], for this is the only religion in which devotion to its god is the same thing as the meanest and most unmitigated selfishness (pp. 592, 594, 596).

(See Robert C. Schweik, 'The "Peace or War" Passages in Tennyson's "Maud"', *Notes and Queries* NS 7 (1960), 457–8.)

6 21–4
21 the blessings of Peace] The expression occurred in the Declaration of the causes of war, delivered in the House of Commons on 22 March 1854 and published in the *London Gazette*, 28 March 1854 (Supplement, p. 1007): 'It is with deep regret that Her Majesty announces the failure of Her anxious and protracted endeavours to preserve for Her people and for Europe the blessings of peace.'

21 we have made them a curse] Malachi 2.2: 'saith the Lord of hosts, I will even send a curse upon you, and I will curse your blessings' (and also, for example, Genesis 27.12, Deuteronomy 23.5, Nehemiah 13.2).

23 Cain] Who slew his brother 'Because his own works were evil, and his brother's righteous' (Genesis 4.4–8, I John 3.12).

7 25–8
26 tradesman's ware or his word] Cf. 'Rifle Clubs!!!' 17–18:
'Some love Peace for her own dear sake, / Tradesmen love her
for gain'.

27 Is it peace or war? Civil war] 'Is it peace?' is the question
reiterated in 2 Kings 9.17–22 (Patrick Scott, *T.R.B.*, 3 (1978),
83). On 'Civil war', H.T. comments:

> What the hero in *Maud* says is that the sins of the nation,
> "civil war" as he calls them, are deadlier in their effect than
> what is commonly called war, and that they may be in a
> measure subdued by the war between nations, which is an
> evil more easily recognised. (*Eversley*, pp. 279–80, *Memoir* I,
> 401.)

The idea occurs in *Essay on the Classification of the Insane* (1837;
T.'s copy in TRC) by Matthew Allen, T.'s occasional doctor
and erstwhile friend:

> One part of society, as well as one part of the mind, is at
> war with another . . . . it is not so much these exciting
> causes, or even the sad effects of these feverish and wasting
> passions, that are in themselves so dreadful and fatal, as
> they are when accompanied or followed by the conflicts and
> condemnations of conscience.

8 29–32
30 golden age] The present age of selfish materialism, in
contrast to the golden age of classical antiquity.

31 make my heart as a millstone, set my face as a flint] Job
41.24: 'His heart is as firm as a stone; yea, as hard as a piece of
the nether millstone'; Isaiah 50.7: 'therefore shall I not be
confounded: therefore have I set my face like a flint, and I
know that I shall not be ashamed.'

9 33–6
Inside the Crystal Palace in 1851 a gigantic olive tree was
planted as a symbol of international concord, the theme of the

Great Exhibition being 'Peace' (see Asa Briggs, *The Age of Improvement 1783–1867*, 1959, pp. 376–7).

The stanza is anticipated in T.'s patriotic poems: 'Rifle Clubs!!!' 2–4: 'Sweet Peace can no man blame, / But peace of sloth or of avarice born, / Her olive is her shame'; 'Hands All Round!' 20: 'Too much we make our Ledgers, Gods'; 'Suggested by Reading . . .' 46–7: 'Sneering bedridden in the down of Peace, / Over their scrips and shares, their meats and wine'. Also cf. Micah 4.3–4: 'neither shall they learn war any more. But they shall sit every man under his vine and under his fig tree.'

34 When the poor are hovell'd and hustled together, each sex, like swine] The moral degeneracy which resulted from the overcrowded conditions in the dwellings of the poor was the object of public attention during the 1840s and 1850s, the period during which several government commissions inquired into sanitation and housing. The newspapers carried countless reports of actual cases; for example, *The Times* investigated the condition of the peasants in Dorset (25 June 1846, p. 3):

Another fruitful source of misery, as well as immorality, is the great inadequacy of the number and size of the houses to the number of the population, and the consequently crowded state of their habitations . . . It is by no means an uncommon thing for the whole family to sleep in the same room, without the slightest regard to age or sex, and without a curtain or the slightest attempt at separation between the beds . . . It will be easily imagined that the nightly and promiscuous herding together of young people of both sexes is productive of the most demoralizing effects.

10 **37–40**
Cf. 'Plain Speaking' in a volume owned by T., *Songs of the Present* (London, n.d.; but some poems dated 'April 1854' and 'May 1854', TRC). The poems are 'songs of self-amelioration and self-elevation on the part of the working classes.' Note 'rough brutes' ('ruffian's'), 'tramples a wife', 'murder':

Of all the rough brutes whom this earth has borne,
I know not a fitter mark for scorn
Than the wretch who tramples a wife forlorn,
    Because he's the viler and stronger;
The children's catchpipes should hiss his name,
As the meanest password for guilt and shame,
And Infamy's trump the word should claim
    And echo it deeper and longer.

The sot sits drinking long hour on hour,
Then home he goes in the pride of his power . . .
And her, who would shield her young one's life,
He eyes with a glance with murder rife,
Yells a hideous oath, and then opens his knife . . .

But daily such scenes do our giant-towns view! . . .
Have Englishmen lived a password to be
For the vilest and coarsest brutality?
Don't the nations sneer, when they call us free,
While our daily deeds disgust them?
(1–10, 13–15, 17, 21–4)

The poem following 'Plain Speaking', 'One Word More', also
condemns working men who beat their wives.

37 vitriol madness] Vitriol-throwing became a public
menace during the 1840s, years of civil disobedience in
Ireland and of social unrest in England.

**39–40 chalk and alum and plaster are sold to the poor for
bread . . . means of life]** The sale of adulterated foodstuffs
and poisonous drugs (44) had caused widespread complaint
since the eighteenth century. The publication in 1820 of
Friedrich Accum's *Adulterations of Food and Culinary Poisons*
fomented public interest and initiated further scientific
investigations, notably by Dr Arthur Hill Hassall. His
'Records of the Analytical Sanitary Commission of *The Lancet*'
were published in that journal from 1851 to 1854 and as a
book, *Food and its Adulterations*, in 1855. His findings, the

results of microscopic analyses of hundreds of foods and beverages, were disseminated by the popular press. *Household Words*, for example, ran a series of articles in 1850–1 describing the effects caused by adulterating substances ('Death in the Teapot', 'Death in the Bread-Basket', 'Death in the Sugar Plum', 2: 277, 323, 426–7). The addition of chalk, alum and plaster of Paris to inferior flour gave bread a white appearance and lightened it. Other foodstuffs commonly adulterated were milk and cream, coffee, tea, beer, gin, honey and sweetmeats. Hundreds of cases of poisoning resulted and an untold number of people died. The victims were generally the poor. Parliament was urged to regulate the manufacture of foods and the selling of poisonous drugs. Hassall was the chief witness before the Commons Select Committee on Foods in July 1855. The first Adulteration of Foods Act was passed in 1860 but disappointed radical reformers.

II 41–4
41 centre-bits] A tool used by burglars to cut cylindrical holes (see *Oliver Twist* ch. 19).

43–4 another is cheating the sick ... as he sits / To pestle a poison'd poison] Chemists and drug merchants ground and mixed their own preparations and so could increase their profits by adulterating the pure medicines. The 'poison' referred to here is undoubtedly opium, the cheap and popular remedy for a wide variety of ailments. It was identified as a poison and required to be marked as such. Nevertheless, it was openly sold in various forms (such as crude opium, opium lozenges and laudanum) by chemists, grocers and public houses. Opium was the chief constituent of the most common children's medicines. The result was that many children, mostly of the poor, died from overdoses. A *Household Words* article of 1850 expressed the growing concern over the ready availability of the potentially lethal drug: 'It is easy to perceive that the druggists are driving a good trade – that the quiet homes of the poor reek with narcotics' ('Protected Cradles', 26 October 1850, 2: 108). For children's deaths from arsenic poisoning, see note II v *6* 300–1.

***12* 45–8**

45 a Mammonite mother kills her babe for a burial fee]
Regular payments into 'burial clubs' enabled the working
class to cover the expenses of a decent funeral and so avoid the
indignity of a pauper's funeral performed by the parish. The
sum accumulated frequently tempted the desperate to premature collection, the chief victims being children, particularly
girls (John Morley, *Death, Heaven and the Victorians*, 1971,
p. 120). Reports of infanticide appeared frequently in the
press in the 1850s (see especially 'Human Kittens and Blind
Puppies', *Punch*, 23 (31 July 1852), 65). The trial of four
persons accused of the murder of two children at the Cheshire
Assizes in 1841 (*The Times*, 4–6 August 1841) provided
Carlyle (who used licence with some details) with an anecdote
in *Past and Present* about the mother and father

> arraigned and found guilty of poisoning three of their
> children, to defraud a 'burial-society' of some £3. 8s. due on
> the death of each child . . . and the official authorities, it is
> whispered, hint that perhaps the case is not solitary, that
> perhaps you had better not probe farther into that
> department of things. (I 1)

(For the suggestion that T. had this passage in mind, see
Stanley Thomas Williams, *Studies in Victorian Literature*, 1923;
rpt. 1967, p. 25.) 'Mammon', which was current in English as
a term of opprobrium from the sixteenth century onwards,
became a vogue word in the mid-nineteenth century. Carlyle's
usage may have helped to popularize the word, but T. had no
need of Carlyle as a source, as is sometimes claimed.

46 Timour] Matthew G. ('Monk') Lewis's 'grand romantic
and equestrian drama', *Timour*, was first performed in 1811 (at
Covent Garden) and later in 1822 (at Richmond). The horse-
spectacle followed the plays by Marlowe, Charles Saunders
and (most popular of all) Nicholas Rowe which adopted as
hero the medieval Turkish conqueror, Timur Beg. The
English stage tradition portrays Tamerlane as a brutal tyrant,
but Lewis's play, while depicting many atrocities, contains no
scene which might have suggested the lines here. Another of

Lewis's works, incidentally, inspired the play by Byron, *The Deformed Transformed* (1824), which features a cruel, Sycorax-like mother who scorns and curses her hunchback son. Deeply rejected, he likens himself to 'Timour the lame Tartar' (I i 322).

13 49–52
'He is wrong in thinking that war will transform the cheating tradesman into a great-souled hero, or that it will sweep away the dishonesties and lessen the miseries of humanity' (T. to Van Dyke, in *Studies in Tennyson*, 1921, p. 221).

14–16 53–64
Added in **1856**, apparently in response to adverse criticism of stanzas *6–13*, as Shannon suggests:

> Thus deliberately he weakened the force of the diatribe on the evils of Mammonism and of the exaltation of war as a corrective, and attempted to clear himself of responsibility for the invective of his *dramatis persona* . . . At the same time, the added lines contributed to the characterization of the hero by showing early that his inclination to rave was hereditary and that his father was actually a suicide. In the original version the reader had been left in uncertainty about the father's end. (pp. 408–9)

17 65–8
66 The dark old place will be gilt by the touch of a millionaire] Perhaps, as Rader suggests (p. 93), Bayons Manor in Lincolnshire, the late-Georgian Tudorized romantic castle built at great expense by T.'s loathed uncle, Charles Tennyson d'Eyncourt, between 1836 and 1842.

67 Maud] For the origins of the name, see Introduction, p. 33.

19 73–6
75 the fiend best knows] The proverb is: 'The Devil knows many things because he is old.'

76 I will bury myself in myself, and the Devil may pipe to his own] From a line in the unadopted stanza following 77–87 in T36/H.

I ii 77–87
This section was originally conceived as the middle part of a sequence which opened with a shortened version of I i and closed with an unadopted stanza (see headnote to I i **1–19** and ii above).

78 savour nor salt] Matthew 5.13: 'Ye are the salt of the earth: but if the salt have lost his savour, wherewith shall it be salted?'

79–87 But a cold and clear-cut face . . . touch of spleen] The description of Maud echoes lines in three sonnets about Rosa Baring, composed in 1835–6: 'I linger'd yet awhile to bend my way', 'Ah, fade not yet from out the green arcades', 'How thought you that this thing could captivate?' (Rader, pp. 34–6).

I iii 88–101
'Visions of the night' (T.).

91 pale] The revision to 'calm' in Berg A is contemporary with the second stage of revision as described in textual notes 100, 101.

98 the tide in its broad-flung shipwrecking roar] 'In the Isle of Wight the roar can be heard nine miles away from the beach' (T.). H.T. adds: 'Many of the descriptions of Nature are taken from observations of natural phenomena at Farring-ford, although the localities in the poem are all imaginary.' Emily's Journal notes that T. would take long walks to Bonchurch, in the south of the island, and back again 'sometimes over the shingly shore' (June 1854).

101 The shining daffodil dead, and Orion low in his grave] The season is late spring. T. told Mangles that a critic had complained that Orion is never 'low down in the west' at this time of year. Mangles records: 'Of course, he meant that Orion was setting over a high hill. I said I thought daffodils were favourites of his. He said they were. He admired very much Wordsworth's daffodils' (*Diary*, 29 March 1871, p. 70). The scene described is identical to the Lincolnshire of 'Locksley Hall' (1842):

> Locksley Hall, that in the distance overlooks the sandy tracts,
> And the hollow ocean-ridges roaring into cataracts.
>
> Many a night from yonder ivied casement, ere I went to rest,
> Did I look on great Orion sloping slowly to the West.
> (5–18)

I iv *1–10* 102–61
Composition: The numbered heading of this section in T36 may perhaps be a clue to T.'s early plans for the opening of the poem. I iv is headed with a roman numeral 'II', emended from an arabic '1'. All the other sections in the T36 series are headed with arabic numerals. Those which immediately follow I iv, for example, I v and I vi, are headed '3' and '4' respectively. The emendation might suggest that at an early stage of composition T. intended to open *Maud* with I iv.

T. comments: 'Mood of bitterness after fancied disdain'.

1 102–7
102–3 A million emeralds break from the ruby-budded lime / In the little grove] In April 1854, Emily's Journal records that T. took her to the 'wilderness' to admire 'the rose-coloured & green sheaths of the lime-leaves as they lay like flowers under the trees.'

2 108–13
109 bubbles o'er like a city, with gossip, scandal, and spite] This line may have been associated in some way with

the lost unadopted section containing the line 'When all the scum of night & hell boils from the cellar & the sewer' (see Introduction, pp. 18–19).

110 as many lies as a Czar] Nicholas I was widely referred to in the press as a liar, hypocrite and charlatan on account of his claim to be fighting a holy war, not a war of aggression. T. remarked in 1878, 'I've hated Russia ever since I was born, and I'll hate her till I die!' (Allingham's *Diary*, p. 265).

4 120–5
122 A wiser epicurean] Lucretius, follower of Epicurus and Roman poet of the 1st century BC, about whom T. published a poem in 1868. The Greek philosopher Epicurus held that one of the goals of life should be peace of mind.

123 For nature is one with rapine, a harm no preacher can heal] Cf. Matthew Arnold, 'To an Independent Preacher, who preached that we should be "In Harmony with Nature"' (1849; rpt. 1877 with a shorter title):

> 'In harmony with Nature?' Restless fool . . .
>
> Nature is cruel, man is sick of blood;
> Nature is stubborn, man would fain adore;
>
> Nature is fickle, man hath need of rest;
> Nature forgives no debt, and fears no grave . . .
>
> Nature and man can never be fast friends.
> (1, 7–10, 13)

124–5 The Mayfly is torn by the swallow . . . a world of plunder and prey] The allusion to Keats, 'Epistle to John Hamilton Reynolds' (1848) (suggested by Green, *PMLA*, 66 (1951), 367) is further supported by the reading in H29: 'rent by the robin':

> I was at home,
> And should have been most happy – but I saw

Too far into the sea, where every maw
The greater on the less feeds evermore. –
But I saw too distinct into the core
Of an eternal fierce destruction,
And so from happiness I far was gone,
Still am I sick of it, and tho', to-day,
I gather'd young spring-leaves, and flowers gay
Of periwinkle and wild strawberry,
Still do I that most fierce destruction see, –
The Shark at savage prey, – the Hawk at pounce, –
The gentle Robin, like a Pard or Ounce,
Ravening a worm . . .

6 132–7
132 monstrous eft] 'The great old lizards of geology' (T.).
Charles Kingsley used the expression in 'The Wonders of the
Shore', *North British Review*, 22 (Nov. 1854), 1–56, a review
article of six books on natural history:

> For, when questions belonging to the most sacred hereditary
> beliefs of Christendom were supposed to be affected by the
> verification of a fossil shell, or the proving that the
> Maestricht "homo diluvii testis" was, after all, a monstrous
> eft, it became necessary to work upon Conchology, Botany,
> and Comparative Anatomy, with a care and a reverence
> . . . which had never before [been] applied to them. (p. 4)

The review was the foundation of the book Kingsley published
the next year, the year *Maud* was published: *Glaucus; or, the
Wonders of the Shore* (in which the passage above appears on
p. 12). Considering T.'s interest in natural history and his
friendship with Kingsley, it seems likely that he would have
read the review. Kingsley may well have coined 'monstrous
eft' and used it for the first time in his review. In this case, the
composition of the section could be ascribed to the winter of
1854 (or later). Alternatively, Kingsley may have coined the
expression and mentioned it to T. months, or even years,
before he used it in print. Alternatively, again, both Kingsley
and T. may have drawn on a mutual source, one well known
at the time. This is certainly possible: dinosaurs were a subject

of immense fascination in the mid-century, and references to them, and to recently discovered fossils, appeared regularly in the news and periodical press. An event widely publicized in 1853 was the construction of replicas of dinosaurs, supervised by the anatomist Richard Owen. These were displayed in the gardens of the Crystal Palace at Sydenham (where they can still be seen). T., who had referred to the monsters in *The Princess*, *In Memoriam* and elsewhere, visited the exhibition in May 1854 and commented: 'I was much pleased with . . . the Iguanodons and Ichthyosaurs' (*Memoir* I, 376) (see Shatto, 'Byron, Dickens, Tennyson and the Monstrous Efts', *Yearbook of English Studies*, 6 (1976), 144–55). In light of other hints that the composition of the section may date from the spring of 1854 (see Introduction, p. 11), there is perhaps as much reason to attribute it to the spring on the basis of T.'s visit to Sydenham as there is to attribute it to the winter on the basis of Kingsley's review.

134–7 Nature's crowning race . . . is he not too base?] The influence of passages in Robert Chambers, *Vestiges of the Natural History of Creation* (1844), which T. read the year it was published, was noticed by W. R. Rutland (*Essays and Studies*, 26 (1940), 23) and John Killham (*Tennyson and 'The Princess'*, 1958, p. 258):

> Are there yet to be species superior to us in organization, purer in feeling, more powerful in device and act, and who shall take a rule over us? . . .

> The gestation of a single organism is the work of but a few days, weeks or months; but the gestation, so to speak, of a whole creation is a matter probably involving enormous spaces of time.

For T.'s understanding of contemporary evolutionary theories, see notes to *In Memoriam* 55, 56 in Shatto and Shaw, pp. 216–20.

7 138–43
139 The passionate heart of the poet is whirl'd into folly and vice] An allusion to the personal details about the life of

Shelley which had been recently disclosed as the result of a literary hoax. In 1852, Tennyson's publisher, Moxon, unwittingly published *Letters of Percy Bysshe Shelley, with an introductory essay by Robert Browning*. All but two of the twenty-five letters were subsequently shown to be fabricated. Whilst editing the volume, Browning came to learn the truth about Shelley's moral failings, mental instability and addiction to laudanum. Shocked and disillusioned, he was forced to withdraw his fervent admiration for the poet. He contrived to write an essay on the distinction between the objective and the subjective poet in the course of which he praises Shelley's poetry while acknowledging his personal weaknesses.

142 not to desire or admire] Horace, *Epistles* I 6 1: 'Nil admirari . . .' ('"Marvel at nothing" – that is perhaps the one and only thing, Numicius, that can make a man happy and keep him so.')

143 sultan of old] The image seems to conflate scenes from the *Arabian Nights* with Song of Solomon 4.16: 'Blow upon my garden, that the spices thereof may flow out. Let my beloved come into his garden, and eat his pleasant fruits'.

8 **144–9**
144 Isis hid by the veil] 'The great Goddess of the Egyptians' (T.). The veiled statue of Truth at the temple of Sais. T. alluded to the familiar myth in *In Memoriam* 56.28 and in his Cambridge essay, 'Ghosts':

> He who has the power of speaking of the spiritual world, speaks in a simple manner of a high matter. He speaks of life and death, and the things after death. He lifts the veil, but the form behind it is shrouded in deeper obscurity. (*Memoir* I, 497)

145–6 Who knows the ways of the world . . . world is wide] Cf. Pope, *An Essay on Man* I 21–8 (noted by John Churton Collins, ed., *'In Memoriam', 'The Princess' and 'Maud'*, 1902, p. 294):

Thro' worlds unnumber'd tho' the God be known,
'Tis ours to trace him only in our own.
He, who thro' vast immensity can pierce,
See worlds on worlds compose one universe,
Observe how system into system runs,
What other planets circle other suns,
What vary'd Being peoples ev'ry star,
May tell why Heav'n has made us as we are.

147 Poland ... Hungary] The Polish insurrection against Russia failed in 1831. T., sympathetic with the Poles, wrote two sonnets on the subject. In 1849, Russia helped Austria suppress the movement for independence in Hungary. For another example of how these events were linked with the Crimean War in the mind of the public, cf. William Cox Bennett, 'To the Besiegers of Sebastopol: June, 1855', in *War Songs* (1855):

> What! shall fresh lands, year by year,
>   Sink beneath the despot's heel!
> Shall we weakly wait our turn
>   Poland's fearful fate to feel!
> Not for us is Finland's doom!
>   Hungary's fall we will not know!
> Foot by foot, and hour by hour,
>   Onward, brave hearts! – forward go!

148 ruled with rod or with knout] Cf. the poem 'War!', *Punch*, 26 (8 April 1854), 146:

> What was Attila's flail of iron to the knout
>   wherewith this Czar,
> A Slave himself, drives on his Slaves from icy
>   steppes afar!
>
> Body and soul he must control who rules as this
>   man rules.
> Down! Kiss the rod! The Czar is God! . . .

A poem published the following week, 'The Right Side of the

Question, The "Bright" Side of the Question', includes the lines (in a stanza mentioning the Czar) 'if it come to the knout, / You may dodge, but don't offer defiance' (15 April, 53).

10 156–61
160 fed on the roses, lain in the lilies] Cf. Marvell, 'The Nymph complaining for the death of her Faun', 81–3:

> For, in the flaxen Lillies shade,
> It like a bank of Lillies laid.
> Upon the Roses it would feed.

I v *1–3* 162–89
1 162–72
'He fights against his growing passion' (T.).

I vi *1–10* 190–284
Composition: Stanzas *4–10* are adaptations of the vitriolic stanzas following I ii 87 in T36/H (see textual notes).

6 229–45
233 curl'd Assyrian Bull] 'With hair curled like that of the bulls on Assyrian sculpture' (T.). The huge statue of the winged bull of Nineveh was excavated by Austen Henry Layard. It was illustrated in his *Nineveh and Its Remains* (1849), of which T. owned a copy (TRC), and widely publicized in the press when acquired by the British Museum in 1853. T. denied the misunderstanding of a reviewer (*Morning Post*, 1 Sept. 1855) that the line referred to Layard himself (*Memoir* I, 405).

235–45 Her brother, from whom I keep aloof ... vote may be gain'd] The depiction of Maud's brother is based on T.'s uncle, Charles Tennyson d'Eyncourt, as Rader suggests (p. 143, n. 7). Charles's assumption of the additional surname (from a distantly related ancestor) was characteristic of his affectations and social pretensions. He adopted it to publicly dissociate himself from the Tennysons at Somersby. He was disappointed in his lifelong expectation of a peerage. He was elected MP for Stamford in 1831, and it is interesting to note that he was accused of unscrupulous and intimidating methods of canvassing by the losing candidate, Lord Thomas Cecil. Charles challenged Cecil to a duel, a romantic thing to do in 1831. Honour was satisfied by an exchange of harmless shots at Wormwood Scrubs, after which the combatants were taken into custody by the police and driven to Paddington Station. They were ridiculed in the London papers for days afterwards, and the Somersby Tennysons delighted to see Charles publicly lampooned. The comic episode is related by Martin, pp. 143–4. The duel described in II i surely owes something to this incident. For the link between dandyism and Charles's friend, Edward Bulwer, see note I x *2* 358.

8 252–67
257–63 Living alone in an empty house . . . its echoing chambers wide] Cf. 'Mariana', 61–8:

> All day within the dreamy house,
>   The doors upon their hinges creak'd;
> The blue fly sung in the pane; the mouse
>   Behind the mouldering wainscot shriek'd,
> Or from the crevice peer'd about.
>   Old faces glimmer'd thro' the doors,
>   Old footsteps trod the upper floors,
> Old voices called her from without.

267 heart half-turn'd to stone] Cf. *Othello* IV 1 178–9: 'my heart is turn'd to stone; I strike it, and it hurts my hand'; and with 268, Ezekiel 11.19: 'I will take the stony heart out of their flesh, and will give them an heart of flesh'.

9 268–75
273–4 her hand, / Come sliding out of her sacred glove] Cf. *Romeo and Juliet* II 2 23–4: 'See how she leans her cheek upon her hand! / O that I were a glove upon that hand'.

I vii *1–4* 285–300
'He remembers his father and her father talking just before the birth of Maud' (T.). Contemporary critics and readers found

this section confusing. D. G. Rossetti described it as 'that incomprehensible section of the two governors getting groggy together'. The addition of I xix in **1856** clarified the obscurities (see M. L. Howe, *Modern Language Notes*, 49 (May 1934), 291; Shannon, pp. 410–11).

3 293–6
The allusion is to 'The Story of Noor Ad Deen Ali and Buddir Ad Deen Houssun' in *The Arabian Nights* (see W. D. Paden, *Tennyson in Egypt*, 1942, p. 93 and *Eversley*, I, 340). The story tells of twin brothers who, while passing the evening in conversation, make an agreement to marry on the same day:

> Suppose both our wives should conceive the first night of our marriage, and should happen to be brought to bed on one day, yours of a son, and mine of a daughter, we will give them to each other in marriage (quoted from *The Arabian Nights Entertainments*, trans. Jonathan Scott (1811), 2.116–17).

The brothers quarrel over the dowry, but the children are born according to plan, and after many adventures eventually marry each other.

I viii 301–13
313 'No surely ... pride'] 'It cannot be pride that she did not return his bow' (T.), referring to I iv *3* 116–17.

I x *1–6* 330–97
Composition: The composition of this section falls into four stages:
Stage 1: T36 (fair copy); seven stanzas: *1*, *2* early version; unadopted stanzas B, C (stanza A inserted later); *3*; *4* early version.
Stage 2: Berg A (fair copy) and P1–3 (but P1 now lost for *1*); eight stanzas: all the above, plus *5*.
Stage 3: **Trial**, **1855**; four stanzas: *1, 2, 3, 5*.
(Omits *2* early version and unadopted stanzas A, B, C, substituting for them *2*; omits *4* early version.)

Stage 4: **1856**–; six stanzas: *1–6*. (Final reading; introduces *4*, *6*.)

The first written stanza was apparently *2* early version, for a fair copy (sixteen lines) comes early on in T36 (f. 34). A revision (nine lines) finds a place in the first sequence of stanzas, Stage 1 (T36, ff. 44–7).

I 330–51

Cf. Keats, 'Isabella', stanzas 14, 15:

> . . . her two brothers . . .
>   Enriched from ancestral merchandize,
> And for them many a weary hand did swelt
>   In torched mines and noisy factories,
> And many once proud-quiver'd loins did melt
>   In blood from stinging whip; – with hollow eyes
> Many all day in dazzling river stood,
> To take the rich-or'd driftings of the flood.

> For them the Ceylon diver held his breath,
>   And went all naked to the hungry shark.

(noted by Fritz Schneider, *Tennyson und Keats*, Weimar, 1916, pp. 27–8).

T.'s favourite aunt, Elizabeth Russell, understood the stanza as an attack on her husband, whose inherited fortune derived from coal mining. T. denied the charge (*Memoir* I, 407–8), but Rader notes T.'s dislike of Matthew Russell and his heir, the 'new-made' Viscount Boyne, and associates the 'gewgaw castle' with the Russells' elaborately reconstructed Brancepeth Castle. Rader suggests a further reference to the rich husband of Rosa Baring, Robert Shafto, who had made his money from coal (pp. 53, 90–3). Another suggested model for the castle is, of course, Bayons Manor (see Jerome Hamilton Buckley, *The Victorian Temper*, 1951, p. 69).

335–40 a blacker pit, for whom / Grimy nakedness dragging his trucks / And laying his trams in a poison'd gloom / Wrought ... And left his coal all turn'd into

gold] The subject was topical: the grim and unhealthy working conditions suffered by coal miners evoked widespread sympathy and shock when the hazards and diseases associated with the industry began to be publicized in the early 1840s. But the lines are perhaps a recollection of the poem by Elizabeth Barrett which was inspired by the investigations of R. H. Horne into the employment of children in mines and factories, 'The Cry of the Children':

> Our knees tremble sorely in the stooping . . .
> For, all day, we drag our burden tiring,
>   Through the coal-dark, underground . . .
> "How long," they say, "how long, O cruel nation,
> Will you stand, to move the world, on a child's heart, –
> Stifle down with a mailed heel its palpitation,
>   And tread onward to your throne amid the mart?
> (*Poems* (1844), 2.130, 131, 135)

341 first of his noble line] Many peerages were created for nineteenth-century captains of industry who had made fortunes from coal mining in the wake of the Industrial Revolution.

344–5 And simper and set their voices lower, / And soften as if to a girl] T. told Mangles that he took these lines from Samuel Rogers, 'who used the expression once at breakfast' (*Diary*, 29 March 1871, p. 70).

351 cockney] The gaudy new castle is derisively associated with a city and looks out of place in the country.

2 352–65
358 a padded shape] The artificial appearances of Maud's brother ('that dandy-despot, he') and her lover identify them as Charles Tennyson d'Eyncourt and his close friend, also loathed by T., Edward Bulwer (Rader, p. 143, n. 7). T. had good reason to hold a grudge against Bulwer (see Introduction, p. 35) who in any case was not a likeable man. Carlyle (among others) had already ridiculed him, and his fashionable novels, in 'The Dandiacal Body', in *Sartor Resartus* (1836). T.

sought revenge in a sarcastic portrait of his enemy, 'The New Timon, and the Poets', published in *Punch* (10 Feb. 1846, 103). Dandyism was virtually passé by the 1840s, and Bulwer's lifelong reputation for affectation in manners and foppery in dress would have made T.'s portrait of him immediately recognizable (other clues aside):

> The padded man – that wears the stays –

> Who kill'd the girls and thrill'd the boys,
>   With dandy pathos when you wrote,
> A Lion, you, that made a noise,
>   And shook a mane en papillotes . . .

> What profits now to understand
>   The merits of a spotless shirt –
> A dapper boot – a little hand –
>   If half the little soul is dirt?

> *You* talk of tinsel! why we see
>   The old mark of rouge upon your cheeks.

Sir Edward Bulwer assumed the surname of Lytton in 1843 (upon the death of his mother). From 1831 until his own death, he was three times an MP. He was elevated to the peerage (as first Baron Lytton) in 1866.

359 a bought commission] The system of purchasing commissions, combined with the conferral of military appointments and promotions on men of social distinction, initiated a middle-class attack upon the aristocracy during the Crimean War. Fuelled by the press (notably *The Times*), the criticism increased during 1854–5 with the exposure of countless examples of administrative and military incompetence. Appointments to high office in civil government were criticized, but the Army in particular was seen to be an aristocratic preserve, its members hidebound by precedent and lacking in practical experience, technical knowledge and organizational abilities. Much publicity was also given at this time to the Northcote–Trevelyan plan to recruit government officials by

THE ROYAL ARMS AS IMPROVED BY THE PEACE SOCIETY.

"I WISH THE BRITISH LION WERE DEAD OUTRIGHT."—John Bright *at Edinburgh.*

4 *Punch*, 25 (29 October 1853), 179. Popular sentiment denounced all that John Bright represented: the Quakers, the Peace Society (the fawning spaniel and timid hare) and the interests of commerce.

open competitive examination (Olive Anderson, *A Liberal State at War*, 1967, pp. 101–28). T.'s sympathies with the movement for administrative reform are most apparent in the unadopted stanzas B and C of this section (see textual notes).

363–4 A wounded thing ... a wretched race] On the addition of these lines in **1856**, see note *4* 382–8 below.

3 **366–81**
'The *Westminster Review* said this was an attack on John Bright. I did not even know at the time that he was a Quaker' (T.). H.T. adds: 'It was not against Quakers but against peace-at-all-price men that the hero fulminates.' T.'s denial of hostility towards Bright is undermined by lines he omitted from two poems published in 1852. In 'The Third of February, 1852',

the line 'Though niggard throats of Manchester may bawl'
originally read: 'Though Bright and niggard Manchester . . .'.
And in 'The Penny-Wise', the original reading of 'O babbling
Peace Societies, / Where many a dreamer trifles' was:
'. . . Where Bright or Cobden trifles!' The present stanza
mimics the pugnacious, denunciatory oratorical style for
which Bright was famous.

John Bright and Richard Cobden were the most prominent
members of the Manchester School. Their opposition to a war
against France in the early 1850s and to the Crimean War was
partly based on the anxiety that commercial development
would be arrested and economic disaster would result. T.
would have sympathized with the treatment of Bright in the
press. In November 1854, *Blackwood's* published an article
which may have influenced this stanza (see note I i *6–13*
above). Bright was regularly assailed by *Punch* during 1853–5
(see Plate 4, for example). A prominent attack was the poem,
'The Right Side of the Question, the "Bright" Side of the
Question' (26, 15 April 1854, 153). The tone and content
anticipate T.'s stanza:

> If the Czar we resist down goes cotton twist;
> Non-resistance is our suggestion . . .
>
> "The Russians sell corn and tallow as well,
> And also hemp and bristles;
> Raise their prime cost, how much is lost,
> Dear payment for warlike whistles!
> Let £. *s. d.* our standard be;
> And every other test shun."
> Oh this is the rule of the Manchester school,
> And "the Bright side of the Question."
>
> "There are worse things far than blood or war,
> Higher things than cotton-spinning;
> Such as Right and Truth, and Honour and Ruth,
> And Glory for the winning! . . .
> Oh this is the voice of England's choice,
> And "the Right side of the Question."

Another possible influence on this stanza is the poem, 'The Muster of the Guards', quoted in note I i *6–13*).

368 play the game] Apparently alluding to the Quakers' policy of appeasement. On 10 February 1854, for example, a deputation of Quakers visited St Petersburg to present to the Czar an address which deplored the coming war.

370 broad-brimm'd hawker of holy things] Bright is compared to the notoriously deceitful travelling priests of the Middle Ages who sold indulgences. Bright never actually wore a Quaker-style broad-brimmed hat, although in the early days of his public career he had worn a Quaker coat and collar. *Punch* regularly caricatured him wearing a Quaker coat and a broad-brimmed hat (Plate 4) (G. M. Trevelyan, *The Life of John Bright*, 1913, p. 107, n. 2).

371 cramm'd] 'Deceived with lies,' a slang expression in T.'s time.

cotton] Cf. 'The Third of February, 1852', 43, 45: 'Though niggard throats of Manchester may bawl . . . / We are not cotton-spinners all'. The term was widely used as a synonym for the Manchester School.

4 382–8
T. added these lines in **1856**, along with *2* 363–4 and *6* 396–7, apparently in response to the reviewers. The additions emphasize the narrator's frenzied nature (363–4), mitigate the satire upon the peace orator (382–8) and reinforce the impression of the jealous, tortured mind (396–7) (Shannon, pp. 409–10). The manuscripts show that *4* is a revision of an early stanza which T. decided to omit only after the proof stage. He adapted the early stanza in **1856** by substituting the narrator for the rival lover.

5 389–95
390 Like some of the simple great ones gone] Cf. Wordsworth, 'Poems Dedicated to National Independence and Liberty', Sonnet XV, 1–4:

Great men have been among us; hands that penned
And tongues that uttered wisdom – better none:
The later Sidney, Marvel, Harrington,
Young Vane, and others who called Milton friend.

T. would have also had in mind Wellington, 'The last great Englishman', and Nelson, 'Mighty Seaman' ('Ode on the Death of the Duke of Wellington', 18, 83).

6 396–7
On the addition of these lines in **1856**, see note *4* 382–8 above.

I xi *1–2* 398–411
T.'s misleading note on the early version of this section in *Memoir* I, 403 was corrected in *Eversley*. He is reported to have 'expressed the longing for love' when he read the section aloud (*Memoir* I, 397). While reciting it to Knowles, he commented: 'The poor madman – he begins to soften', and (of 5–7): 'It's terrible – isn't it?'

1 398–404
402, 404 let come what come may, . . . I shall have had my day] Cf. *Macbeth* I 3 146–7: 'Come what come may, / Time and the hour runs through the roughest day'.

2 405–11
405 sweet heavens] Cf. *King Lear* I 5 43–4: 'O let me not be mad, not mad, sweet heaven! / Keep me in temper; I would not be mad!' (Ricks (1969), p. 1061).

I xii *1–8* 412–43
Composition: For the possibility that the section might have been intended at one time to open the poem, see Introduction, pp. 3–4.

412 high Hall-garden] Two gardens have been proposed as the original: the one at Harrington Hall, the home of Rosa Baring, and the one at Swainston, the house on the Isle of Wight of Sir John Simeon (Rader, pp. 52, 135–6, citing Drummond and Willingham Rawnsley for support; John

Murray Moore, *Three Aspects of the Late Alfred, Lord Tennyson*,
1901, p. 28). But the description may well be merely an echo
of 'Recollections of the Arabian Nights', 8: 'High-walled
gardens green and old'.

414 Maud, Maud, Maud, Maud] 'Like the rooks' caw' (T.).

2 **416–19**
419 blow] 'bloom,' a poeticism.

3 **420–3**
422 Maud is here, here, here] 'Like the call of the little
birds' (T.).

6 **432–5**
434–5 her feet have ... left the daisies rosy] 'Because if
you tread on the daisy ... it turns up a rosy underside' (T.).

8 **440–3**
441 King Charley] a King Charles spaniel. In Plate 4, it is
used to imply the 'fawning' attitude of the Peace Society
towards the Czar; here, merely as a favourite dog of ladies.

I xiii *1–4* 444–88
Composition: T36 contains two drafts (T36a, T36b) which
show three stages of composition. Stage 1 is represented by
T36a, virtually a fair copy. T36a is an early version of *3*,
containing all but three (466, 474, 481) of the lines in the final
reading.
  T. apparently became dissatisfied with this. He deleted it
and composed a new section, slightly longer than the
original stanza, incorporating revisions of some (but not all) of
the lines in Stage 1. The working drafts for Stage 2 are lost (as
they are for Stage 1), but T. transcribed a fair copy into T36.
This draft (T36b) contains abbreviated versions of *1*, *2* and *3*:
at Stage 2 *1* is half as long as in the final reading, and *2* and *3*
are each two-thirds as long as the final reading.
  He then made further major revisions (Stage 3): he
expanded the section by fifteen lines, incorporating the
remainder of the rejected lines from Stage 1 and also adding

new lines; he added a concluding stanza of two lines (*4*); and he made many verbal changes. He superimposed all these revisions on the fair copy of Stage 2, as evidenced by a change of pen (T36b, revision). In other words, Stage 3, which agrees for the most part with the final reading, survives as a layer of revision on top of Stage 2.

T. comments: 'a counter passion – passionate & furious' (to Knowles); 'Morbidly prophetic. He sees Maud's brother who will not recognize him' (*Eversley*).

2 457–65
459 grasp of fellowship] With the reading in Proofs, 'hand of fellowship', cf. Galatians 2.9: 'they gave to me . . . the right hands of fellowship.'

464–5 Gorgonised me . . . With a stony British stare] In Greek mythology, the Gorgons were three hideous sisters. Medusa, the only mortal of the three, was originally beautiful, but when her hair was transformed into hissing serpents, her head became so fearful that everyone who looked at it was changed into stone.

I xiv *1–4* 489–526
Composition: T36 has two drafts. T36a, a fair copy, was revised on a now lost intermediate draft. A fair copy of this was transcribed into H30, presumably in order to develop the early group of sections (Stage A: see Introduction, p. 5). The section was transcribed back into T36 (T36b) as the sequence there developed.

1 489–96
495–6 A lion . . . claspt by a passion-flower] 'A token – I hardly write anything without some meaning of that kind' (T. to Knowles). Cf. 'Lady Clara Vere de Vere' 23–4: 'The lion on your old stone gates / Is not more cold to you than I.'

2 497–510
505–6 a hand, as white / As ocean-foam in the moon] Horace describes the white shoulder of Chloris that 'gleams like the reflection of the unclouded moon in the midnight sea'

('non Chloris albo ... luna mari') (Wilfred P. Mustard, *Classical Echoes in Tennyson*, 1904, p. 113). The allusion to *Odes* II 5, 'Nondum subacta ...' ('Not yet!') is appropriate. The poet advises the passionate lover that his young beloved is not yet ready to 'fulfil the duties of a mate, or endure the vehemence of a lover'. The consolation is that soon she will be ready, with 'eager forwardness', to receive his embraces.

507–8 my Delight / Had a sudden desire ... to glide] 'alludes to the time when she did come out' (T. to Knowles).

I xv 527–36
533–6 Shall I not take care ... some one else] 'He begins with universal hatred of all things & gets more human by the influence of Maud' (T. to Knowles).

I xvi *1–3* 537–70
Composition: T36 originally had 537–55, 560, 561, 567–70 written continuously as one stanza. T. made two later additions: 556–9, in the margin; and 562–6, at the top of the adjacent leaf. But lines 562–6 (probably an early version) have been torn out. Berg A, a fair copy of T36, also lacks 562–6. Like T36, Berg A and P1 have all lines written continuously.

1 537–59
537–8 This lump of earth ... loss of his weight] 'the brother' (T. to Knowles). The lines adapt an Homeric expression which had become an English poeticism.

544 Oread] a woodland nymph. 'She lives on the hill near him' (T. to Knowles).

I xvii 571–98
Composition: The stanza appears among songs from *The Princess* composed in 1849 in a holograph notebook (Camb) which also contains a very early draft of III vi *4*. In 1853, T. recited the stanza to Palgrave, who reported him 'at once pleased and amused by his "red man" and "red babe," as effective points of crimson in that rosy landscape' (*Memoir* II, 504). Contemporary reviewers generally ridiculed it.

I xviii *1–8* 599–683

Composition: The sequence of stanzas in T36 originally ran (in agreement with H30): *1–5, 6* 647–50 only, *8*. Added later were the remaining lines of *6* (644–6) and *7*. Stanzas *2* and *3* are run together as one stanza in P1 and so, presumably, in now lost Berg A.

T. comments: 'Happy. The sigh in the cedar branches seems to chime in with his own yearning.' To Knowles he remarked of *1–3*: 'These might not be divided,' suggesting the stanzas should be run together when read. In 1855 he wrote to George Brimley:

> as to the character of the love, do any of the expressions 'rapturous,' 'painful,' 'childish,' however they may apply to some of the poems, fully characterize the 18th? is it not something deeper?

The section was one of T.'s favourites (with II iii and II iv). H.T. records that when T. read it aloud, 'My father's voice would break down' (*Memoir* I, 397, 398). For the many classical allusions (to Theocritus, Virgil and Lucretius), see Wilfred P. Mustard, *Classical Echoes in Tennyson*, 1904, pp. 39, 80–1, 156.

3 611–26

616 Dark cedar] Allingham records of a walk with T. in the grounds of Farringford that they looked at 'a cedar, a huge fern, an Irish yew. The dark yew [*sic*] in *Maud* "sighing for Lebanon" he got at Swainston, – Sir John Simeon's' (*Diary*, 4 Oct. 1863, p. 88).

620–1 And haunted by the starry head ... changed my fate] Cf. 'The Lover's Tale' 82–9:

> Trust me, long ago
> I should have died . . .
> But from my farthest lapse, my latest ebb,
> Thine image, like a charm of light and strength
> Upon the waters, push'd me back again
> On these deserted sands of barren life.

4 627–38
T. comments:

The *sad astrology* is modern astronomy, for of old astrology was thought to sympathise with and rule man's fate. The stars are 'cold fires,' for tho' they emit light of the highest intensity, no perceptible warmth reaches us. His newer astrology describes them (verse viii) as 'soft splendours.'

6 644–50
648 It seems that I am happy] 'Isn't that a change for the man?' (T. to Knowles).

7 651–9
651 Not die; but live a life of truest breath] 'This is the central idea – the holy power of Love' (T.).

658 'The dusky strand of Death inwoven here] 'Image taken from the coloured strands inwoven in coloured ropes, *e.g.* in the Admiralty rope' (T.).

8 660–83
669 May nothing there her maiden grace affright] In T36 the line is surrounded by round brackets which have been crossed out, suggesting that T. considered deleting the line.

678 *I* have climb'd nearer out of lonely Hell] 'a wonderful line, surely!' (T. to Knowles).

I xix *1–10* 684–786
Composition: The section was first published in **1856**. That it appears in H30 in numerous drafts but not at all in T36 might suggest that T. was dissatisfied with it and decided not to publish it. But as the drafts come at the end of H30, it is more likely that he returned to using the notebook after the publication of **1855**, encouraged by the reviewers (as Shannon suggests, pp. 410–11) to compose a new section which would clarify some obscurities of plot.

H30 shows the section in an early stage of composition: the stanzas are in no particular order, and most are drafted several times: *4* has four drafts; *5* and *9* have three drafts each; and *6* and *10* have two drafts each. The arrangement of *9* and *10* in H30a suggests they were originally conceived as one stanza. H31 originally ran: *1, 2, 4–7, 9, 10*. Added to this sequence were *3* and *8*, two of the three stanzas not in H30.

(Regarding *4* and *5*: between these stanzas in what is described as 'the present *Harvard* draft for *Maud*', Ricks (1969) (p. 1071) locates a passage of ten lines (the first four from a song in *The Princess* and describes it as preceding 760–7 (*8*). This description unfortunately conflates the contents of two different manuscripts, H30 (f. 23v) and 760–7 in H31 (f. 17r). The passage quoted as preceding 727 should consist of five lines (see the five deleted lines quoted in the textual notes to this stanza in the present edition), not four. The lines are in H31 (f. 18v).)

4 709–26
The stanza of course responds to the reviewers' criticism of obscurity in I vii by elaborating the details there which T. founded on a tale in the *Arabian Nights* (see note). What is interesting is the manner of response. T. may have been prompted to reiterate the idea by reading 'The Betrothed Children' in *Household Words* (10, 23 Sept. 1854, 124–9). The story, which is set in Egypt, adapts the traditional motif of two friends who betroth their unborn children but then quarrel. The girl's parents also quarrel (like the parents of Maud); her father loses all his money (like the father of the narrator); and she herself is beautiful, proud and contemptuous. In the end, as usual, the grown children are happily united and their fathers reconciled.

I xx *1–4* 787–836
1 787–808
790 The Sultan] 'the brother' (T.), who is thus twice more derided: 'with the Sultan's pardon' (*4* 825); 'if he had not been a Sultan of brutes' (II v *8* 319). Paden is right, of course, to associate the epithet with 'the old image of the Turkish Beys, tyrannical, lecherous, and indolent' (*Tennyson in Egypt*, 1942, p. 93). So it is ironic to recall that in the Crimean War, the Sultan of Turkey (who was regularly mentioned in the press)

was the ally of Britain, who declared war on Russia ostensibly to protect Turkey from Russian aggression.

805 gipsy bonnet] A style of large straw hat, suggesting simplicity and artlessness, fashionable from the 1790s to the 1830s.

2 809–16
815 titmouse] i.e., tit; figuratively used since the sixteenth century for a small, petty or insignificant person.

4 824–36
832–6 Come out to your own true lover ... all her splendour] 'The verse should be read here as if it were prose – Nobody can read it naturally enough!' (T. to Knowles).

I xxii *1–11* 850–923
Composition: The earliest surviving draft (T36a) shows the section consisting of only *1* and *2*. A later draft (T36/H) shows the section expanded to first seven stanzas and then to the final eleven. The original sequence in T36/H runs *1–3, 8–11*, the stanzas being headed ['1'] to '7' consecutively. The fair copy was revised to include *4–7*, T. renumbering the headings accordingly.

The section shows the influence of Persian poetry, particularly of a lyric by the poet Hafiz whom T. may well have read in the original or in translation (see J. D. Yohannan, *Modern Language Notes*, 52 (1942), 83, 89 and W. D. Paden, *Tennyson in Egypt*, 1942, p. 653). T. denied that he knew how to read Persian or that the section was influenced by FitzGerald's yet unpublished *Rubaiyat of Omar Khayyam* (see T.'s marginalia in John Churton Collins, *Cornhill Magazine*, 41 (Jan. 1880), 36–50; TRC). Such denials of influence by T. are common and cannot always be believed. In this instance, for example, there is the evidence of his letter to John Forster on 29 March 1854 explaining that he had hurt his eyes while 'reading or trying to read small Persian text.' And on 25 May, his wife recorded in her Journal:

Mr FitzGerald came & stayed about a fortnight . . . In the evening he translated Persian odes for A. who had hurt his eyes . . . by poring over a small-printed Persian Grammar . . . with other Persian books whose type seemed to be trying.

H.T. adds that at least the Grammar, 'with Hafiz and other Persian books had to be hidden away', for T. had begun to see '"the Persian letters stalking like giants round the walls of his room"' (*Memoir* I, 374). In T.'s library were *A Grammar of the Persian Language* (1841) and a volume which belonged to his father, a Persian, Arabic and English Dictionary (1806). There was a translation of Hafiz, but in an edition published too late for it to have been that read by T. in 1854 (all TRC). The section has many stylistic similarities to T.'s early poem, 'Recollections of the Arabian Nights'.

T. told Mangles that the section 'had, & was intended to have, a taint of madness,' and also that he 'Hated the valse to which "Come into the Garden, Maud," was made to dance. Nothing fit for it but the human voice' (*Diary*, 29 March 1871, pp. 69–71). Harold Nicolson noticed with disdain that the rhythm was that of a Victorian polka. John Killham, on the other hand, justifies the rhythm as being appropriate to the situation (see *Tennyson*, 1923, pp. 232–3; *Critical Essays on the Poetry of Tennyson*, 1960, p. 225).

Of T.'s reading the section aloud, H.T. records:

Joy culminates in 'Come into the garden, Maud,' and my father's eyes, which were through the other love-passages veiled by his drooping lids, would suddenly flash as he looked up and spoke these words, the passion in his voice deepening in the last words of the stanza. (*Memoir* I, 397)

1 850–5
854 woodbine] T. pronounced it 'wood *bin*' (Mangles' *Diary*, 29 March 1871, p. 69).

2 856–61
857 planet of Love] Venus, the morning star.

859 On a bed of daffodil sky] Emily's Journal (November 1853) describes her first visit to Farringford, crossing with T. by rowing-boat from Lymington: 'It was a still November evening. One dark heron flew over the Solent backed by a daffodil sky.'

3 862–7
T. once commented after reading this stanza aloud: 'Many have written as well as that, but nothing that ever sounded so well' (*The Autobiography of Margot Asquith*, 1920, p. 198).

8 894–901
894–5 The slender acacia ... on the tree] T36/H shows these lines added after the completion of the rest of the stanza.

10 908–15
909 passion-flower at the gate] See note I xiv *1* 495–6.

914 The larkspur listens] Because it has 'ear-like hoods' (R. J. Mann, *Tennyson's 'Maud' Vindicated* [1856], p. 52). Mangles asked T. how he had thought of this line and T. replied that someone had suggested it to him (*Diary*, 29 March 1871, p. 70).

11 916–23
923 And blossom in purple and red] Mangles describes looking at some heath and heather with T.: 'I said I thought he must have meant the heaths, when he wrote "Blossom in purple & red." He smiled & said he supposed he meant "Blood."' (*Diary*, 4 Sept. 1870, p. 40).

Part II

II i *1–2* 1–48
Composition: In the two drafts of this section in T36, *1* and *2* are written as one stanza.

***1* 1–35**
For the origins of this scene in the duel between Charles Tennyson d'Eyncourt and his political rival in 1831, see note I vi *6* 235. Duelling was a felony: a duellist who killed his adversary would be tried for murder and, if found guilty, sentenced to be hanged. The subject was topical in the late 1840s. Duelling had been widely discouraged since the turn of the century and was in decline. In 1843 the Anti-Duelling Association was established to denounce it and encourage its abolition. In 1844 duelling among army officers was prohibited. During the next few years, duelling became virtually defunct on account of the pressure of public opinion and the ridicule of the press.

1–3 'The fault was mine . . . on the hill] 'He has fled to the top of the next hill after the duel' (T. to Knowles). H.T. comments on T.'s recitation of the stanza: 'Then we heard after the duel the terrible wail of agony and despair . . . . read with slow solemnity' (*Memoir* I, 398).

5–6, 33–4 And there rises ever a passionate cry / From underneath in the darkening land, And there rang . . . a brother's blood] Genesis 4.10–11:

> What hast thou done? the voice of thy brother's blood crieth unto me from the ground. And now art thou cursed from the earth, which hath opened her mouth to receive thy brother's blood from thy hand.

12–14 When her brother ran in his rage . . . disgrace] The situation is paralleled in 'Edwin Morris' by the 'Trustees and

200

Aunts and Uncles' who interrupt the lovers' embrace, banish Edwin and marry Letty to 'sixty thousand pounds' (118–29).

26 the Christless code] Matthew 5.38–9:

> Ye have heard that it hath been said, An eye for an eye, and a tooth for a tooth: But I say unto you, That ye resist not evil: but whosoever shall smite thee on thy right cheek, turn to him the other also.

2 36–48
'It all has to be read like passionate prose' (T. to Knowles).

II ii *1–9* 49–131
Composition: That this lyric was composed in the 1830s and then laid aside was the recollection of Douglas Heath (quoting Spedding) in 1894 (Charles Tennyson's Notebooks, TRC). The statement has been understood to refer to all nine stanzas, but the organization and rearrangement of the stanzas in T36 (no manuscripts of any stanzas survive from the 1830s), in addition to internal evidence, suggest a different conclusion: the original lyric composed in the 1830s consisted of only a few stanzas, most likely *1–3*; these were revised and supplemented when T. returned to the lyric, probably in December 1854 (see note *5* 78–80).

T36 has early drafts of *9*, *5* and *6* respectively (f. 36ᵛ); *5* is headed '1', *6* '2', and *9* '3'. T36 probably also once contained early drafts of some of, and possibly all, the other stanzas (in a gathering following f. 36 now torn out). Originally it also contained a fair copy of the entire section with all the stanzas in the final order, except that *7* was added later. The leaf having *6*, *8* and *9* (f. 42) has, however, been mostly torn out. The surviving evidence is therefore: early drafts of *5*, *6* and *9* and later drafts of *1–5*, *7*. One stanza, *8*, has no surviving drafts.

'In Brittany. The shell undestroyed amid the storm perhaps symbolises to him his own first and highest nature preserved amid the storms of passion' (T.). The influence on the opening stanzas of Charles Lyell, *Principles of Geology* (1830–3), has been suggested by Paul Turner (*Tennyson*, 1976, p. 134):

It sometimes appears extraordinary when we observe the violence of the breakers on our coast . . . that many tender and fragile shells should inhabit the sea in the immediate vicinity of this turmoil.

T. read Lyell in 1837 (*Memoir* I, 162).

2 57–60
57–8 a learned man / Could give it a clumsy name] The scientists and taxonomists who identified and named with compound words coined from Greek and Latin the thousands of new species of plant and animal life discovered by amateur and professional naturalists in the first half of the nineteenth century, the heyday of popular interest in botany and geology.

5 78–90
78–80 Breton, not Briton; here / Like a shipwreck'd man . . . fable and fear] Emily's Journal notes (2 December 1854): 'We hear of the dreadful storm at Balaclava in November . . . Souvestre's account of the Bretons interests us very much.' This account is no longer among T.'s books, but it could have been any one of several of Émile Souvestre's many works on Brittany. None of the probable ones had yet been translated into English: *Le Foyer breton, traditions populaires* (Paris, 1845); *Le Foyer breton, contes et récites populaires*, 2 vols. (Paris, 1853); *Les Derniers Bretons*, 2 vols. (Paris, 1843; 1854). (Published in English in 1855 was *Brittany and La Vendée; Tales and Sketches*, but none of its eight stories could be described as an 'account of the Bretons'.) In July 1855, T. wrote to the Breton poet, Hippolyte Lucas:

> Si jamais je fais un voyage en Bretagne, j'aurai l'honneur et le plaisir de vous faire une visite. Votre province est riche en légendes poétiques de toute espèce, et par cela même particulièrement chère aux Anglais. J'espère la voir un jour, et vous en même temps. (*Memoir* I, 385 n.)

A disastrous storm in the Black Sea on 14 November drove ashore and wrecked thirty-two English transport ships which had just arrived at Balaclava laden with a large body of troops and an immense quantity of stores for the winter. More than a thousand men died. The connection between the Journal entry and lines 78–80 suggests that *5* and probably also *4, 6–9* were composed in December 1854.

6 91–6
96 Lamech] T.'s *Eversley* gloss quotes the words of Lamech to his wives: 'I have slain a man to my wounding, and a young man to my hurt' (Genesis 4.23).

8 106–18
116–18 one of his many rings ... his mother's hair] Hairwork, fashioned into rings, brooches, lockets and so on was the most sentimental form of mourning jewellery. The vogue reached its height in the 1840s and 1850s.

II iii 132–40
Composition: E.T. wrote to Edward Lear on 30 August 1855: 'It is strange Ally had written the saddest possible little poem before we heard the bad news, and it was "alone" that was its burthen as far as feeling goes' (TRC). The 'bad news', received on 11 August, was the death of Henry Lushington in Paris (Emily's Journal).

T. told Knowles: 'Here he comes back to England and London. There was another poem about London & the streets at night . . .' (see Introduction, pp. 18–19). He told Mangles that he inserted the stanza 'because people would not understand that Maud was dead' (*Diary*, 29 March 1871, p. 70). Shannon quotes several reviewers who were perplexed about the fate of Maud (pp. 411–12). The *Court Journal* presumed she had 'gone out as a nurse to the hospital at Scutari.' And the *Morning Post* inquired:

> But what has become of the young woman herself? Has she jilted Villikins, or is she waiting for him in maiden constancy till the war is over? Whi is she – what is she – where is she? . . . What has become of her? 'Who knows?' Nobody knows, and nobody cares. All we know about her is that she is as mad as a March hare.

T. comments: 'He felt himself going mad.' He would recite this lyric 'with slow solemnity,' and it was one of his three favourites (with I xviii and II iv) (*Memoir* I, 398).

132 heart of stone] See note I vi *8* 267.

135 for ever alone] 'Here he learns her death' (T. to Knowles).

II iv *1–13* 141–238

Composition: For the role of this section in the genesis of *Maud*, see Introduction, pp. 1, 2–5, 32. The history of composition of the section is for the most part that of the poem entitled 'Stanzas' published in *The Tribute: a Collection of Miscellaneous Unpublished Poems, by Various Authors*, ed. Lord Northampton (1837), pp. 244–50 and, with minor variants, in *The Annual Register . . . of . . . 1837*, pp. 402–4 (see Plate 5 and Appendix A).

The period of composition of the lyric spans twenty-two years:

stanzas corresponding to:

1833–4: *1–3, 5, 7, 10, 13*
1837:   *4, 8, 9, 11, 12*
1855:   *6*

The 1833–4 stanzas were composed in response to the death of Arthur Hallam in September 1833 and echo in several places sections from *In Memoriam* composed at the same time (see George O. Marshall, Jr, *PMLA*, 78 (1963), 288–9). The lyric was first published as a result of Richard Monckton Milnes soliciting T. for a poem for *The Tribute*. T. initially refused to contribute to a fashionable publication, explaining: 'To write for people with prefixes to their names is to milk he-goats: there is neither honour nor profit.' But he later acquiesced:

> these two poems have been causing me confounded bother to get them into shape. One [unidentified] I cannot send: it is too raw, but as I made the other double its former size, I hope it will do. I vow to Heaven I never will have to do with these books again. So never ask me.

The full account is given in *Memoir* I, 157–60 and in James Pope-Hennessy, *Monckton Milnes, The Years of Promise*, 1949, pp. 92–5.

T. sent Lord Northampton a poem of sixteen stanzas, having lengthened the original poem by adding three stanzas subsequently incorporated in *Maud* ('It leads me forth,' 'Then I rise,' 'Would the happy spirit') and four stanzas not incorporated (see textual notes and Appendix A).

The use of manuscript evidence: a note

In drawing conclusions from manuscript evidence, it is understandably easy to err unless all the relevant manuscripts have been collated. With T.'s manuscripts, a complete collation has only been possible since 1969. To support his suggestion that T. 'continued to think of his poem as incomplete' after publication in 1837, Rader relied on what he described as 'a fair copy, dated April, 1838, in which it ['Oh! that 'twere possible'] has been returned to its pre-1837 form' (p. 6). The manuscript referred to, H21, is in fact a transcript by James Spedding (inscribed 'copied April 1838') which is witness to a now lost autograph contemporaneous with H13 1st reading (c. 1833) but antedating H13 2nd reading. Ricks (1969, p. 598) quotes Rader on this point and inadvertently perpetuates the error. T. may have thought of his poem as incomplete after 1837, but there is no evidence to suggest this.

The foundation of Ricks's collation of 'Oh! that 'twere possible' and of II iv is two drafts in the John M. Heath Commonplace Book, Fitzwilliam Museum, Cambridge University (Heath A, Heath B in Ricks). These are scribal transcripts of the autographs H13 and T21 respectively and have no authority.

The section was one of T.'s favourites (with I xviii and II iii). It has been much admired by critics, notably by Swinburne in 1876, who praised it as

> what seems to certain readers the poem of deepest charm and fullest delight of pathos and melody ever written even by Mr Tennyson; since recast into new form and refreshed with new beauty to fit it for reappearance among the crowning passages of *Maud*. (*The Swinburne Letters*, ed. Cecil Y. Lang, 1959–62, III, 125).

Several verbal echoes of Shelley are noted by Ricks (1969, pp. 1083–5). Stanzas 7, 9, 10 and 13 show the influence of Hood, 'The Dream of Eugene Aram, the Murderer' (see Introduction, p. 34).

1 141–14
With the stanza and also 153, cf. a famous sixteenth-century lyric (noted by C. W. and M. P. DeVane (eds.), *Selections from Tennyson*, 1940, p. 452):

> Westron winde, when wilt thou blow,
> The smalle raine downe can raine?
> Christ if my love were in my armes,
> And I in my bed againe.

3 151–6
151 A shadow flits before me] 'Haunted (after Maud's death)' (T. to Knowles, on the section as a whole).

153–6 Ah Christ, that it were possible . . . where they be]
Cf. Webster, *The Duchess of Malfi* IV 2 27–31 (noted by Swinburne, *The Complete Works of Algernon Charles Swinburne* (1925–7), XIV, 337–8):

> O that it were possible we might
> But hold some two days' conference with the dead!
> From them I should learn somewhat, I am sure,
> I never shall know here. I'll teach thee a miracle;
> I am not mad yet, to my cause of sorrow.

4 157–62
157 It leads me forth at evening] 'In London' (T. to Knowles).

6 171–83
'His dream still' (T. to Knowles).

174 turrets and the walls] 'Of the old hall' (T. to Knowles).

7 184–95
185–90 My bird with the shining head . . . . shakes the city] This passage was added in proof, doubtless to introduce the reference to the murder of Maud's brother.

187–9 But there rings . . . thunder is roll'd] 'Perhaps the

sound of a cab in the street suggests this cry of recollection'
(T. to Knowles).

**191–5 And I wake, my dream is fled . . . abiding phantom
cold]** Cf. Hood, 'The Dream of Eugene Aram, The Murderer':

> "But Guilt was my grim Chamberlain
>   That lighted me to bed;
> And drew my midnight curtains round,
>   With fingers bloody red! . . .
> "Oh, God! that horrid, horrid dream
>   Besets me now awake! . . .
> "The horrid thing pursues my soul, –
>   It stands before me now!"
> (141–4, 199–200, 207–8)

9 **202–7**
Cf. 'The Dream of Eugene Aram':

> "Heavily I rose up, as soon
>   As light was in the sky,
> And sought the black accursed pool
>   With a wild misgiving eye;
> And I saw the Dead in the river bed,
>   For the faithless stream was dry!
> (163–8)

10 **208–14**
**213–14 And on my heavy eyelids / My anguish hangs like
shame]** Cf. 'The Dream of Eugene Aram':

> "All night I lay in agony,
>   In anguish dark and deep;
> My fever'd eyes I dared not close
>   But stared aghast at Sleep.
> (145–8)

12 **221–8**
228 To the regions of thy rest] For the four stanzas which
followed on in *The Tribute* but were not adopted in *Maud*, see
Appendix A.

13 229–38
**233–7 And the faces . . . I long to creep . . . cavern deep
. . . to weep, and weep, and weep]** Cf. 'The Dream of Eugene
Aram':

> "Then down I cast me on my face,
>   And first began to weep,
> For I knew my secret then was one
>   That earth refused to keep:
> Or land or sea, though he should be
>   Ten thousand fathoms deep.
> (187–92)

235–8 Always I long to creep . . . out to thee] 'I've often
felt this in London' (T. to Knowles).

II v *1–11* 239–342
Composition: Composed February 1855, according to Emily's
Journal (1 February): 'A. reads some Edgar Poe Poems to me
two or three evenings. Then the beginning of Maud & the
Mad scene and one night all Maud.' The original sequence of
stanzas in T36 ran: *1*; *3*; *4* and *7* written as one stanza; *8*; *10*; *11*.
Added later were *2* and *9*; *5* and *6* are not included in T36.
     They would have read Poe in the first three volumes
(1850–3) of the edition by Griswold (4 vols.; New York,
1850–6). The set (TRC) was a gift from F. G. Tuckerman, an
American poet who stayed at Farringford in mid-January.
Emily wrote on 8 February to thank him for the books just
received (letter, TRC). This section, especially stanza *11*,
shows the influence of the tale, 'The Premature Burial' (in
volume I, 325–38). The narrator describes how he had once
read so many accounts (which he in turn recounts) of persons
buried alive that he became obsessed by this happening to
himself. With the help of his friends, he took elaborate
precautions to prevent such an accident. But one night, away
from home and asleep in the narrow berth of a boat laden with
garden mould, he awoke and imagined himself buried alive,
his precautions having failed:

> The conclusion was irresistible . . . I had fallen into a
> trance while absent from home – while among strangers –

when, or how, I could not remember – and it was they who had buried me as a dog – nailed up in some common coffin – and thrust, deep, deep, and for ever, into some ordinary and nameless *grave*.

As this awful conviction forced itself, thus, into the innermost chambers of my soul, I once again struggled to cry aloud. And in this second endeavour I succeeded. A long, wild, and continuous shriek, or yell, of agony, resounded through the realms of the subterrene Night.

With Poe's tale fresh in his mind, and perhaps actually in front of him, the speed with which T. composed the section (according to his own account) hardly seems remarkable:

The whole of the stanzas where he is mad in Bedlam, from 'Dead, long dead' to 'Deeper, ever so little deeper,' were written in twenty minutes, and some mad doctor wrote to me that nothing since Shakespeare has been so good for madness as this.

The mad doctor he refers to was J. C. Bucknill, physician and editor of the *Asylum Journal of Mental Science*, who reviewed *Maud* for the *Journal* in October 1855 (pp. 95–100). He praised it as 'a remarkable sketch of poetic mental pathology' and 'true to psychological probabilities.' T.'s experience of mental instability and insane asylums was unfortunately intimate: his violent, depressive father died of alcoholism; one brother was an opium addict; two other brothers, one of whom was an alcoholic, spent periods as voluntary patients in asylums; another brother, completely insane, lived for fifty-seven years in an asylum in York, where he died. T.'s three sisters were very odd. T. himself suffered recurrent breakdowns during the late 1830s and throughout the 1840s, years when he was especially prey to the family melancholia, hypochondria and fear of inherited epilepsy. He made several visits to different water-cures and was himself an occasional voluntary patient at the private asylum in Epping Forest owned by Dr Matthew Allen. He was also familiar with contemporary writings on abnormal pathology, among them, Matthew Allen's *Essay on the Classification of the Insane* (1837; TRC).

With such a personal history, and with Poe's tale in mind, T. perhaps needed no further source for this section. There is nevertheless a musical curiosity which he may well have known (his wife was a talented pianist, and Edward Lear often gave song recitals after dinner at Farringford): 'The Maniac', a song by the contemporary composer and popular singer, Henry Russell (1812–1901). Russell gave public recitals in London and elsewhere throughout the 1840s and 1850s. He specialized in dramatic narratives, often based on social issues. He was a good actor and his own presentation was highly dramatic. One of his most popular songs was 'The Maniac' (composed 1840), about wrongful imprisonment in madhouses and the inhumane treatment of the insane, both contemporary issues. The lyrics were inspired by Matthew G. ('Monk') Lewis:

> Hush! 'tis the night-watch, he guards my lonely cell;
> Hush! hush, he comes to guard, to guard my lonely cell;
> He comes this way!
> Yes! 'tis the night-watch, his glim'ring lamp I see!
> Hush! 'tis the night-watch, softly he comes. Hush! Hush!

> No! by Heaven, no, by Heav'n! I am not mad.
> Oh! release me, oh! release me,
> No! by Heaven, no, by Heav'n! I am not mad.

> I loved her sincerely, I loved her too dearly,
> I loved her in sorrow, in joy, and in pain;
> But my heart is forsaken, yet ever will waken,
> The mem'ry of bliss which will ne'er come again.
> Oh! this poor heart is broken.

> I see her dancing in the hall, I see her dancing in the hall!
> I see her dancing in the hall, she heeds me not;
> No! by Heaven, &c.

> He quits the grate, he turns the key;
> He quits the grate; I knelt in vain;
> His glim'ring lamp, still, still I see,
> And all is gloom again.

Cold, bitter cold; no life, no light;
Life, all thy comforts once I had,
But here I'm chained this freezing night;
   No! by Heaven, &c.

I see her dancing in the hall, I see her dancing in the hall!
She heeds me not; come; come; she heeds me not . . .

Aye! Laugh, ye fiends – laugh, laugh, ye fiends!
Yes, by Heaven – yes, by Heav'n, they've driven me mad!

I see her dancing in the hall, I see her dancing in the hall!
Oh! release me, oh! release me,
She heeds me not;
Yes! by Heaven – yes, by Heav'n, they've driven me mad!

(The editor is indebted to Philip Collins for the suggestion and the information.)

1 239–58
'Here he is mad in Bedlam' (T.). Cf. the opening of *The Old Curiosity Shop* (1840–1) (noted by J. C. Maxwell, quoted in Ricks (1969), p. 1087):

> That constant pacing to and fro, that never-ending restlessness, that incessant tread of feet wearing the rough stones smooth and glossy – is it not a wonder how the dwellers in narrow ways can bear to hear it! Think of a sick man . . . listening to the footsteps . . . think of the hum and noise being always present to his senses, and of the stream of life that will not stop, pouring on, on, on, through all his restless dreams, as if he were condemned to lie dead but conscious, in a noisy churchyard, and had no hope of rest for centuries to come.

243–5 And my bones . . . beneath the street] In conjunction with II iv *13* and the note there on 'The Dream of Eugene Aram', cf. 195–8:

Ay, though he's buried in a cave,
And trodden down with stones,
And years have rotted off his flesh, –
The world shall see his bones!

The situation of the corpse in Hood's poem would seem transferred to that of the narrator in *Maud*.

2 259–67
260–4 They cannot even bury a man ... There is none that does his work] Abuses surrounding interment in metropolitan churchyards and burial grounds had been a notorious scandal since the early 1840s. Sanitary reformers, parliamentary reports and works such as *Bleak House* (1852–3) combined to keep the subject before the public throughout the 1850s. The abuses chiefly affected the poor, who could not afford burial fees sufficient to ensure a decent and Christian burial. The pauper funerals provided by the parish were usually hasty affairs neglectful of religious observance. Undertakers and clergymen alike were involved in unscrupulous practices concerning burial fees, funeral expenses, speculation in burial grounds and the sale of corpses for dissection. The overcrowding in many graveyards was an abomination: bodies recently buried were disinterred to make room for later ones; there were mass graves left open to save the gravediggers work; and coffins were crammed against each other, the topmost within a foot or two of the surface (see *Household Words*, 1 (8 June 1850), 241–2 and 6 (27 November 1852), 241–5; John Morley, *Death, Heaven and the Victorians*, 1971, *passim*).

266–7 But the churchmen fain would kill their church, / As the churches have kill'd their Christ] Two tendencies within the established church, sectarianism and Anglo-Catholicism, worried T. most of his life. His often expressed attitudes towards the growth of religious sects were summarized by his son:

He thought, with Arthur Hallam, that 'the essential feelings of religion subsist in the utmost diversity of forms,' that 'different language does not always imply different opinions, nor different opinions any difference in *real* faith.' (*Memoir* I, 309)

He was also suspicious and afraid of Catholicism, like most Englishmen of the time. He was writing during the period of what was called the 'papal aggression': the restoration of the Catholic bishoprics to England. The sentiments behind these lines in *Maud* are elaborated in one of his political poems of 1852, 'Suggested by Reading an Article in a Newspaper', 67–78:

> Alas, our Church! alas, her growing ills,
> And those who tolerate not her tolerance,
> But needs must sell the burthen of their wills
> To that half-pagan harlot kept by France!
> Free subjects of the kindliest of all thrones,
> Headlong they plunge their doubts among old rags
> and bones.
>
> Alas, church-writers, altercating tribes –
> The vessel of your church may sink in storms;
> Christ cried, Woe, woe, to Pharisees and scribes;
> Like them, you bicker less for truth than forms.
> I sorrow when I read the things you write,
> What unheroic pertness! what unchristian spite!

3 268–78
270 a lord of all things] 'I put "a God Almighty" first, which is a usual form of madness' (T. to Knowles). T. alludes to a draft preceding T36 which does not survive.

272–3 a statesman there, betraying / His party-secret, fool, to the press] See note *4* 283–5 below.

274 a vile physician] 'the doctor of the madhouse' (T. to Knowles). This would seem to be T.'s revenge on Matthew Allen, a scoundrel and a con-man in spite of his benign treatment of the insane. In 1840 Allen persuaded T. and his family to invest £8000 in a project to make wood-carvings by steam-driven machine. The scheme collapsed in 1842, the Tennysons lost their money and T. broke off relations with Allen. Private madhouses, such as Dr Allen's, were run on a commercial basis and licensed by the Commissioners in Lunacy. They flourished in the nineteenth century because of the lack of county asylums. Managed by medical doctors or by laymen, the madhouses offered a variety of accommodation. Most sought to maintain the atmosphere of a country house or gentleman's residence, for the patients were primarily middle and upper class.

277–8 a world that loves him not, / For it is but a world of the dead] 'A glance at the whole world' (T. to Knowles).

4 279–90
280–8 the prophecy given of old ... top of the house] Luke 12.3:

> Therefore whatsoever ye have spoken in darkness shall be heard in the light; and that which ye have spoken in the ear in closets shall be proclaimed upon the housetops.

283–5 Not let any man think for the public good . . . . a private affair] Here and above (272–3) the issues are scandal-mongering and national security, preoccupations T. expressed in 'Suggested by Reading an Article in a Newspaper', 19–24:

> And you, dark Senate of the public pen,
>   You may not, like yon tyrant, deal in spies.
> Yours are the public acts of public men,
>   But yours are not their household privacies.
> I grant you one of the Great Powers on earth,
> But be not you the blatant traitors of the hearth.

Jowett told H.T.:

> Your father was very sensitive and had an honest hatred of being gossiped about. He called the malignant critics and chatterers 'mosquitoes.' He never felt any pleasure at praise

(except from his friends), but he felt a great pain at the injustice of censure. (*Memoir* I, 93 n.)

The danger of the press breaching national security in time of war was an important public issue. For example, in 'Peace and War: A Dialogue', T. could have read (apropos the battle of Alma):

> The worst of our popular press is, that by it the country or Government thinks aloud; and even though it adopts the better counsel, and does the right thing at last, it gets little credit, because it is so inconveniently communicative of passing thoughts of meanness or wickedness. If individuals thought aloud in the same way, the most strait-laced gentlemen . . . would appear guilty of most of the sins of the Decalogue. (*Blackwood's*, 76 (Nov. 1854), 589–98)

290 *him*] 'the brother' (T.).

5 291–4
291 gray old wolf] Maud's father (I xiii *3* 471).

294 Crack them . . . and die] 'For his son is, he thinks, dead' (T.).

6 295–302
296–7 the British vermin, the rat . . . he came in the Hanover ship] 'The Norwegian rat has driven out the old English rat' (T.). H.T. explains: 'The Jacobites asserted that the brown Norwegian rat came to England with the House of Hanover, 1714, and hence called it "the Hanover rat."'

300–1 Arsenic, arsenic, sure, would do it, / Except that now we poison our babes] Cf. the mad King Lear's 'Peace, peace: this piece of toasted cheese will do it' (IV 6 88; noted by W. C. and M. P. DeVane (eds.), *Selections from Tennyson*, 1940, p. 453). Arsenic, as arsenite of copper or Scheele's green, was a constituent in the colouring of cheap confectionery. The children of the poor were the principal victims of this type of poisoning, for the penny-a-dozen sweetmeats were hawked about the streets and sold in the shops of poor neighbourhoods. The dangers of arsenic and the deaths of children from poisoned sweetmeats received much publicity in the 1850s, largely on account of the published reports of the Analytical Sanitary Commission (A. H. Hassall, *Food and its Adulterations*, 1855, p. 605; 'Death in the Sugar Plum', *Household Words*, 2 (25 Jan. 1851), 426–7; *The Lancet*, I (25 Jan. 1851), 89; and see note I i *10* 39–40). Arsenic was readily available as a powder sold in two-ounce packets by grocers and chemists. It was widely used to poison rats, to cure sheep of scabies and to prevent smut in wheat. Because it was colourless, flavourless and odourless, its being sold alongside foodstuffs and drugs led to countless accidental poisonings, and in cases of wilful poisoning arsenic was used more often than oxalic acid or laudanum ('Poison Sold Here!', *Household Words*, 2 (9 November 1850), 155–71). It was arsenic which poisoned the children in the widely publicized trial of four persons for infanticide, the case on which Carlyle based the anecdote in *Past and Present* which influenced I i *12* 45–8 (see note).

7 303–9
303 Tell him now] 'her old Father . . . [tell him] how we met in the garden' (T. to Knowles).

8 310–20
317 the keeper] 'the brother' (T.).

318 He linkt a dead man there to a spectral bride] 'that is, himself in his fancy' (T.). A reversal of the situation in the celebrated ballad of Leonore by Gottfried Bürger (1747–94). Leonore is carried off on horseback by the spectre of her dead lover and forced to marry him at the graveside. Walter Scott translated and imitated the ballad in 'The Chase and William and Helen'.

9 321–6
321 the old man] 'Maud's father. The second corpse is Maud's brother, the lover's father being the first corpse, whom the lover thinks that Maud's father murdered' (T.).

10 327–33
For T.'s attitude towards Quakers ('The Society of Friends')
and the Peace Society, see note I x *3*.

**323–3 I swear to you, lawful and lawless war / Are
scarcely even akin]** 'He feels that he is getting a little too
sensible in this remark' (T. to Knowles).

11 334–42
T. is reported as having given an impression of 'delirious
madness' when reciting this stanza (*Memoir* I, 398).

Part III

III vi *1–5* 1–59
Composition: 'Written when the cannon was heard booming
from the battleships in the Solent before the Crimean War'
(T., of *1–4*). Emily's Journal (20 Feb. 1854) notes: 'in the
kitchen garden facing the down . . . we heard the sound of the
cannon practising for the Crimea. Their booming sounded
somewhat knell-like.' The Baltic fleet embarked from Spithead
on 11 March. Parliament declared war against Russia on 22
March. For the implications of the date of composition,
see Introduction, pp. 9–10. T. apparently overlooked the renumbering of sections when the division into three parts was
introduced in **1865**.

1 1–14
'Sane, but shattered' (T.). 'The poem is to show what love
does for him. The war is only an episode' (T. to Van Dyke).

**6–8 the Charioteer / And starry Gemini hang . . . Over
Orion's grave low down in the west]** The season is late
spring. T. told Mangles that a critic had complained that
Orion is never 'low down in the west' at this time of year.
Mangles records: 'Of course, he meant that Orion was setting
over a high hill. I said I thought daffodils were favourites of
his. He said they were. He admired very much Wordsworth's
daffodils' (*Diary*, 29 March 1871, p. 70).

**13–14 Mars / As he glow'd like a ruddy shield on the
Lion's breast]** Emily's Journal (16 March 1854) notes: 'Our
Lionel born. A. when he heard of it was watching in the little
study under the bedroom and saw Mars in the Lion
culminating' (the planet Mars is in the constellation of the
lion).

2 15–28
19 a war would arise in defence of the right] The popular

218

sentiment that the Allied defence of Turkey against Russian aggression was a righteous and just cause was reiterated in the British press throughout the course of the war. Cf., for example, 'God Defend the Right!' (*Punch* 26 (4 March 1854) 85), a poem contemporaneous with the composition of Part III:

> Who said that peace had eaten out the manhood from
>   our race?
> That love of gain, and fear of pain, for valour left no
>   place?
> That leave to spin and gold to win, was Englishmen's
>   sole prayer –
> Which so we got it mattered not how all besides might
>   fare? . . .
>
> 'Tis not so now; the knee we bow, as those who,
>   kneeling, see
> That war's event is ever bent by an all-wise decree,
> That we who fight for truth and right, must win,
>   whate'er betide,
> For that the God of battles goes forth upon our side.
>
> That right is old which we uphold, and call God to
>   defend.

25 watch her harvest ripen, her herd increase] Cf. 'The Penny-Wise' (composed January 1852), on the threat of an invasion by France:

> O big-limbed yeomen, leave awhile
>   The fattening of your cattle;
> And if indeed ye long for peace,
>   Make ready to do battle –
> (37–40)

27 the cobweb woven across the cannon's throat] A classical image of desolation and disuse; cf., for example, Theocritus XVI 96: 'May spiders weave their delicate webs over martial gear' (Wilfred P. Mustard, *Classical Echoes in Tennyson*, 1904, p. 23).

3 29–37

29 as months ran on and rumour of battle grew] The dispute between the Greek and Latin churches concerning the holy places at Jerusalem began in December 1852 and developed into a dispute between Russia and Turkey. Russia, under the guise of defending the rights of the Greek church in Turkey, sought to seize control of the straits of the Bosporus and the Dardanelles and the remainder of the shipping route from the Black Sea to the Mediterranean. Britain and France perceived a threat to the integrity of the Ottoman Empire and to the balance of power in Europe. In January 1853 Russian troops advanced to the Danube and hostilities began. In October Turkey declared war on Russia but lost its entire fleet in a Russian bombardment in November. The attack outraged British public opinion and war fever seized the nation. In February 1854 the Emperor of Russia issued a manifesto of war, and a month later England and France declared war on Russia.

34 I stood on a giant deck] Perhaps, as Rader suggests (p. 8), HMS *Duke of Wellington*, a wooden steam- and sail-powered battleship launched in 1852 which served as the flagship for the Baltic expeditions of 1854 and 1855. She weighed 3700 tons and carried 131 guns on three decks and a crew of 1100 (Lawrence James, *1854–56: Crimea*, 1981, p. 186). Rader notes that newspaper accounts described her as 'a giant ship' and 'the largest ship in the world', but the Spithead embarkations included a number of 'gigantic transports' (see Joseph Irving, *The Annals of Our Time*, 1869, 22 Feb. 1854, p. 264).

35 a loyal people shouting a battle cry] Identified by Rader, quoting the *Morning Chronicle*, as the cheers of the troops being reviewed by the Queen on 12 March (p. 8). The *Chronicle* described the 'thrilling and ungoverned burst of enthusiastic loyalty', 'a remarkable cheer – one which may be heard once, but never forgotten in a lifetime.'

36 dreary phantom] 'Of Maud' (T. to Knowles).

37 the North] Synonymous with Russia throughout the war. *Punch*, for example, referred to the Czar as 'The Wizard of the North' (26 (6 May 1854), 184). Cf. 'To the Rev. F. D. Maurice', composed January 1854 and published in the same volume as *Maud*:

> We might discuss the Northern sin
> Which made a selfish war begin;
>   Dispute the claims, arrange the chances;
> Emperor, Ottoman, which shall win.
> (29–32)

4 38–53
'Take this with the first where he railed at everything – He is not quite sane – a little shattered –' (T. to Knowles). This stanza, the original conclusion to *Maud*, was described by *The Times* as 'the strangest anti-climax that we ever remember to have read' (25 August 1855, p. 8).

45 a giant liar] 'The Czar' (T. to Knowles). 'Liar' was the epithet most frequently applied by the press to Nicholas I, on account of his claim to be fighting a holy war, not a war of aggression. *Punch*, for example, made weekly (and weak) jokes about the lies of the Czar.

50 the peace, that I deem'd no peace] The first reading, 'the long, long canker of peace,' quotes Falstaff, *1 Henry IV* IV 2 32: 'The cankers of a calm world and a long peace.' T. revised the reading apparently in response to hostile criticism, notably from George Eliot in the *Westminster Review* and from *Tait's Edinburgh Magazine*. George Eliot cited the line as proof of the poem's 'hatred of peace and the Peace Society . . . and faith in War as the unique social regenerator' (8 NS, Oct. 1855, 601). *Tait's* (22, Sept. 1855, 531–9) essentially criticized T.'s false logic in condemning peace itself rather than the social evils which had occurred during a time of peace (see Shannon, pp. 403, 408).

51 the Black] Russia's refusal to relinquish supremacy in the

Black Sea was one of the major obstructions preventing a negotiated settlement of the war.

5 54–9

Added in **1856**. Shannon suggests that its late insertion, together with I xiv–xvi and eleven lines in I x, represents T.'s attempt to clarify his much criticized attitudes towards the war (p. 410).

Appendices

THE

T R I B U T E :

A COLLECTION OF

MISCELLANEOUS UNPUBLISHED POEMS,

BY

𝔙arious 𝔄utĵor𝔰.

***

EDITED BY LORD NORTHAMPTON.

***

LONDON:

JOHN MURRAY, ALBEMARLE STREET;

AND

HENRY LINDSELL, WIMPOLE STREET.

MDCCCXXXVII.

5   Title-page, *The Tribute*, 1837

STANZAS,

BY ALFRED TENNYSON, ESQ.

———

Oʜ! that 'twere possible,
    After long grief and pain,
To find the arms of my true-love
    Round me once again!

2] When I was wont to meet her
    In the silent woody places
      Of the land that gave me birth,
    We stood tranced in long embraces,
Mixt with kisses sweeter, sweeter,
      Than any thing on earth.

3] A shadow flits before me—
   Not thou, but like to thee.
Ah God! that it were possible
   For one short hour to see
The souls we loved, that they might tell us
   What and where they be.

4] It leads me forth at Evening,
   It lightly winds and steals
In a cold white robe before me,
   When all my spirit reels
At the shouts, the leagues of lights,
   And the roaring of the wheels.

5] Half the night I waste in sighs,
   In a wakeful dose I sorrow
For the hand, the lips, the eyes—
   For the meeting of to-morrow,
      The delight of happy laughter,
The delight of low replies.

6] Do I hear the pleasant ditty,
    That I heard her chant of old?
        But I wake—my dream is fled.
Without knowledge, without pity—
    In the shuddering dawn behold,
        By the curtains of my bed,
        That abiding phantom cold.

7] Then I rise: the eave-drops fall
    And the yellow-vapours choke.
        The great city sounding wide;
The day comes—a dull red ball,
    Wrapt in drifts of lurid smoke,
        On the misty river-tide.

8] Thro' the hubbub of the market
    I steal, a wasted frame;
It crosseth here, it crosseth there—
Thro' all that crowd, confused and loud,
    The shadow still the same;
And on my heavy eyelids
        My anguish hangs like shame.

9] Alas for her that met me,
    That heard me softly call—
Came glimmering thro' the laurels
    At the quiet even-fall,
In the garden by the turrets
    Of the old Manorial Hall.

10] Then the broad light glares and beats,
    And the sunk eye flits and fleets,
And will not let me be.
    I loathe the squares and streets,
And the faces that one meets,
    Hearts with no love for me;
Always I long to creep
To some still cavern deep,
And to weep, and weep and weep
    My whole soul out to thee.

11]   Get thee hence, nor come again
            Pass and cease to move about—
      Pass, thou death-like type of pain,
            Mix not memory with doubt.
      'Tis the blot upon the brain
            That *will* show itself without.

12]   Would the happy Spirit descend
            In the chamber or the street
                As she looks among the blest;
      Should I fear to greet my friend,
            Or to ask her, " Take me, sweet,
                To the region of thy rest."

13]   But she tarries in her place,
      And I paint the beauteous face
            Of the maiden, that I lost,
                In my inner eyes again,
      Lest my heart be overborne
      By the thing I hold in scorn,
            By a dull mechanic ghost
                And a juggle of the brain.

14] I can shadow forth my bride
     As I knew her fair and kind,
       As I woo'd her for my wife;
   She is lovely by my side
     In the silence of my life—
     'Tis a phantom of the mind.

15] 'Tis a phantom fair and good;
   I can call it to my side,
     So to guard my life from ill,
   Tho' its ghastly sister glide
     And be moved around me still
  With the moving of the blood,
     That is moved not of the will.

16 Let it pass, the dreary brow,
     Let the dismal face go by.
  Will it lead me to the grave?
     Then I lose it: it will fly:
  Can it overlast the nerves?
     Can it overlive the eye?
  But the other, like a star,
  Thro' the channel windeth far
     Till it fade and fail and die,
  To its Archetype that waits,
  Clad in light by golden gates—
  Clad in light the Spirit waits
     To embrace me in the sky.

Appendix B
Descriptions of the Manuscripts and Printed Texts

1 MANUSCRIPTS

The manuscripts described are autographs unless otherwise stated. The descriptions of the Harvard University manuscripts have been compiled partly with the help of the 'Revised Index and Calendar' to the Tennyson Papers, a typescript list of these manuscripts in the Houghton Library.

[Berg A] Henry W. and Albert A. Berg Collection, The New York Public Library, Astor, Lenox and Tilden Foundations

Description   10 ff. (16 pp.) survive of the original 34 ff.; blue laid writing demi-quarto folded once, giving leaves 25 cm × 19 cm; no watermark. The folds have been cut and the leaves are now pasted down along the left margin to sheets 29.2 cm × 23 cm mounted in a dark-blue, gold-tooled leatherbound book 30.5 cm × 24.5 cm (not contemporary). The inside front cover bears the bookplate of Jerome Kern.

Contents   Tennyson foliated the leaves in the upper right corners of the rectos: '4', '10', '12', '13', '16', '19', '23', '24', '32', '33'. On the basis of the foliation and contents of the surviving leaves, the original contents of Berg A can be reconstructed:

surviving ff.	lost ff.	contents	heading
	[1, 2]	I i *1–13,* *17–19*	['1']
	[3]	I ii	['2']
4^r		I iii	'3'
4^v		blank	
	[5]	I iv	['4']
	[6]	I v	['5']
	[7–9]	I vi	['6']
10^r		I vii	'7'
10^v		I viii	'8'
	[11]	I ix	['9']

12^r		I x *2* early version	'10'
12^v		*2* early version, unadopted stanzas A, B, C	
13^r		I x *3–5*	
13^v		blank	
	[14]	I xi	['11']
	[15]	I xii	['12']
16^r		I xiii	'13'
16^v		I xiii con.	
	[17]	I xiv	['14']
	[18]	I xv	['15']
19^r		I xvi	'16'
19^v		blank	
	[20]	I xvii	['17']
	[21, 22]	I xviii	['18']
23^r		I xx	'19'
23^v		I xx con.	
24^r		I xxi	'20'
24^v		blank	
	[25, 26]	I xxii	['21']
	[27]	II i	['22']
	[28, 29]	II ii	['23']
	[30, 31]	II iv	['24']
32^r		II v	'25'
32^v		II v con.	
33^r		II v con.	
33^v		II v con.	
	[34]	III vi	['26']

Notes The printer's copy for P1. Tennyson transcribed it for the most part from T36 between 25 April and 7 July 1855 (*Memoir* I, 384–5). It originally contained all twenty-six sections printed in proofs and Trial and published in **1855**. Most of the surviving drafts are fair copies; the rest have light revisions.

The leatherbound book in which Berg A is mounted also contains Berg B. These manuscripts are preceded by a blue-laid sheet on which Tennyson has written 'Maud.' At the end of the book are a portrait of Tennyson and a collection of newspaper clippings concerning the sale of Tennyson holographs by Sotheby, Wilkinson, and Hodge in June 1889 at which Berg A and Berg B (then unbound) were sold as one item for £111. *The Times*, referring to this as 'the MS of *Maud*', briefly described it: 'It begins with the lines written on the back sheets of old letters, which have been torn off, and is continued on thin blue folio size folded into quarto' (17 June 1889, p. 6). The *Times* reporter expressed amazement that the Poet Laureate should write on 'common notepaper . . . such as is to be bought in any stationer's shop.'

The newspapers speculated as to how these holographs and others (of poems published in **1855**) could have come on to the market during Tennyson's lifetime. It is possible that Moxon never returned them to Tennyson and so they eventually found their way into the saleroom. Alternatively, as in the case of 'The Lover's Tale', they may well have been returned, and Tennyson may have given them to a friend who in turn sold them.

[Berg B] Henry W. and Albert A. Berg Collection, The New York Public Library, Astor, Lenox and Tilden Foundations

Description   5 ff. (5 pp.); 18 cm × 11.2 cm; white laid paper, no watermark. The leaves are tipped in to the same book containing Berg A.

Contents   I xix *1–10*. Tennyson foliated the leaves in the upper right corners of the rectos: 'I'-'V'. The versos are blank.

f. 'I':   heading 'XIX'; *1–3* 695–707; stanzas headed '1'–'3'
f. 'II':   *3* 708; *4, 5* 727–33; stanzas headed '4', '5'
f. 'III':*5* 734–9; *6, 7* 750–6; stanzas headed '6', '7'
f. 'IV': *7* 757–9, *8, 9*; stanzas headed '8', '9'
f. 'V':   *10*; headed '10'

Notes   The printer's copy for the addition of I xix in **1856**. Of the five leaves, two ('III', 'V') are fair copies and the rest are only lightly revised.

[BM] British Library BM Add. MS 45741

Description   2 ff. (4 pp.) numbered (by H.T.?) '278', '279', 21 cm × 13.3 cm, torn off along left margin; greyish wove paper, no watermark.

Contents
f. 278^r: I xii *1–6*
f. 278^v: I xv
f. 279^r: I xii *7, 8*; I xi ['BMa'; see BM Add. MS 49977]
f. 279^v: I xiv.

Notes   The drafts are contemporaneous with those in H30. The leaves are among those given to F. T. Palgrave; the recto of 278 is inscribed by Tennyson: '6 July 1855 / fr. A.T.' (see T. J. Brown, *Book Collector*, 12 (Spring 1963), 61).

[BM] British Library BM Add. MS 49977

Description 1 f. (2 pp.) 20.5 cm × 13.2 cm, torn off along left margin; grey wove paper, no watermark.

Contents I vi *9, 10* (recto); I xi ['BMb'] (verso)

Notes Fair copies. The draft of I xi is transcribed from BMa (see above). The leaf is among those given by Tennyson to F. T. Palgrave; the recto bears the same inscription as BM Add. MS 45741, f. 278^r.

[Camb] Cambridge University Library MS add. 6346

Description A notebook of which 36 ff. survive, with numerous stubs; 19 cm × 12 cm; wove paper watermarked 'Webster'.

Contents I xvii (571–95 only: Tennyson intentionally broke off in the middle of 595), on f. 16^r.
      III vi *4*, on f. 146^v.

Notes The draft of I xvii is a fair copy. It appears among songs from *The Princess* which were composed in 1849. The draft of III vi *4* has many intentional blanks, showing the stanza at an early stage of composition. It appears among passages of Arthurian material.

[H13] Houghton Library, Harvard University MS Eng 952 (13)

Description A notebook of which 20 ff. survive, with numerous stubs; 18.3 cm × 11.3 cm; plain white wove paper, no watermark.

Contents II iv (six stanzas only), on f. 20 (inverted):
f. 20^r: II iv *1–3*
f. 20^v: *5* and *6* conflated, *10, 13*

Notes Originally a fair copy, then revised. The earliest surviving holograph of 'Oh! that 'twere possible'. It can be dated 1833 on the basis of a transcript of it in the John M. Heath Commonplace Book, pp. 110–12 (Fitzwilliam Museum, Cambridge University). The transcript (in an unidentified hand) is inscribed '1833'. Most of the other poems in H13 are known to have been composed that year. The transcript is headed '(An incomplete fragment)' and has been revised in accordance with the revisions in H13. It has no authority. Disregarding the inaccurate date in a comment by Wise, 'A MS of *Stanzas* written in 1832 is still extant' (I, 305), he might refer to either the Heath transcript or to H13.

[H20] Houghton Library, Harvard University MS Eng 952 (20)

Description A notebook of which 19 ff. survive, with numerous stubs;

18.3 cm × 11.9 cm; plain, bluish wove paper, no watermark.

Contents I xiv *1* 489–90 only, on f. 15^v.

[H21] Houghton Library, Harvard University MS Eng 952 (21)

Description A notebook of which 43 ff. survive, with some stubs; 25.7 cm × 21.4 cm; plain white wove paper, gilt-edged, watermarked 'J. Green & Son | 1836)'. The notebook is in the hand of James Spedding. The verso of the front flyleaf is inscribed 'Harriet Anne Rees, from S.M. [Savile Morton]. Mary Isabella Irwin Brotherton to Hallam Tennyson. [sideways:] The Laureate – 21st June 1873.'

Contents II iv (six stanzas only), on f. 24:
f. 24^r: II iv *1–3, 5* and *7* conflated: 163, 164, 167, 169
f. 24^v: *5* and *7* conflated: 183, 184, 191–5, *10, 13*

Notes A fair copy, headed by Spedding: '(Copied April 1838)'. H21 is witness to a now lost holograph which agreed with H13 first reading. It might be conjectured that Tennyson kept the lost holograph even after the publication of **1837** with a view to expanding the poem and, liking it, he allowed Spedding to copy it into the notebook containing his transcripts of other Tennyson poems.

[H27] Houghton Library, Harvard University MS Eng 952 (27)

Description A notebook of which 42 ff. survive, with some stubs; plain white laid paper watermarked 'I & GB' with a large oval enclosing a figure of Britannia.

Contents I i *1* 1–4, on f. 16^r.
II ii *9* 119–31, on f. 31^v (inverted)

Notes Early drafts of both stanzas. The draft of II ii *9* is a fair copy. The other poems in the notebook are known to have been composed in 1851–5.

[H29] Houghton Library, Harvard University MS Eng 952 (29)

Description A notebook of which 25 ff. survive, with numerous stubs; 7.5 cm × 11.9 cm; plain white wove paper, no watermark.

Contents I iv (six stanzas only), on ff. 1–6 (versos blank):
f. 1^r: I iv *9*
f. 2^r: *8*
f. 3^r: *5*
f. 4^r: *7*
f. 5^r: *10*

f. 6^r: *4*

Notes All the drafts are fair copies.

[H30] Houghton Library, Harvard University MS Eng 952 (30); British Library Add. MS 45741

Description A notebook of which 26 ff. survive sewn in, with numerous stubs; 2 ff. have become detached (British Library Add. MS 45741, ff. 278, 279); 20.5 cm × 13.2 cm; plain bluish wove paper, no watermark.

Contents I xi, I xii, I xiv, I xv, I xvii (fragment), I xviii *1–6, 8*, I xix *2, 4–7, 9, 10*, I xx, III vi *1–4*, on the detached leaves and ff. 1–18. Originally, the detached leaves ([1], [2]) immediately preceded the leaves still intact:

f. [1]^r: I xii *1–3, 5, 4, 6*
f. [1]^v: I xv
f. [2]^r: I xii *7, 8*; I xi
f. [2]^v: I xiv *1–4* 516–20
f. 1^r: *4* 521–6, I xvii 571–8 only (leaf torn away)
f. 1^v: blank
f. 2^r: I xviii *1–3*
f. 2^v: blank
f. 3^r: *4–6*
f. 3^v: blank
f. 4^r: I xviii *8* first draft and second draft
f. 4^v: blank
f. 5^r: blank
f. 5^v: I xx *1* second draft
f. 6^r: I xx *1* first draft, *2*
f. 6^v: blank
f. 7^r: I xx *3, 4*
ff. 7^v–10^v: blank
f. 11^r: heading '20': III vi *1, 2* 15–27
f. 11^v: blank
f. 12^r: III vi *2* 28, *3, 4*
ff. 12^v–13^v: blank
f. 14^r: I xix *5* second draft
f. 14^v: I xix *5* 734 only
f. 15^r: I xix *2, 4* first draft, *5* second draft
f. 15^v: I xix *6* first draft, *9* first draft, *10* first draft
f. 16^r: I xix *9* second draft
f. 16^v: I xix *4* fourth draft
f. 17^r: I xix *4* third draft

f. 17^v: I xix *4* second draft, I xix *5* third draft
f. 18^r: I xix *6* second draft, *7*
f. 18^v: I xix *9* third draft, *10* second draft

Notes The significance of H30 in the composition of the poem is discussed in the Introduction, pp. 3–5, 32. The drafts of I xix (published in **1856**) are late additions: Tennyson returned to using the notebook after the publication of **1855**. H30 also contains drafts of *The Princess*, 'The Charge of the Light Brigade' and 'Merlin and Vivien'. The detached leaves are part of a collection of papers given by Tennyson to F. T. Palgrave (see K. W. Gransden, 'Some Uncatalogued Manuscripts of Tennyson', *Book Collector*, 4 (Summer 1955), 159–62).

[H31] Houghton Library, Harvard University MS Eng 952 (31), bMS Eng 952.1 (147), (149)

Description A notebook of which 20 ff. survive sewn in, with numerous stubs; 2 ff. have become detached (bMS Eng 952.1 (147), (149)); 19 cm × 11.3 cm; plain white laid paper watermarked 'Johnson | 1855'.

Contents The two detached leaves (the notebook gives no indication as to where these were located):
I i *14*, *15*, unadopted stanza, *16*, on bMS Eng 952.1 (149), 1 p.
II iii, on bMS Eng 952.1 (147), 1 p.
    The leaves sewn in:
I xix, on ff. 15^v–20^r (inverted):
f. 20^r: I xix *2* 687 second reading, *3* 695–704 only (leaf torn away)
f. 19^v: *1*, *2*, *4* 709–16
f. 18^v: *4* 717–23, *5*, five unadopted lines deleted, 727–36
f. 18^r: blank
f. 17^v: *5* 737–9, *6*, *7* 750–6
f. 17^r: *8*, *10* 782, 783 second reading
f. 16^v: *7* 757–9, *9*, *10* 779–84
f. 16^r: sketch of the head of a man in profile
f. 15^v: *10* 785, 786, sketch of the head of a man sleeping

Notes The drafts can be dated 1855 on the basis of the watermark and publication of the stanzas in **1856**. The draft of II iii (on the second of the detached leaves) is the only surviving draft of this section. It is a fair copy with no significant variants from **1856** and may have been the printer's copy. The draft of I xix was originally a fair copy having the stanzas headed ['1'] '2^1–'8'. The draft was then revised and expanded (by the insertion of *3* and *8*), and the stanza headings corrected accordingly.

[H148] Houghton Library, Harvard University bMS Eng 952.1 (148)

Description   1 f. (1 p.) 21.3 cm × 13.4 cm; plain bluish wove paper, no watermark.

Contents   I x *2, 3* 366 (first two words only), *5* 389 (first six words only)

Notes   The drafts come between proofs and Trial, so they can be dated 1855. The draft of I x *2* is a fair copy.

[Simeon MS] MS in the possession of Sir John Simeon, Vancouver, British Columbia

Description   Only a photocopy of a photograph of the manuscript has been examined. The manuscript comprises 2 ff. (2 pp.) of what appears to be a sheet folded once. No other information is available.

Contents
left side: II v *7* and *8*, an early version headed 'prophecy'
right side: II v *1*, fifteen lines only (the published stanza has twenty), some of which are transposed. The editor has seen only a fragment of the draft.

Notes   Both drafts antedate the T36 drafts of the stanzas. The leaves may have become detached from T36 (they appear to be the same size as those in the notebook).

[T18] Trinity College, Cambridge MS 0.15.18

Description   A notebook of which 38 ff. survive, with numerous stubs; 18.4 cm × 11 cm; cream wove paper watermarked 'J Whatman Turkey Mill 1825'; front paste-down inscribed 'A Tennyson Louth Jan 10 1828'.

Contents   I xx *1* 802–8 (early version), on f. 37^v which is mostly torn away.

Notes   The notebook for the most part contains early drafts of poems published in 1830. The fragment of I xx, however, is doubtless contemporary with H30 (1854) which has a later draft of these lines. (Tennyson frequently drafted new poems in old notebooks.)

[T21] Trinity College, Cambridge MS 0.15.21

Description   A notebook of which 9 ff. and 2 paste-downs survive, with numerous stubs; 18.3 cm × 11 cm; cream wove paper, no watermark.

Contents   II iv (ten stanzas only), on ff. 7ᵛ–9ʳ:
f. 7ᵛ: *4*
f. 8ʳ: *1–3*
f. 8ᵛ: *5* and *7* conflated, *8, 10*
f. 9ʳ: *11, 13, 9*

Notes   A fair copy. The disposition of the stanzas on the pages as well as Tennyson's marks made to indicate insertions show that the stanzas originally ran: *1–3, 5* and *7* conflated, *8, 10, 11, 13*, with *4* and *9* added later. To the earlier surviving drafts of II iv (H21, H13), T21 adds *4, 8, 9* and *11*.

The stage in the composition of this section which T21 represents suggests that the draft may well be the one referred to by James Spedding in a letter to Tennyson on 19 September 1834: 'I have also the alterations of "Oh that it were possible," improvements I must admit though I own I did not think that could have been' (*Letters*, p. 118).

A transcript of T21 in an unidentified hand exists in the John M. Heath Commonplace Book, pp. 172–5 (Fitzwilliam Museum, Cambridge University). It has no authority. A transcript (hand unidentified) of this transcript is among the Harvard Tennyson Papers (bMS Eng 952.1 (146)).

[T36] Trinity College, Cambridge MS 0.15.36, and six detached leaves (T36/H)

Description   A notebook of which 60 ff. survive sewn in, with numerous stubs; 6 ff. have become detached (see T36/H below); 21.1 cm × 13.8 cm; white wove paper, no watermark.

Contents   (Note: Tennyson inverted the notebook, so it has been foliated (by Trinity College) from back to front. Some of the heading numbers are late additions by Hallam Tennyson. These are not described.)

Inside back board: Inscription by Hallam Tennyson: '*Maud* 1.' Evidence of many leaves having become detached. Three of these are HM 19496 (T36/H), containing:
[1]ʳ: heading '1': I i *1–6*
[1]ᵛ: blank
[2]ʳ: I i *7–13*
[2]ᵛ: I i *18* and *19* written as one stanza with unadopted lines, stanza of five further unadopted lines
[3]ʳ: I i *17*, I ii, stanza of eight unadopted lines
[3]ᵛ: blank

ff. 1–2r: ['To the Rev. F. D. Maurice']
f. 2v: Inscription by Hallam Tennyson: '"O that twere possible" is an early MSS | Nos XIV & XXII'
f. 3r: II i *1* first draft[1]
f. 3v: blank
f. 4r: II i *2* early version of only seven lines[2]
f. 4v: blank
f. 5r: I xiv *1, 2* first drafts[3]
f. 5v: blank
f. 6r: I xiv *4* first draft[3]
f. 6v: blank
f. 7r: heading 'II': I iv *1–3*
f. 7v: blank
f. 8r: I iv *4–7*
f. 8v: blank
f. 9r: I iv *8–10*
f. 9v: I v *1–3* first drafts
f. 10r: heading '3': I v *1, 2* second drafts
f. 10v: blank
f. 11r: I v *3* second draft
f. 11v: blank
f. 12r: heading '4': I vi *1, 2*
f. 12v: blank
f. 13r: I vi *3–5*
f. 13v: blank
f. 14r: I vi *6, 7*
f. 14v: blank
f. 15r: I vi *8, 9*
f. 15v: blank
f. 16r: I vi *10*; I viii
f. 16v: blank
f. 17r: heading '6': I xi *1, 2*
f. 17v: heading '5': I ix
f. 18r: heading '7': I xii *1–4*
f. 18v: heading '8': I xiii first draft
f. 19r: I xii *5–8*
f. 19v: I xiii *1–3* second draft
f. 20r: I xiii *4*, heading '9': I xiv *1, 2 497–504* second drafts[4]
f. 20v: blank
f. 21r: I xiv *2 505–10, 3, 4* second draft[1]
f. 21v: blank

---

[1] Second draft on ff. 35r, 36r.
[2] Second draft on f. 36r.
[3] Second drafts on ff. 20r, 21r.
[4] First drafts on f. 5r.

f. 22^r: heading '10': I xv
f. 22^v: I xvi *1–3*
f. 23^r: top quarter torn out: it contained I xvi *2* 562–6, or an early
version, [heading '11' on torn out fragment?]: I xvii 571–94
f. 23^v: blank
f. 24^r: I xvii 595–8
f. 24^v: blank
f. 25^r: heading '12': I xviii *1–3* 611–16
f. 25^v: I xviii *6* 644–7 (647 is deleted)
f. 26^r: I xviii *3* 617–26, *4, 5*
f. 26^v: I xviii *7*
f. 27^r: I xviii *6* 647–50, *8*
f. 27^v: blank
f. 28: blank
f. 29^r: heading '13': I xx *1*
f. 29^v: blank
f.30^r: I xx *2–4*
f.30^v: blank
f. 31^r: heading '14': I xxii *1, 2*^{2}
f. 31^v: blank
f. 32^r: I xxi third draft^3
f. 32^v blank
f. 33^r: blank
f. 33^v: I vii *2, 1, 4* first drafts
f. 34^r: I vii *1–4* second drafts
f. 34^v: I x *2* early version first draft^4
f. 35^r: heading 15: II i *1* 1–30 second draft^5
f. 35^v: blank
f. 36^r: II i *1* 31–5, *2* second draft^2

---

[1] First draft on f. 6^r.
[2] The second draft, HM 19495 (T36/H), is now detached. It would have
been located in the middle or towards the end of T36. It contains:
f. 1^r: heading '14': I xxii *1–4* 868–73
f. 1^v: *4* 874–5, *5–7*
f. 2^r: *8–10*
f. 2^v: blank
f. 3^r: *11*
f. 3^v: blank
Tennyson emended the heading numbers to incorporate *4–7*
[3] First draft of entire section on f. 51^v, second draft on f. 52^r.
[4] Second draft on f. 45^r.
[5] First draft on f. 3^r.
[6] First draft on f. 4^r.

f. 36^v: II ii *9, 5* first draft[3], *6*
stubs of one gathering (eight leaves): contents doubtless included
    II iv headed '18'.
f. 37^r: heading '19': II v *1*
f. 37^v: II v *2*
f. 38^r: II v *3, 4* and *7* written as one stanza
f. 38^v: II v *8* second draft, *9*
f. 39^r: II v *8* first draft, *10, 11*
f. 39^v: blank
f. 40^r: heading '16': II ii *1–3*
f. 40^v: blank
f. 41^r: II ii *4, 5* second draft[2]
f. 41^v: II ii *7*
f. 42:   stub: recto has fragments of II ii *6, 8, 9*; verso is blank.
twenty-three blank stubs: contents doubtless included III vi *1–4*
headed '20', as in H30.
f. 43:   stub having fragments of writing twelve blank stubs
f. 44^r: I x *1*
f. 44^v: I x unadopted stanza A
f. 45^r: I x *2* early version second draft[3], unadopted stanza B
f. 45^v: blank
f. 46^r: I x unadopted stanza C
f. 46^v: I x *3* second draft
f. 47^r: I x *3* first draft, I x *4* early version
f. 47^v: blank
one blank stub
f. 48^r: I iii first draft[4]
f. 48^v: blank
f. 49^r: I iii
f. 49^v: I i *18* and *19* written as one stanza with unadopted lines
f. 50^r: I iii second draft[5], bottom half of leaf torn out
f. 50^v: blank
blank stubs
f. 51^r: blank: the top and bottom are torn out
f. 51^v: I xxi first draft: fragmentary, the leaf being torn away
f. 52^r: I xxi second draft[6]: fragmentary, the leaf being torn away
f. 52^v: blank
seventeen blank stubs
f. 53:   stub: recto is blank, verso has fragments of writing, inverted

---

[1] Second draft on f. 41^r.   [2] First draft on f. 36^v.
[3] First draft on f. 34^v.   [4] Second draft on f. 50^r.
[5] First draft on ff. 48^r, 49^r.   [6] Third draft on f. 32^r.

f. 54: both sides have sketches of men in profile
f. 55: both sides have sketches of men in profile, inverted
six blank stubs
f. 56^r: blank
f. 56^v: ['Sir John Oldcastle'] 50–76 (early draft), inverted
f. 57: blank
f. 58^r: blank
f. 58^v: ['Sir John Oldcastle'] 28–34, inverted
f. 59^r: blank
f. 59^v: ['Sir John Oldcastle'] 11–23, inverted
f. 60^r: blank
f. 60^v: ['Sir John Oldcastle'] 1–10, inverted
one stub
stub of front endpaper
inside front board

Notes T36 originally contained every section printed in proofs and Trial and published in **1855**, except for three stanzas: I x 5, II v 5, 6. The significance of T36 in the composition of the poem is discussed in the Introduction, pp. 5, 8–10, 13, 16.

Tennyson's first entry in T36 was an early draft of 'Sir John Oldcastle'. The almost empty notebook being at hand when he decided to begin gathering together sections of *Maud*, he inverted it, as he was accustomed to do, and started at the other end.

[T36/H] Henry E. Huntington Library and Art Gallery HM 19495, HM 19496

Description 6 ff. (4 pp.) detached from T36.

Contents See p. 243 fn.[2]

[1855US] British Library c.60.f.1

Description A copy of *Maud, and Other Poems* (Boston: Ticknor and Fields, 1855) having Tennyson's autograph revisions.

Contents Revision of III vi 4 50, on p. 105
Three drafts of III 5, on p. 106.

Notes The volume contains the only surviving holograph of III 5. The third draft agrees with **1856**, except for minor variants.

[1855Va] Alderman Library, University of Virginia

Description A copy of *Maud, and Other Poems* (London: Moxon, 1855) having Tennyson's autograph revisions.

Contents   Insertion of 'or the Madness' after the title heading the poem, on p. [1].

> Insertion of I i *14–16*, on p. 9.
> Emendations to I x *2*, *3*, on p. 37.
> Insertion of I x *4*, on p. 38.

Notes   The revisions of Part I were introduced in **1856**. For Tennyson's considering the addition of a subtitle, see Introduction, p. 22 and note.

2   PRINTED TEXTS

Introductory note
The list is confined to the proofs, the Trial issue and the first two editions. Most of the so-called 'editions' of *Maud, and Other Poems* published by Tennyson are in fact reissues having some revisions or corrections, or (in some cases) new impressions of reissues.

[P1, P2, P3] Proofs, Henry W. and Albert A. Berg Collection, The New York Public Library, Astor, Lenox and Tilden Foundations

Description   Gatherings in fours of 222 pages. Some of the gatherings are duplicates.

Contents   The twenty-six sections, including unadopted stanzas, contained in Berg A.

Notes   The proofs were set from Berg A. They represent three stages of revision: P1, the first proofs; P2, proofs later than P1; P3, proofs later than P2, used to set the Trial issue. Proofs of every stage no longer survive for many of the stanzas. P3 is Tennyson's own set of proofs, but with one inconsequential exception it is uncorrected. Because most of the sections no longer survive in Berg A, it is impossible to know how many significant variants the proofs introduce. In regard to the sections which do survive in Berg A, the proofs introduce significant variants in twelve places. The proofs in the Berg Collection are those described by Wise as once belonging to Sir John Simeon (II, 151).

[Trial] The private printing, Tennyson Research Centre, Lincoln Central Library

Formula   Foolscape 8°: A^2 B–I^8 K^8 L^4 M (one leaf tipped in); 77 leaves
pp. *i–iv*, *1* 2–100 *101* 102–13 *114 115* 116–18 *119–21* 122–36 *137* 138–44 *145* 146–8 *149* 150 *151* 152–3 *154*.

Contents Inscription by Hallam Tennyson, p. *i*; pp. *ii–iv* blank; twenty-six sections, pp. *1* 2–100; 'THE BROOK; | AN IDYL.', pp. *101* 102–13; p. *114* blank; 'THE LETTERS.', pp. *115* 116–18; separate title 'ODE | ON THE DEATH OF | THE DUKE OF WELLINGTON.', p. *119*; p. *120* blank; 'ODE ON THE DEATH | OF | THE DUKE OF WELLINGTON.', pp. *121* 122–36; 'THE DAISY.', pp. *137* 138–44; 'TO THE REV. F. D. MAURICE.', p. *145* 146–8; 'WILL.', pp. *149* 150; 'THE | CHARGE OF THE LIGHT BRIGADE.', pp. *151* 152–3; the printer's imprint, above which Tennyson has written a variant of lines 50–5 (printed in Ricks, 1969, p. 1036), p. *154*.

Notes Trial was set from P3. It introduces substantive verbal changes in twenty-six places. In addition it revises I x *2* and omits the three unadopted stanzas following the early version of the stanza. H148 contains the final reading of I x *2* and so comes between P3 and Trial.

The TRC copy is the only one known to survive. It has Tennyson's corrections of punctuation in three places (in addition to many corrections in the miscellaneous poems).

The Trial copy owned by Coventry Patmore was examined by R. H. Shepherd and later burnt by Patmore.[1] Shepherd transcribed its variants from **1855** into an interleaved copy of the edition (Henry E. Huntington Library and Art Gallery, 129100). He also transcribed into the volume the variants from a set of proofs (P1). Presumably these also belonged to Patmore. On a preliminary sheet interleaved into his **1855**, Shepherd describes his originals as 'the Author's first proofs' and 'the Revises', respectively. He quoted some of the variants in 'The Genesis of Tennyson's "Maud" ', *North American Review*, 139 (1884), 356–61.

Wise's own description of what he calls the 'pre-natal edition' is misleading because he never examined a copy, as he admits. He errs in stating that Trial was entitled *Maud; or, the Madness* (a misunderstanding of the reference in *Memoir* I, 402). The TRC copy has no

---

[1] The authority for Patmore's copy of Trial being the one which Shepherd examined is Wise (I, 126); Shepherd does not state his source. In burning his copy, Patmore was probably following the advice of Tennyson. When preparing *In Memoriam* for publication, Tennyson wrote to Aubrey de Vere at Curragh Chase promising to send him a Trial copy of the poem

> on the condition that when the book is published, this vaunt courier of it shall be either sent back to me, or die the death by fire in Curra[g]h Chase. I shall print about 25 copies and let them out among friends under the same condition of either return or cremation.
> (*Letters*, p. 321)

title or half-title. He also errs in stating that ('[s]o far as can now be ascertained') the Trial issue of *Maud* was printed on its own, the Trial sheets of the other poems published in **1855** being gathered in at a later stage. The TRC copy has continuous pagination and signatures.

The TRC copy is the one which, bound with the Trial sheets of *In Memoriam*, was bought for £100 at a Sotheby's sale in 1891 by G. L. Craik of Macmillans. He returned it to Tennyson, who replied: 'I thank you and the Macmillans for your chivalrous gift. I value this more especially as showing your abhorrence of the sale of proof-sheets' (*Memoir* II, 393, transcribed by Hallam Tennyson on the verso of the front endpaper of TRC Trial). Tennyson and his son referred to privately-printed issues as 'proofs'. Macmillans rebound both the *In Memoriam* and the *Maud* before presenting them. The *Maud* volume (16.5 cm × 10.5 cm) is bound in crushed brown Morocco with all edges gilt, gilt tooling on both boards, and the spine lettered in gilt 'TENNYSON'S | MAUD. | REVISES. | 1855.' with gilt rules and ornaments.

[1855]

Formula Foolscap 8°: A^4 B–I^8 K^8 L^4 M^2; 82 leaves, pp. *i–viii, 1* 2–100 *101* 102–13 *114 115* 116–18 *119–21* 122–36 *137* 138–44 *145* 146–8 *149* 150 *151* 152–4 *155 156.*

Contents Half-title 'MAUD, | AND OTHER POEMS.', p. *i*; p. *ii* blank; title (see Plate 1), p. *iii*; the printer's imprint, p. *iv*; contents list, p. *v*; p. *vi* blank; separate title 'MAUD.', p. *vii*; p. *viii* blank; twenty-six sections, pp. *1* 2–100; 'THE BROOK; | AN IDYLL.', pp. *101* 102–13; p. *114* blank; 'THE LETTERS.', pp. *115* 116–18; separate title 'ODE | ON THE DEATH OF | THE DUKE OF WELLINGTON.', p. *119*; p. *120* blank; 'ODE ON THE DEATH | OF | THE DUKE OF WELLINGTON.', pp. *121* 122–36; 'THE DAISY.', pp. *137* 138–44; 'TO THE REV. F. D. MAURICE.', p. *145* 146–8; 'WILL.', pp. *149* 150; 'THE | CHARGE OF THE LIGHT BRIGADE.', pp. *151* 152–4; publisher's advertisement for Tennyson's poems, p. *155*; p. *156* blank.

Notes The first edition, published 28 July (*Athenaeum*, No. 1448 (28 July 1855), 859). The publisher's copies measure 17.8 cm × 11 cm and are bound in green linen-texture cloth with covers decorated in blind and the spine ruled in blind and lettered in gilt 'MAUD.'

It introduces five significant variants from the Trial issue and nine minor variants. The sections are numbered consecutively 'I'–'XXVI', the poem not yet being divided into parts.

[1856]

Formula Foolscap 8°: *A*⁴ B–I⁸ K–L⁸ M²; 86 leaves, pp. *i–viii 1* 2–110 *111* 112–23 *124 125* 126–8 *129–31* 132–46 *147* 148–54 *155* 156–8 *159* 160 *161* 162–4.

Contents Half-title as in **1855**, p. *i*; p. *ii* blank; title 'MAUD, | AND OTHER POEMS. | BY | ALFRED TENNYSON, D.C.L., | POET LAUREATE. | A NEW EDITION. | LONDON: | EDWARD MOXON, DOVER STREET. | 1856.', p. *iii*; the printer's imprint, p. *iv*; contents list, p. *v*; p. *vi* blank; separate title 'MAUD.', p. *vii*; p. *viii* blank; twenty-eight sections, pp. *1* 2–110; 'THE BROOK; | AN IDYL.', pp. *111* 112–23; p. *124* blank; 'THE LETTERS.', pp. *125* 126–28; separate title 'ODE | ON THE DEATH OF | THE DUKE OF WELLINGTON.', p. *129*; p. *130* blank; 'ODE ON THE DEATH | OF | THE DUKE OF WELLINGTON.', pp. *131* 132–46; 'THE DAISY.', pp. *147* 148–54; 'TO THE REV. F. D. MAURICE.', p. *155* 156–8; 'WILL.', pp. *159* 160; 'THE | CHARGE OF THE LIGHT BRIGADE.', pp. *161* 162–4.

Notes The second edition. It introduces two sections, I xix and II iii; six stanzas, I i *14–16*, I x *4, 6*, III vi *5*; and two lines, I x *2* 363–4. It also introduces seven verbal changes and twelve changes in punctuation. The sections are numbered consecutively 'I'–'XXVIII', the poem not yet being divided into parts. Wise describes a 'Second Edition' which comes between **1855** and **1856** (I, 131), but there is no evidence to support his claim. Moreover, the first edition which the publisher described by number rather than as 'A New Edition' is **1866A**, the 'Eleventh Edition'. If Wise's statement were true, **1866A** would have been the 'Twelfth Edition'.

Editions after **1856** Only two are of interest. In **1859**, a reissue of **1856**, the poem is divided into two parts and the sections accordingly renumbered: 'I i–xxii', 'II i–vi'. **1865** further divides the poem into three parts. The final section of Part II becomes Part III but retains the heading 'vi'. This is almost certainly an oversight resulting from **1865** being a reissue of **1859**. From **1859** up to and including **1889**, Tennyson made few changes in the text: there are changes in diction in sixteen places and forty-seven changes in punctuation. Occasionally the changes were introduced in the texts of the collected editions before appearing in the single-volume editions.

Appendix C

Minor Variants in the Text (excluding proofs)

I i *1* 1–4]

1   wood,] Trial–; wood T36/H

2   blood-red] Trial–; bloodred T36/H

     heath,] Trial–; heath T36/H

3   red-ribb'd] Trial–; redribb'd T36/H

     blood,] Trial–; blood T36/H

4   'Death.'] Trial–; 'Death' T36/H

I i *2* 5–8]

5   found,] Trial–; found T36/H

6   life . . . well?—] Trial–; *no punctuation in* T36/H

7]   Trial–; *no punctuation in* T36/H

I i *3* 9–12

9–12] Trial; *no terminal punctuation in* T36/H

I i *4* 13–16

13   time,] Trial–; time T36/H

14   fright,] Trial–; fright T36/H

I i *5* 17–20

17   One says,] Trial–; one says T36/H

18   be] T36/H *has* by, *an error in transcription*

     maintained:] **1865**–; maintained T36/H; maintain'd: Trial–
     1864

19]   Trial–; *no punctuation in* T36/H

I i *6* 21–4

21 Peace?] Trial–; Peace: T36/H
    curse,] Trial–; curse T36/H
22 own;] Trial–; own T36/H
23] Trial–; *no punctuation in* T36/H
24 hearthstone?] Trial–; hearthstone T36/H

I i *7* 25–8]

25 mind,] Trial–; mind T36/H
26 tradesman's] Trial–; tradesmans T36/H
    word?] Trial–; word T36/H
27 Civil] Trial–; civil T36/H

I i *8* 29–32]

30 trust;] Trial–; trust T36/H
31 flint,] Trial–; flint T36/H
32 cheated,] Trial–; cheated T36/H

I i *9* 33–6]

33] Trial–; *no punctuation in* T36/H
34 hovell'd] Trial–; hovel'd T36/H
    together . . . swine,] Trial; *no punctuation in* T36/H
35 lives,] Trial–; lives T36/H
    when] *interlineated in* T36/H
    lie;] Trial–; lie T36/H
36 —yes!—] Trial–; —yes— T36/H
    wine.] Trial–; wine T36/H

I i *10* 37–40]

37 head,] Trial–; head T36/H
38 by-lane] Trial–; bylane T36/H
    wife,] Trial–; wife T36/H
39 alum] T36/H 2nd reading–; alumn T36/H 1st reading

plaster] Trial–; plaister T36/H
bread,] Trial–; bread T36/H

40   life,] **1864**–; life T36/H; life. Trial–**1862**

I i *11* 41–4]

41   arm'd,] Trial–; arm'd T36/H
centre-bits] Trial–; centre bits T36/H

42   nights,] Trial–; nights T36/H

44   lights.] Trial–; lights T36/H

I i *12* 45–8]

45   Mammonite] Trial–; mammonite T36/H
fee,] Trial–; fee T36/H

46   bones,] Trial–; bones— T36/H

47   better, war!] Trial–; better war; T36/H
sea,] Trial–; sea T36/H

48]   Trial–; *no punctuation in* T36/H

I i *13* 49–52]

40   hill,] Trial–; hill T36/H

50   three-decker] Trial–; threedecker T36/H
foam,] Trial–; foam T36/H

51   smooth-faced] **1865**–; smoothfaced, T36/H; smoothfaced Trial–
1864

till,] Trial–; till T36/H

52   home.—] **1856**–; home. T36/H–**1855**

I i *14* 53–6]

55   made,] **1855Va, 1856**–; made H31

I i *15* 57–60]

57–8] **1855Va, 1856**–; *no terminal punctuation in* H31

59] **1855Va, 1856**–; *no punctuation in* H31

I i *16* 61–4]

63   pain,] **1855Va, 1856**–; pain H31

64   fear?] **1855Va, 1856**–; fear. H31

I i *17* 65–8]

65   Hall!—] **1862**–; Hall: T36/H–**1861**

       abroad;] **1856**–; abroad T36/H; abroad, Trial, **1855**

66   millionaire:] **1889**; millionaire T36/H; millionnaire: Trial–**1884**

67   Maud;] **1856**–; Maud T36/H; Maud, Trial–**1855**

68   I] *failed to print in* Trial

       child;] Trial–; child: T36/H

I i *18* 69–72]

69   escapes,] T36b–; escapes T36a

70   Hall,] Trial–; hall, T36a, b

71   purse-mouth] T36b–; purse mouth T36a

       grapes,] T36b–; grapes T36a

72   mother,] Trial–; mother T36a, b

       moon-faced] Trial–; moonfaced T36a, b

       all,—] Trial–; all T36a, b

I i *19* 73–6]

74   moor;] T36b–; moor: T36a

       alone.] Trial–; alone T36a; alone; T36b

75   worse.] Trial–; worse T36a, b

I ii 77–87]

77   calm:] Trial–; calm; T36/H

78   Maud,] Trial–; Maud; T36/H

78   salt,] Trial–; salt T36/H

79   past,] Trial–; past— T36/H

80   beautiful:] Trial–; beautiful— T36/H

84   rose,] Trial–; rose T36/H

I iii 88–101]

90   Pale] Berg A–; Pale, T36b

91   profound;] Trial–; profound T36b; profound, Berg A

92   Womanlike,] Trial–; Womanlike T36b, Berg A

93   beauty,] Trial–; beauty T36b, Berg A

94   Growing] Berg A–; Growing, T36b
      sound,] T36b, Trial–; sound Berg A

96   growing,] T36b, Trial–; growing Berg A
      more,] T36b, Trial–; more Berg A

97   'garden ground,] Berg A–; gardenground T36b

I iv *1* 102–7]

103   ah,] Trial–; ah T36

104   bland,] Trial–; bland T36

105   clime,] Trial–; clime T36

107   marriage ring] Trial–; marriage-ring T36
      land?] Trial–; land. T36

I iv *2* 108–13]

108   village,] Trial–; village T36
      small!] Trial–; small T36

109   o'er] Trial–; oer T36
      city, . . . spite;] *no punctuation in* T36

110   Czar;] Trial–; Czar T36

111   side,] Trial–; side T36
      rock,] Trial–; rock T36
      Hall;] Trial–; hall, T36

112   Hall-garden] Trial–; hall-garden T36
      .light;] Trial–; light T36

113   star!] Trial–; star. T36

I iv *3* 114–19]

115   brother,] Trial–; brother T36

bow'd:] **1870 Mini**, **1872**, **1875**; bow'd T36; bow'd; Trial *all
single-volume editions from* **1855** *to* **1884**.

116   moor;] Trial–; moor T36

117   face.] Trial–; face T36

I iv *4* 120–5]

121   smile,] Trial–; smile H29, T36

stoic,] Trial–; Stoic H29, T36

122   epicurean,] Trial–; Epicurean H29, T36

way:] Trial–; way H29, T36

123   heal;] Trial–; heal H29, T36

124   Mayfly] H29, Trial–; mayfly T36

shrike,] Trial–; shrike H29, T36

I iv *5* 126–31]

126   puppets,] T36–; puppets H29

Man] Trial–; man H29, T36

pride,] T36–; pride H29

flower;] Trial–; flower H29, T36

128   board,] Trial–; board H29, T36

succeed?] Trial–; succeed H29, T36

129] Trial–; *no punctuation in* H29, T36

130] Trial–; *no punctuation in* H29, T36

131] T36–; *no punctuation in* H29

I iv *6* 132–7]

132   Master] Trial–; master T36

Earth,] Trial–; Earth T36

133–6] Trial–; *no punctuation in* T36

I iv *7* 138–43]

139 well-practised] Trial–; well practised H29; well-practiced T36
140 whirl'd] T36–; whirld H29
     vice.] Trial–; vice H29, T36
141] Trial–; *no punctuation in* H29, T36
142 it,] T36–; it H29
143 sultan] Trial–; Sultan H29, T36
     spice.] T36–; spice H29

I iv *8* 144–9]

144–5] T36–; no punctuation in H29
146 wide.] T36–; wide H29
147 fall?] T36–; fall, H29
     fail?] T36–; fail H29
148 civilisation] Trial–; civilization H29, T36
     knout?] T36–; knout H29
149] T36–; *no punctuation in* H29
     He] T36–; he H29

I iv *9* 150–5]

152 lies;] Trial–; lies, T36
153 long-neck'd] Trial–; longneckd H29; long neck'd T36
154 and, . . . not,] Trial–; *no punctuation in* H29, T36
155 flies.] Trial–; flies H29, T36

I iv *10* 156–61]

156 love,] T36–; love H29
157 poison-flowers] Trial–; poison flowers H29, T36
     ill.] Trial–; ill H29, T36
158 Maud,] T36–; Maud H29
     fawn, . . . wife.] Trial–; *no punctuation in* H29, T36
159 in marble] **1862** *and* **1864** *read* is marble, *a misprint*

above;] Trial–; above H27, T36

160   London,] T36–; London H29

      will;] Trial–; will H27, T36

161   roses] H29, T36, **1889**; roses, Trial–**1884**

      life.] Trial–; life H29, T36

I v *1* 162–72]

162   tree] T36a, b, **1878**–; tree, Trial–**1877**

163   Hall!] T36b–; hall: T36a.

165   A] T36a *has* And *revised to* A (*error in transcription*)

      gay,] Trial–; gay T36a, b

166   call! [Trial–; call— T36a, b

167   life,] T36b–; life T36a

168   May,] T36b–; May— T36a

172   death,] Trial–; death T36a, b

      land.] T36a–; land T36b

I v *2* 173–9]

173–4] Trial–; *no punctuation in* T36a, b

176   grace,] Trial–; grace T36a, b

177   Death,] Trial–; Death T36a, b

      die,] T36b–; die T36a

I v *3* 180–9]

180   voice!] T36b–; voice T36a

182   rejoice,] T36b–; rejoice T36a

183   find.] Trial–; find: T36a, b

184   more,] T36b–; more T36a

187   grass,] T36b–; grass T36a

      adore,] Trial–; adore T36a, b

189   Not her,] **1884** *has* Not her., *a misprint*

I vi *1* 190–5]

192   cloud,] Trial–; cloud T36

I vi *2* 196–203]

197   night,] Trial–; night T36

201   sweet,] **1889**; sweet T36–**1884**

I vi *3* 204–11]

207–8] Trial–; *no punctuation in* T36

209   the] *interlineated in* T36 (*error in transcription?*)

210   faded,] Trial–; faded T36

I vi *4* 212–19]

212–13] Trial–; *no punctuation in* T36

215   deceit,] Trial–**1866A, 1867**–; deciet, **1866B**

I vi *5* 220–8]

220–1] Trial–; *no punctuation in* T36

223   twenty-five?] Trial–; twenty-five? T36

226   dream'd,] Trial–; dream'd T36

228   sweet.] **1878** *and* **1884** *have* sweet, *probably a result of stereotyping*

I vi *6* 229–45]

229   tho'] Trial–; tho T36

231   dandy-despot, he,] Trial–; dandy-despot he T36

234   insolence,] Trial–; insolence T36

235   brother,] Trial–; brother T36

237] Trial–; *no punctuation in* T36

241   feign'd,] Trial–; feign'd T36

244   lies,] Trial–; lies T36

I vi *7* 246–51]

246] Trial–; *no punctuation in* T36

247 ward, *(terminal)*] Trial–; ward T36

248 tool.] Trial–; tool: T36

249 Yea, too,] **1889**; Yea too T36; Yea too, Trial–**1884**
     guard,] Trial–; guard T36

251 fool.] Trial–; fool T36

I vi *8* 252–67]

252–8] Trial–; *no punctuation in* T36

260–5] Trial–; *no punctuation in* T36

I vi *9* 268–75]

268–74] Trial–; *no punctuation in* BM, T36

275 lip?] Trial–; lip. BM, T36

I vi *10* 276–84]

276 child;] Trial–; child BM, T36

277 it] *interlineated in* T36 *(error in transcription)*

278–84] Trial–; *no punctuation in* BM, T36

I vii *1* 285–8]

287 ago,] Trial–; ago T36a–Berg A

288 arm-chair?] Trial–; armchair T36a, b; armchair? Berg A

I vii *2* 289–92]

290 me;] Trial–; me T36a, b; me, Berg A

291–2 'Well, . . . be.'] Berg A–; Well . . . be. T36a; Well . . . be T26b

291 girl,] Berg A–; girl T36a, b

I vii *3* 293–6]

294 delight,] Berg A–; delight T36b

296 night?] Berg A–; night T36b

I vii *4* 297–300]

297 Strange,] Berg A–; Strange T36a, b

299   'Well,] Trial–; Well T36a, b; Well, Berg A
     girl,] Berg A–; girl T36a, b

300   be.'] Berg A–; be. T36a, b

I viii 301–13]

301   church,] Trial–; church. T36 2nd reading; church Berg A

302   alone;] Trial–; alone, T36 2nd reading, Berg A

304   her,] Trial–; her T36 2nd reading, Berg A
     stone;] Trial–; stone. T36 2nd reading; stone Berg A

305   once, . . . once,] Trial–; once . . . once T36 2nd reading, Berg A

306   suddenly,] Berg A–; Suddenly T36 2nd reading

307   own;] Berg A–; own T36 2nd reading

308   suddenly, sweetly,] Trial–; Suddenly sweetly T36 2nd reading;
     suddenly, sweetly Berg A

309   thicker,] Berg A–; thicker T36 2nd reading

311   intone;] T36 2nd reading, Trial–; intone Berg A

312   thought,] Trial–; thought T36 2nd reading, Berg A
     is . . . pride,] Trial–; 'is . . . pride' T36 2nd reading; is . . . pride
     Berg A

313   pride.'] Berg A–; pride' T36 2nd reading

I ix 314–29]

314–15] Trial–; *no punctuation in* T36

316   look'd] Trial–; lookt T36

317   moor,] Trial–**1884**, *this edition*; moor T36, **1889** (*misprint*)

319–21] *Trial–; no punctuation in* T36

323–7] Trial–; *no punctuation in* T36

323   flash'd] Trial–; flashd T36

I x *1* 330–51]

331   not one of] Berg A *has* not ~~of~~ one of (*error in transcription*)

332   new-made] Berg A–; newmade T36
      lord,] Berg A–; lord T36
333   head?] Trial–; head T36–; head— Berg A
334   grandfather] T36, **1889**; grand-father Berg A–**1884**
      died,] Berg A–; died T36
339   shire,] Berg A–; shire T36
341   line,] Trial–; line T36, Berg A
343   adore,] Berg A–; adore T36
348   title,] Berg A–; title T36
      year,] Trial–; year T36, Berg A
349   perky] Berg A *has* peaky *revised to* perky (*error in transcription*)
351   ear.] Berg A–; ear T36

I x *2* early version]
      out, T36b; out Berg A
      he T36b; he, Berg A
      hall T36b; Hall Berg A
      too . . . doubt T36b; too, . . . doubt, Berg A
      shape T36b; shape, Berg A
      half grain T36b; half-grain Berg A
      Straw colour'd T36b; Straw-colour'd Berg A
      agape T36b; agape. Berg A

I x unadopted stanzas A, B, C]
[A]
  3)   Captain! Berg A
  4)   ball T36; ball; Berg A
  5)   bantam-cockrel T36, Berg A
  6)   land T36; land, Berg A
  7)   gains T36; gains, Berg A

8)   applause T36; applause, Berg A

9)   second hand T36; second-hand Berg A

10) remains T36; remains. Berg A

[B]

12) throne T36, Berg A

13) lunge— T36; lounge, Berg A

      she T36; she, Berg A

14) knows— T36; knows, Berg A

[C]

17) Tho Berg A

      smile T36; smile, Berg A

20) routine T36, Berg A

21) great *interlineated in* Berg A (*error in transcription*)

      reels T36; reels, Berg A

22) dirt T36; dirt, Berg A

I x *2* 352–65]

352 What,] Trial–; What H148

      out?] H148, **1855**–; out, Trial (*Lincoln copy has Tennyson's revision to* out?)

353 side] H148, **1855**–; side, Trial (*Lincoln copy has Tennyson's revision to* side)

354 Hall,] **1855**–; Hall H148, Trial (*Lincoln copy has Tennyson's revision to* Hall,)

355 Hall,] **1855**–; Hall H148, Trial

357 too,] Trial–; too H148

      doubt] H148, **1889**; doubt, Trial–**1884**

358 shape,] Trial–; shape H148

360 agape—] Trial–; agape. H148

362 therefore] Trial–; therefore, H148

363 rancorous] **1870 Mini**, **1872**, **1875**, **1889**; rancourous *all single-volume editions from* **1855** *to* **1884**

I x *3* 366–81]

370 broad-brimm'd] **1865**–; broad brim'd Berg A; broad-brim'd
Trial–**1864**

375 Hell!] Berg A–; Hell T36a

376 ambition,] Berg A–; ambition T36a

pride,] Berg A–; pride T36a

379 too,] Trial–; too T36a, Berg A

fireside,] Berg A–; fireside T36a

380 and] Berg A *has* fo *revised to* & (*error in transcription*)

ear,] Berg A–; ear T36a

I x *4* early version]

3) me T36; me, Berg A

morning T36; morning, Berg A

4) battle song T36; battle-song, Berg A

7) men T36; men. Berg A.

I x *4* 382–8]

386 wrong,] **1862**–; wrong **1855Va–1861**

I x *5* 389–95]

389 hand,] Trial–; hand Berg A

391 by,] Trial–; by Berg A

I x *6* 396–7]

397 be!] **1878** *and* **1884** *have* be? (*printer's error*)

I xi *1* 398–404]

401–2] Trial–; *no punctuation in* BMa–T36

404 day.] BMa–H30, Trial–; day T36

I xi *2* 405–11]

408 me;] Trial–; me BMa–T36

I xii *1* 412–15]

412   Hall-garden] Trial–; hall garden BM, H30; hall-garden T36

413   falling,] Trial–; falling BM–T36

414]   BM, H30, Trial–; *no punctuation in* T36

415   calling.] BM, H30, Trial–; calling T36

I xii *2* 416–19]

416   wood;] BM, H30, Trial–; wood T36

417   her,] Trial–; her BM–T36

418   lilies,] BM, H30, Trial–; lilies T36
        together.] BM, H30, Trial–; together T36

I xii *3* 420–3]

421   valleys,] **1889**; vallies BM–T36, **1859**, **1862**, **1869A**, **B**; vallies,
        Trial–**1858**, **1860**, **1861**, **1864–1867**, **1870–1884**

422   here] T36, Trial–; here, BM, H30

423   lilies.] Trial–; lilies BM–T36

I xii *4* 424–7]

424   hand,] Trial–; hand BM–T36

425   sedately;] Trial–; sedately BM, H30; sedately. T36

I xii *5* 428–31]

429   favour!] T36–; favour BM, H30

430   Heaven] T36–; heaven BM, H30

I xii *6* 432–5]

433   posy,] Trial–; posy BM–T36

434   touch'd] T36–; touchd BM, H30

435   rosy.] T36–; rosy BM, H30

I xii *7* 436–9]

436   Hall-garden] Trial–; hall-garden BM–T36

437   her,] Trial–; her BM, H30; her. T36

438   Maud?] **1889**; Maud T36; Maud, BM, H30, Trial–**1884**

I xii *8* 440–3]

440 Look,] T36–; Look! BM, H30
    door,] Trial–; door BM, H30, T36

441 snarling,] Trial–; snarling BM–T36

442 back, . . . lord,] BM, H30, Trial–; back . . . lord T36
    moor,] Trial–; moor. BM, H30; moor T36

I xiii *1* 444–56]

444 Scorn'd,] Stage 3, Trial–; Scorn'd Berg A
    scorn,] Trial–; scorn Stage 3, Berg A

448 pride!] Berg A–; pride Stage 3

449 him,] Berg A–; him Stage 3
    lands;] stage 3, Trial–; lands Berg A

450 aside;] Trial–; aside Stage 3, Berg A

451] Trial–; *no punctuation in* Stage 3; . . . spite Berg A

452 broad-blown] Trial–; broad blown Stage 3, Berg. A
    comeliness, . . . white,] Trial–; *no punctuation in* stage 3, Berg A

453 six feet two,] Berg A–; 6 feet 2 Stage 3
    think,] Berg A–; think Stage 3
    stands;] Trial–; stands Stage 3, Berg A

I xiii *2* 457–65]

461 Stopt,] Stage 3, Trial–; Stopt Berg A
    riding whip] Berg A, Trial–; riding-whip Stage 3

464 Gorgonised] Trial–; Gorgonized Stage 3, Berg A

I xiii *3* 466–86]

466 chair?] Berg A–; chair. Stage 3

467 place:] Berg A–; Place. Stage 3

469] Trial–; *no punctuation in* stage 3, Berg A

470 face,] Berg A–; face Stage 3

477 side;] Trial–; side Stage 3, Berg A

479   allied.] Berg A–

483] Stage 3 *and* Berg A *(no comma)*, Trial–; **1878** *and* **1884** *have no comma (misprint)*

485   race,] Trial–; race Berg A

486   All,] Berg A–

I xiii *4* 487–8]

487   spirit,] Berg A–; spirit Stage 3

      be! Berg A–; be. Stage 3

I xiv *1* 489–96]

489   roses] H20, H30–; roses, T36a

490   lawn;] Trial–; lawn H20; lawn. T36a–T36b

491   state] T36a–**1862**, **1869A**–; state, **1864–1867**

492   bower,] **1866A**–; bower. T36a, b; bower: BM, H30; bower;
      Trial, **1855**, **1864**, **1865**; bower **1856–1862**

494   garden-gate;] Trial–; garden-gate. T36a; garden gate: BM,
      H30; garden-gate: T36b

495   top,] T36b–; top. T36a; top BM, H30

496   claspt] T36a, T36b–; clasp'd BM, H30

      passion-flower.] T36b–; passion flower. T36a; passion flower:
      BM, H30

I xiv *2* 497–510]

500   herself,] BM–; herself T36a

501   books] T36a–T36b, **1889**; books, Trial–**1884**

504   garden-gate:] T36a, **1864**–; garden-gate; BM, H30; garden
      gate. Trial; garden gate: T36b, **1855–1862**

506   ocean-foam] T36b–; oceanfoam T36a; Ocean-foam BM, H30

      moon,] Trial–; moon T36a–T36b

507   Delight] T36b–; delight T36a, BM, H30

508   desire,] Trial–; desire BM, H30, T36b 2nd reading

      ghost,] Trial–; ghost T36b 2nd reading

      glide,] T36b 2nd reading, **1856**–; glide Trial, **1855**

509 side,] Trial–; side H30, T36b 2nd reading

I xiv *3* 511–15]

511 mind,] Trial–; mind BM, H30, T36b

512 overbold;] T36b–; overbold. BM, H30

513 me,] BM, H30, Trial–; me T36b

514 kind] T36b–; kind, BM, H30

I xiv *4* 516–26]

520 dim-gray dawn;] T36b–; dimgray dawn: T36a; dim-gray dawn
  BM, H30

521 round,] T36b–; round T36a, H30

522 death-white] Trial–; deathwhite T36a, H30; death white T36b
  drawn;] T36b–; drawn. T36a; drawn: H30

523 creep,] T36b–; creep T36a, H30

524 breath,] T36b–; breath; T36a; breath H30

525 death-white] Trial–; deathwhite T36a, b; death white H30
  sleep,] T36b–; sleep T36a, H30

I xv 527–36]

527–9] Trial–; *no punctuation in* BM–T36

530 fear;] Trial, **1855**, **1859**–; fear BM–T36, **1856–1858**

531–5] Trial–; *no punctuation in* BM–T36

534 ev'n] T36–; even BM, H30

I xvi *1* 537–59]

538 weight;] Trial–; weight. T36; weight, Berg A

540 Pleasure] Berg A–; pleasure T36

542 year] Berg A–; year, T36

544 down,] Berg A–; T36 *has* down: *revised to* down

546 creature,] T36, Trial–; creature Berg A
  I] Berg A–; I, T36

547 way;] T36 2nd reading–; way: T36 1st reading

548   sweet,] Berg A–; sweet T36

550   dread,] T36, Trial–; dread Berg A

553   peacock,] Trial–; peacock T36, Berg A
       head,] T36 2nd reading–; head. T36 1st reading

554   not:] Berg A–; not— T36
       O, . . . it,] Berg A–; *no punctuation in* T36

556   it] Berg A *has* it, *revised to* it *(error in transcription)*

557   yet young] Trial–; yet-young T36, Berg A
       Time,] Berg A–; Time T36

558   crime,] Berg A–; crime T36

I xvi *2* 560–6]

560   fool lord,] Berg A–; fool-lord, T36

I xvi *3* 567–70]

568   eye,] Berg A–; eye: T36

570   die.] T36, Trial–; die Berg A

I xvii 571–98]

571] T36–; *no punctuation in* Camb, H30

572   fields,] Trial–; *no punctuation in* MSS

573   T36–; *no punctuation in* Camb, H30

574   yields.] Trial–; *no punctuation in* MSS

575   West,] T36–; west Camb, H30

576   South,] Trial–; south MSS

577   cheeks,] T36–; cheeks Camb, H30

578   mouth.] T36, Trial, **1855**–; mouth Camb, H30; Eversley *and*
       1884 *(error)*

579   Yes] Trial–; yes Camb, T36

580   lips,] Trial–; lips H30, T36

583   seas,] Trial–; seas Camb, T36

584   rest,] T36–; rest Camb

586   thro'] T36–; thro Camb
       West;] Trial–; west Camb; West T36

588 cedar-tree,] **1889**; cedar tree Camb, T36; cedar tree, Trial–
     1884
589 man's] T36–; mans Camb
590–4] Trial–; *no punctuation in* Camb, T36
594 thro'] T36–; thro Camb
595–7] Trial–; *no punctuation in* T36

I xviii *1* 599–604]
599 friend.] Trial–; friend T36; *torn away in* H30
600 none.] Trial–; none H30, T36
603 end,] H30, Trial–; end T36

I xviii *2* 605–10]
606 dry-tongued] T36–; drytongued H30
     laurels'] Trial–; laurel's H30, T36
607 walk,] Trial–; walk H30, T36
608 more;] Trial–; more T36; *torn away in* H30
609 door,] Trial–; door H30, T36
610 closed,] Trial–; closed H30, T36

I xviii *3* 611–25]
611 none.] T36–; none H30
612 deceased.] T36–; deceased H30
613 O,] Trial–; O H30, T36
614 East,] Trial–; East T36; *torn away in* H30
615 Lebanon,] H30, Trial–; Lebanon T36
616 increased,] Trial–; increased T36; *torn away in* H30
617–19] Trial–; *no punctuation in* H30, T36
621 fate,] Trial–; fate H30, T36
622 altar-flame;] Trial–; altar flame H30; altar-flame T36
626 snow-limb'd] T36–; snowlimbd H30
     Eve] T36–; Eve, H30

I xviii *4* 627–38]

627–30] Trial–; *no punctuation in* H30, T36

632 labour] T36–; labour, H30

hand,] T36–; hand H30

I xviii *5* 639–43]

639] Trial–; *no punctuation in* H30, T36

642 madness,] Trial–; madness H30, T36

I xviii *6* 644–50]

646 world,] Trial–; world T36

'tis] Trial–; tis T36

live.] Trial–; live; T36

648 happy,] T36–; happy H30

649 grass,] Trial–; grass H30, T36

I xviii *7* 651–9]

651 die;] Trial–; die, T36

breath,] Trial–; breath T36

652 wrongs.] Trial–; wrongs T36

653 Love,] Trial–; Love T36

drinking-songs,] Trial–; drinking-songs T36

655] Trial–; *no punctuation in* T36

656 kiss,] Trial–; kiss T36

657 this?] Trial–; this T36

I xviii *8* 660–83]

661 bay?] Trial–; bay; T36

663 white,] Trial–; white T36

666 hand,] Trial–; hand T36

667 fancies] Trial–; Fancies T36

669 affright!] Trial–; affright T36

671 delight,] T36–; delight H30b

672 own,] T36–**1855**, **1872**, **1875**, **1889**; own H30b, **1856–1884**, **1870 Mini**

farewell;] **1856**–; farewell. H30b–**1855**

673 go:] Trial, **1855**, **1889**; go. H30b, T36; go **1856**

675 night!] Trial–; night. H30b, T36

677 bright?] Trial–; bright. H30b, T36

679 below,] Trial–; below H30b, T36

680 tell,] Trial–; tell. H30b; tell T36

682 so:] Trial–; so H30b, T36

I xix *1* 684–5]

684 to-night,] Berg B–; to-night H31

I xix *2* 686–94]

690 youth,] Berg B–; youth H30, H31

692 mine:] Berg B–; mine? H30; mine. H31

I xix *3* 695–708]

699 talk,] Berg B–; talk H31

703 thin,] Berg B–; thin H31

705 debt:] Berg B–; debt; H31

706 wet,] **1856**–; wet H31, Berg B

707 sighing] Berg B–; sighing, H31

I xix *4* 709–26]

716 torn:] H31, **1856**–; torn. H30d; torn; Berg B

717 said,] Berg B–; said H30d, H31

721 other,] H31–; other H30d

722 wine,] H31–; wine H30d

723 born;] H31–; born. H30d

725 Mine,] Berg B–; Mine H31

726 Mine, mine—] Berg B 2nd reading (Mine mine—), **1856**–; Mine; H31; Mine— Berg B 1st reading

I xix *5* 727–39]

728   bond,] Berg B–; bond. H31

730   beyond,] Berg B–; beyond H31

731   desire] Berg B–; desire, H31

      child,] Berg B–; child H31

733   friends] Berg B–; friends, H31

      reconciled;] Berg B–; reconciled! H31

734   doom,] Berg B–; doom H31

I xix *6* 740–9]

740   then] H30a, b, Berg B–; then, H31

741   Abroad,] H30b–; Abroad H30a

      Florence,] H30b–; Florence H30a

      Rome,] H30b–; Rome H30a

742   me] H30a, b, Berg B–; me, H31

I xix *7* 750–9]

750   Maud,] H31–; Maud H30

751   mind,] H31–; mind H30

752   see] H30, Berg B–; see, H31

      him,] H31–; him H30

753   kind,] H31–; kind H30

754   him,] H31, **1856**–; him H30, Berg B

755   me,] H31, **1856**–; me H30, Berg B

756   once,] H31–; once H30

      worse,] H31, **1856**–; worse H30, Berg B

757   play,] Berg B–; play H30, H31

I xix *8* 760–7]

762   kind?] H31, Berg B 2nd reading–; kind, Berg B 1st reading

764   still.] **1856**–; still: H31; still; Berg B

766   kind;] Berg B–; kind: H31

      why] **1865**–; why, H31, Berg B, **1856–1864**

I xix *9* 768–78]

768   Maud,] Berg B–; Maud H30c, H31

     true,] H31–; true H30c

769   endures] H30c, Berg B–; endures, H31

770   debt,] H31–; debt H30b, c

771   pay;] H31–; pay, H30b; pay H30c

774   yours;] Berg B–; yours H30b; yours, H30c; yours— H31

776   forget,] H30b, H31–; forget H30c

778   yet!] H30c–; yet. H30b

I xix *10* 779–86]

780   hate,] H31–; hate H30b

782   weight,] H31 2nd reading–; weight H30b, H31 1st reading

784   merry;] H31–; merry H30a, b

786   Hall] H30a, H31–; hall H30b

     to-night.] **1856**–; tonight H30a, H31; tonight. H30b, Berg B

I xx *1* 787–808]

793   folly:] H30b, Berg A–; folly H30a, T36

797   due?] Trial–; due T36; due, Berg A

799   manners,] H30a, T36–; manners H30b

800   dresses?] Trial–; dresses, H30a; dresses H30b; dresses! T36;
     dresses: Berg A

801   two,] Trial–; two H30a, T36, Berg A

802   it] T36–; it, H30a

804] Trial–; . . . habit, H30a; *no punctuation in* T36, Berg A

806   completer;] Trial–; completer H30a, T36, Berg A

I xx *2* 809–16]

809   to-morrow,] **1889**; tomorrow T36, Berg A; to morrow, Trial–
     1884

     live,] Trial–; live T36, Berg A

813   jewels,] H30, Trial–; jewels T36, Berg A

816   her] T36 *has* his (*error in transcription*)

I xx *3* 817–23]

818   acres,] Trial–; acres H30–Berg A

819   Tory,] T36, **1855**–; Tory; H30; Tory Berg A; Tory,— Trial

821   marriage-makers,] **1855**–; marriage-makers; H30; marriage-makers T36–Trial

823   glory.] H30, T36, Trial–; glory Berg A

I xx *4* 824–36]

825] T36–; *no punctuation in* H30

827   rose-garden,] Trial–; rose-garden H30–Berg A

831] Trial–; *no punctuation in* H30–Berg A

     For] H30 *has* Tha *revised to* For (*error in transcription*)

834   also,] H30, Trial–; also T36, Berg A

835   darling,] Trial–; darling H30–Berg A

836   Maud] H30–Berg A, **1855**–; Maud, Trial

     splendour.] H30, T36, Trial–; splendour Berg A

I xxi 837–49]

837   Rivulet] T36c–; Rivulet, T36b; *torn away in* T36a

     ground,] T36b, Berg A–; ground T36a, T36c

838   Hall] T36c, Trial–; hall Berg A; *torn away in* T36b

839   garden-rose] T36a, Trial–; garden rose, T36b; garden rose T36c, Berg A

     found,] Berg A–; found T36a, T36c; *torn away in* T36b

843   sea;] Trial–; sea T36a, T36b; sea, Berg A; *torn away in* T36b

844   Hall,] Trial–; Hall T36a, T36c; hall, Berg A; *torn away in* T36b

847   me,] Berg A–; me T36c

848   colour,] Trial–; colour T36c, Berg A; *torn away in* T36b

I xxii *1* 850–5]

850   Maud,] T36a, Trial–; Maud; T36/H

851   flown,] Trial–; flown T36a; flown. T36/H

852   Maud,] T36a, Trial–; Maud; T36/H

853–4] T36/H–; *no punctuation in* T36a

I xxii *2* 856–61]

856 moves,] T36/H–; moves T36a

857 Love] T36/H–; love T36a

      high,] Trial–; high T36a, T36/H

858 that] *interlineated in* T36/H (*error in transcription*)

859 sky,] Trial–; sky T36a, T36/H

860 sun] T36/H–; Sun T36a

      loves,] T36/H–; loves T36a

861 light,] Trial–; light T36a, T36/H

      to] *not in* T36/H (*error in transcription*)

      die.] T36/H–; die T36a

I xxii *4* 868–75]

868–9] Trial–; *no punctuation in* T36/H

868 'There] Trial–; There T36/H

875 away.] Trial–; away T36/H

I xxii *5* 876–81]

876 rose,] Trial–; rose T36/H

      'The] Trial–; the T36/H

878 those,] Trial–; those T36/H

879 thine?] Trial–; thine T36/H

881 'For] Trial–; For T36/H

I xxii *6* 882–7]

883 hall;] Trial–; hall, T36/H

884 garden lake] Trial–; garden-lake T36/H

886 wood,] **1867** *omits comma* (*probably a result of stereotyping*)

I xxii *8* 894–901]

895 tree;] Trial–; tree T36/H

896 lake] **1865**–; lake; T36/H; lake, Trial–**1864**

I xxii *9* 902–7]

906   head,] Trial–; head T36/H

I xxii *10* 908–15]

912   cries,] Trial–; cries T36/H
      'She . . . near;'] Trial–; 'she . . . near' T36/H
913   weeps,] Trial–; weeps T36/H
      'She . . . late;'] Trial–; 'she . . . late. T36/H
914   listens,] Trial–; listens T36/H
      hear,] Trial–; hear T36/H
      hear;'] Trial–; hear' T36/H
915   whispers,] Trial–; whispers T36/H

I xxii *11* 916–23]

917   tread,] Trial–; tread T36/H

II i *1* 1–35]

1   mine'—] T36b–; mine' T36a
3   wild-flower] Trial–; wildflower T36a, b
      hill?—] T36b–; hill? T36a
4   hand!—] T36b–; hand! T36a
7   it,] T36b–; it T36a
8   sky,] Trial–; sky T36a, b
9   sun,] Trial–; sun; T36a, b
10   Hate;] T36b–; hate; T36a
12   gate,] T36b–; gate T36a
13   babe-faced] T36b–; babefaced T36a
      lord;] T36a, Trial–; Lord; T36b
14   Heap'd] T36b–; Heapt T36a
      disgrace,] T36b–; disgrace; T36a
15   wept,] T36b–; wept T36a

20 by:] Trial–; by; T36a, b

22 woe;] T36b–; woe T36a

23 stood,] Trial–; stood T36b

25 red-ribb'd] Trial–; red-ribbed T36b

30 mine,'] Trial–; mine' T36b
 whisper'd,] Trial–; whisper'd T36b

34 blood:] Trial–; blood, T36a; blood; T36b

35 ears,] T36b–; ears T36a
 die.] Trial–; die T36a, b

II i *2* 36–48]

37 brain?] Trial–; brain: T36b

40 land.] Trial–; land; T36b

41 rain,] Trial–; rain T36b

44 forgive:] Trial–; forgive— T36b

47 dust;] Trial–; dust, T36b

II ii *1* 49–56]

52 Frail,] Trial–; Frail T36

I ii *3* 61–8]

63 shore.] Trial–; shore: T36

66 push,] Trial–; push T36
 uncurl'd,] Trial–; uncurl'd T36

II ii *4* 69–77]

70 finger-nail] Trial–; fingernail T36
 sand,] Trial–; sand! T36

71 divine,] Trial–; divine! T36

72 withstand,] Trial–; withstand T36

75 three decker's] **1870 Mini**, **1872**, **1875**, **1889**; threedecker's
 T36; three-decker's Trial, *all single-volume editions from* **1855** *to*
 1884

II ii *5* 78–90

85   eye,] Trial–; eye T36b

II ii *7* 97–105]

98   ever,] Trial–; ever T36

99   she,] Trial–; she T36

      still;] Trial–; still T36

101   me,] Trial–; me T36

103   heart,] Trial–; heart T36

II ii *8* 106–18]

109   eye,—] **1855**–; eye, Trial

II ii *9* 119–31]

120–1] Trial–; *no punctuation in* T36

123   her, . . . her,] T36 (first line), Trial–; her, . . . her T36 (second line)

      good,] Trial–; good T36

124   sea!] Trial–; sea. T36

125   by,] Trial–; by T36

126   her] T36 (second line), Trial–; her, T36 (first line)

      high,] T36 (first line), Trial–; high T36 (second line)

127   me!] Trial–; me. T36

130] Trial–; *no punctuation in* T36

131   her] Trial–; her, T36

II iii 132–40]

132] **1856**–; *no punctuation in* H31

134   canst] **1856**–; cans't H31

136   stone.—] **1856**–; stone: H31

137–40] **1856**–; *no punctuation in* H31

II iv *1* 141–4]

141 O] Trial–; Oh! H21–**1837**, **AR**

possible] H21–T21, Trial–; possible, **1837**, **AR**

142 pain] H21–T21, Trial–; pain, **1837**; pain; **AR**

143 true love] H21–T21, **AR**, Trial–; true-love **1837**

144 again!] **1837**–; again. H21, T21; again H13

I iv *2* 145–50]

147 birth,] **1837**–; birth H21–T21

148 embraces] H21–T21, Trial–; embraces, **1837**; embraces. **AR**

149 sweeter sweeter] Trial–; sweeter—sweeter— H21; sweeter, sweeter H13, T21; sweeter, sweeter, **1837**, **AR**

150 anything] **AR**, **1889**; any thing H21–**1884**

earth.] H13, **1837**–; Earth. H21; earth T21

II iv *3* 151–6]

151 me,] Trial–; me H21–T21; me— **1837**, **AR**

152 thou,] H21, **1837**–; thou— H13, T21

thee:] **1889**; thee. H21, T21, **1837**; thee, **AR**; thee H13; thee; Trial–**1884**

155 loved,] **1837**–; loved H21–T21

156 be.] H21, **1837**–; be H13, T21

II iv *4* 157–62]

157 evening,] **AR**, Trial–; evening T21; Evening, **1837**

159–62] **1837**–; *no punctuation in* T21

II iv *5 and 7* (*early version of* 163–70, 184–95)

169 laughter, H21, H13; laughter T21

184 chaunt H13 1st reading, T21; chant H13 2nd reading, H21

old. H21, H13; old T21

191 fled H13, fled— H21; fled. T21

193 knowlege, H13, T21; knowledge H21

195 cold. H13, T21; cold— H21

II iv *5* 163–70]

166   doze] Trial–; dose **1837**, **AR** (*errors*)

167   eyes,] Trial–; eyes— **1837**, **AR**

II iv *6* 171–83]

180   meadow] **1889**; meadow, Trial–**1884**

II iv *7* 184–95]

191   wake,] Trial–; wake–**1837**, **AR**
      fled;] Trial–; fled. **1837**, **AR**

192   dawn] Trial–; dawn **1837**, down **AR** (*error*)

193   pity,] Trial–; pity— **1837**, **AR**

194   bed] Trial–; bed, **1837**, **AR**

II iv *8* 196–201]

196   hence,] **1837**–; hence T21
      again,] **AR**, Trial–; again T21, **1837**

197   doubt,] **AR**, Trial–; doubt T21; doubt. **1837**

198   Pass,] **1837**–; Pass T21
      deathlike] T21, Trial–; death-like **1837**, **AR**
      pain,] **1837**–; pain T21

199   about!] **1865**–; about. T21; about— **1837**; about; **AR**; about, Trial–**1864**

200   'Tis] **1837**–; Tis T21

201   without.] **1837**–; without T21

II iv *9* 202–7]

202   rise,] Trial–; rise— T21; rise: **1837**, **AR**
      eavedrops] T21, Trial–; eave-drops **1837**, eave drops **AR**
      fall,] Trial–; fall T21, **1837**, **AR**

203   yellow vapours] T21, **AR**, Trial–; yellow-vapours **1837**
      choke] T21, **1837**, Trial–; choke, **AR**

204   wide;] **1837**–; wide T21

205 comes,] Trial–; comes T21; comes— **1837, AR**

ball] T21, Trial–; ball, **1837**; ball; **AR**

206 smoke] T21, Trial–; smoke, **1837, AR**

207 river-tide.] **1837**, Trial–; rivertide T21; river tide. **AR**

II iv *10* 208–14]

209 steal,] H13, **1837**–; steal— H21; steal T21

frame,] H13, Trial–; frame H21, T21; frame; **1837, AR**

210 here,] H13, **1837**–; here— H21, T21

there,] Trial–; there H21–T21, **AR**; there— **1837**

211 crowd] H21, T21, Trial–; crowd, H13, **1837, AR**

loud,] H13, **1837**–; loud H21, T21

212 shadow] H21, T21–; shadow, H13

same;] **1837**–; same. H21, H13; same T21

214 shame.] H21, **1837**–; shame H13, T21

II iv *11* 215–20]

215 Alas] T21, **1837**, Trial–; Alas! **AR**

me,] **1837**–; me— T21

216 call,] Trial–; call— T21, **1837, AR**

218 evenfall,] T21, Trial–; even-fall, **1837**; even fall **AR**

220 manorial hall.] **AR**, Trial–; manorial Hall T21; Manorial Hall. **1837**

II iv *12* 221–8]

221 spirit] **AR**, Trial–; Spirit **1837**

descend,] Trial–; descend **1837, AR**

223 street,] **AR**, Trial–; street **1837**

224 blest,] Trial–; blest; **1837, AR**

225 friend] Trial–; friend, **1837, AR**

226 'Forgive] **1889**; 'forgive Trial–**1884**

227 'Take] **1889**; "Take **1837, AR**; 'take Trial–**1884**

sweet,] **1837**, Trial–; sweet. **AR**

228   rest'?] **1889**; rest." **1837**, **AR**; rest?' Trial–**1884**

II iv *13* 229–38]

229   beats,] **1837**–; beats T21

230   fleets] T21, Trial–; fleets, **1837**, **AR**

231   be;] **1837**–; be— T21; be, **AR**

232   streets,] **1837**–; streets H21–T21

233   the] *omitted in* H21 (*error in transcription*)
      meets,] H13, **1837**–; meets H21, T21

234   me:] Trial–; me H21–T21; me; **1837**, **AR**

236   deep,] **1837**–; deep H21–T21

237   weep, and weep,] **AR**, Trial–; weep & weep H21, T21; weep,
      and weep H13, **1837**

II v *1* 239–58]

239   Dead,] Berg A–; Dead T36

241   dust,] Trial–; dust T36, Berg A

242   head,] Trial–**1864**, **1866A**–; head T36, Berg A; head; **1865**

244   thrust,] Trial–; thrust T36, Berg A

245   street,] Berg A–; street T36

246   beat, beat,] Berg A–; beat, beat T36

247–9] Trial–; *no punctuation in* T36, Berg A

250] Trial–; *no punctuation in* T36; Driving, hurrying, marrying, bury-
      ing Berg A

252   bad,] Berg A–; bad T36

253   peace,] Berg A–; peace T36
      so;] Trial–; so T36, Berg A

254   grave,] Berg A–; grave T36

255   fro,] Trial–; fro T36, Berg A

II v *2* 259–67]

259   age,] Berg A–; age T36

Time] Berg A–; time T36

began,] Trial–; began! T36, Berg A

260   man;] Berg A–; man. T36

264   one;] Berg A–; one. T36

265   sufficed,] Trial–; sufficed T36, Berg A

266   church,] Berg A–; church T36

II v *3* 268–78]

268   sobbing,] Trial–; sobbing T36, Berg A

269   distress;] T36, Trial–; distress Berg A

274   physician,] Trial–; physician T36, Berg A

II v *4* 279–90]

282   foretold;] Trial–; foretold T36; foretold, Berg A

283] Berg A (*no punctuation*), Trial–

284–5] Berg A–

286] Berg A (. . . mouse), Trial–

287] Berg A–; *no punctuation in* T36

II v *5* 291–4]

292] Trial–; *no punctuation in* Berg A

293   o'ergrown] Trial–; oergrown Berg A

crack;] Trial–; crack Berg A

294   yourself, . . . howl,] Trial–; yourself . . . howl Berg A

II v *6* 295–302]

296   vermin,] Trial–; vermine Berg A

297   ship,] Trial–; ship Berg A

299   holes:] Trial–; holes; Berg A

II v *7* 303–9]

307   us,] Berg A–; us: T36

divine;] Trial–; divine T36, Berg A

308   dead,] Berg A–; dead T36

II v *8* 310–20]

316   roses,] Trial–; roses T36a, b, Berg A
       blood;] Trial–; blood: T36b; blood T36a, Berg A
319   brutes,] Trial–; Brutes T36b; brutes T36a, Berg A
320   side?] T36a, b, Trial–; side. Berg A

II v *9* 321–6]

321   say?] Berg A–; say T36
323   day;] Trial–; day T36; day: Berg A
324   it;] Trial–; it T36, Berg A
326   pit?] Berg A–; pit T36

II v *10* 327–33]

328   low,] Trial–; low T36, Berg A
330   sin;] Berg A–; sin T36
332   akin.] Berg A–; akin T36

II v *11* 334–42]

334   enough?] Trial–; enough T36, Berg A
337   half-dead;] Berg A–; half dead T36
338   dumb;] Berg A–; dumb T36
339   head] T36, **1870 Mini**, **1872**, **1875**, **1889**; head, Berg A–Trial,
       all single-volume editions from **1855** *to* **1884**
340   somebody,] Trial–; somebody— T36; somebody Berg A

III vi *1* 1–14]

2   fear,] Trial–; fear H30
6   Charioteer] Trial–; charioteer H30
11   wars—] Trial–; wars H30
13   thee,'] Trial–; thee' H30

III vi *2* 15–28]

16   dream,] Trial–; dream H30
       fair,] Trial–; fair H30

17 bright;] Trial–; bright: H30

18 dream,] Trial–; dream H30

19 right,] Trial–; right H30

21 height,] Trial–; height H30

22 millionaire:] H30–**1855, 1889**; millionnaire: **1856–1884**

23 all,] Trial–; all H30
    Peace] Trial–; peace H30

24 note,] Trial–; note H30

25 increase,] Trial–; increase H30

26 shore,] Trial–; shore H30

27 throat] H30, **1856**–; throat, Trial, **1855**

III vi *3* 29–37]

29 grew,] Trial–; grew H30

31 true),] Trial–; true) H30

32 eye,] Trial–; eye H30

34 mix'd] Trial–; mixt H30

35 cry,] Trial–; cry H30

37 North,] Trial–; North H30
    battle,] Trial–; battle H30

III vi *4* 38–53]

39–40] Trial–; *no punctuation in* H30

42 unroll'd!] Trial–; unroll'd. H30

43 darken,] Trial–; darken H30

44 claims,] Trial–; claims H30

45 liar;] Trial–; liar, H30

46 leap,] Trial–; leap. H30

48 freër] H30, **1865**–; freer Trial–**1864**

49 desire;] Trial–; desire, H30

50 done,] **1856**–; done H30–**1855**

51 deep,] Trial–; deep H30

53   blood-red] Trial–; bloodred H30

     fire.] Trial–; fire H30

III vi 5 54–9]

54   fade,] **1856**–; fade **1855US**

     wind,] **1856**–; wind. **1855US**

55   still,] **1856**–; still. **1855US**

56   mind;] **1856**–; mind. **1855US**

57   good] **1855US, 1889**; good, **1856–1884**

     ill;] **1856**–; ill. **1855US**

58   kind,] **1856**–; kind **1855US**

59   God,] **1856**–; God **1855US**

Select index to the Introduction, Commentary and Appendices

References to *Maud* and to 'Oh! that 'twere possible' are not indexed. T.'s personal relationships and literary associations are indexed under the name of the other person involved. For T.'s attitudes towards particular subjects (e.g., politics), and for his knowledge and experience (e.g., of asylums), see under 'Tennyson, Alfred'.

Index of first lines